PRZEDMOWA

Praktyczny samouczek języka angielskiego to książka, która stanowi owoc naszych wieloletnich doświadczeń w nauczaniu języka angielskiego, naszej wieloletniej praktyki nauczycielskiej w polskich szkołach różnego stopnia, z uczniami w różnym wieku i o zróżnicowanych potrzebach. Zauważyłyśmy, że niezależnie od wieku i stopnia zaawansowania, wielu naszych uczniów ma podobne problemy z językiem angielskim i popełnia podobne błędy. Postanowiłyśmy wyjść naprzeciw tym typowym dla polskich uczniów problemom i opracować dla nich **szybkie i skuteczne powtórki**. Dobór przedstawionych struktur zgodny jest z nowym programem polskiej szkoły. Każdy rozdział naszej książki składa się z krótkiego omówienia danego, kłopotliwego problemu językowego, podania prawidłowych form oraz przykładów użycia, a także uwypuklenia typowych dla Polaków błędów. Druga część każdej **lekcji** to ćwiczenia utrwalające prawidłowe formy. Klucz do ćwiczeń znajduje się u dołu strony.

Książka nasza ma charakter samouczka, gdy trzeba szybko **nadrobić braki** lub choćby tylko **sprawdzić, co umiemy**, np. **przed klasówką lub egzaminem**, ale można z niej korzystać również **w codziennej nauce**, w grupie szkolnej. Polecamy ją także jako materiał uzupełniający dla Polaków uczących się języka angielskiego na kursach.

Zakładamy, że korzystające z naszej książki osoby wybiorą po prostu te zagadnienia, które chcą powtórzyć i utrwalić. Książka nie wymaga czytania „od deski do deski". Jeśli masz problem z jakimś zagadnieniem gramatycznym, po prostu odszukaj w spisie treści odpowiedni rozdział (**unit**).

Stopień trudności omawianych zagadnień oznaczono symbolem umieszczonym w prawym górnym rogu. Rozdziały opatrzone symbolem >b – to poziom podstawowy (**basic**), a rozdziały oznaczone symbolem >i – poziom średnio zaawansowany (**intermediate**). Każdy 25-ty rozdział to test zwany **CONSOLIDATION**, sprawdzający opanowanie materiału w poprzednich 24 jednostkach. Kolejna część, opatrzona symbolem e to dodatkowe ćwiczenia utrwalające (**exercises**).

W 11 rozdziałach tematycznych zostało zebrane ponad 60 ćwiczeń, poświęconych tym zagadnieniom gramatycznym, które sprawiają najwięcej trudności. Na końcu zamieszczono klucz z prawidłowymi rozwiązaniami.

Na końcu książki zamieściłyśmy **zadania egzaminacyjne typu maturalnego** dla dwóch poziomów – **podstawowego** i **zaawansowanego**, listę najczęściej spotykanych **czasowników frazowych** oraz wykaz najważniejszych **czasowników nieregularnych** wraz z ich polskimi odpowiednikami.

Mając nadzieję, że nasza książka okaże się pomocna w opanowaniu przez polskich uczniów zawiłości gramatyki angielskiej, życzymy sukcesów wszystkim uczącym się tego pięknego i tak popularnego w świecie języka.

Autorki

SPIS TREŚCI

przedmowa 3
spis treści 4

b BASIC

Unit 1 **three books/two women** REGULAR AND IRREGULAR NOUNS 8
Unit 2 **an apple/some advice** COUNTABLE AND UNCOUNTABLE NOUNS 10
Unit 3 **Jenny's book/my sister's jacket** SAXON GENITIVE 12
Unit 4 **an apple/the apple/apples** ARTICLES A/AN/THE/ZERO ARTICLE 14
Unit 5 **I/me/my/mine** PERSONAL PRONOUNS POSSESSIVES 16
Unit 6 **long/longer/the longest beautiful/more beautiful/the most beautiful** COMPARISON OF ADJECTIVES 18
Unit 7 **quickly/easily ADVERB** 20
Unit 8 **in/on/at/between/among** PREPOSITIONS OF TIME AND PLACE 22
Unit 9 **I am/you are** BE PRESENT SIMPLE 24
Unit 10 THERE IS/THERE ARE 26
Unit 11 **I have/I have got** PRESENT SIMPLE 28
Unit 12 **I do/I work** PRESENT SIMPLE 30
Unit 13 **I am doing/I am working** PRESENT CONTINUOUS 32
Unit 14 **now/always/often** TIME EXPRESSIONS PRESENT SIMPLE & PRESENT CONTINUOUS 34
Unit 15 **I was/they were** PAST SIMPLE 36
Unit 16 **I had/I didn't have** PAST SIMPLE 38
Unit 17 **I did/I worked** PAST SIMPLE 40
Unit 18 **I was doing/I was working** PAST CONTINUOUS 42
Unit 19 **I have worked/I have done/I have been** PRESENT PERFECT 44
Unit 20 **I did & I have done** PAST SIMPLE & PRESENT PERFECT 46
Unit 21 **I will do/I will be** FUTURE SIMPLE 48
Unit 22 **be going to** 50
Unit 23 **I can do** CAN 52
Unit 24 **must/have to/have got to do** 54
Unit 25 **CONSOLIDATION** 56

i INTERMEDIATE

Unit 26 **two coffees/coffee** NOUNS: COUNTABLE OR UNCOUNTABLE? 58
Unit 27 **scissors/door/family/police** SINGULAR OR PLURAL 60
Unit 28 **a swarm of bees/the homeless** GROUP NOUNS 62
Unit 29 **a film star/a T-shirt/sunglasses** COMPOUND NOUNS 64
Unit 30 **going/doing/swimming** GERUND 66
Unit 31 **the Pacific/the British Isles/the USA** THE ARTICLE PRECEDING GEOGRAPHICAL NAMES 68
Unit 32 **in prison, in the prison** ARTICLES WITH PLACES 70
Unit 33 **the one on the right** PRONOUNS ONE, ONES 72

Unit 34 myself/ourselves/yourself/yourselves REFLEXIVE PRONOUNS 74
Unit 35 another/the second/other/the other/others/the others 76
Unit 36 all/whole/every 78
Unit 37 every/each/each of 80
Unit 38 each other/one another 82
Unit 39 both (of)/either (of)/neither (of) 84
Unit 40 IT as a subject 86
Unit 41 IT as a subject/THERE as a subject 88
Unit 42 (a) little/(a) few 90
Unit 43 more/less/fewer/the most/the least/the fewest 92
Unit 44 enough/too 94
Unit 45 A nice large new house ORDER OF ADJECTIVES 96
Unit 46 Good-looking man/high-heeled shoes COMPOUND ADJECTIVES 98
Unit 47 as...as/not so...as 100
Unit 48 like/as 102
Unit 49 So/such/so that 104
Unit 50 CONSOLIDATION 106
Unit 51 do/let's do THE IMPERATIVE 108
Unit 52 need/don't need/needn't 110
Unit 53 must/need/have to/have got to NEGATION 112
Unit 54 should/ought to 114
Unit 55 can do/could do/may do/might do 116
Unit 56 must be/can't be/could be/may be/might be EXPRESSING SUPPOSITIONS: PRESENT AND FUTURE 118
Unit 57 I have been doing PRESENT PERFECT CONTINUOUS 120
Unit 58 I had done/I had worked PAST PERFECT 122
Unit 59 I had been doing/I had been working PAST PERFECT CONTINUOUS 124
Unit 60 He does/He will do PRESENT HABITS 126
Unit 61 used to do/would do PAST HABITS AND STATES 128
Unit 62 used to do/be used to do/get used to do 130
Unit 63 to do/to be doing/to have done/to be done/to have been done THE INFINITIVE 132
Unit 64 was invented/is being made THE PASSIVE (1) 134
Unit 65 I was told/We were given THE PASSIVE (2) 136
Unit 66 He is said to be bossy/It is said that THE PASSIVE (3) 138
Unit 67 to have something done THE PASSIVE (4) CAUSATIVE HAVE 140
Unit 68 One/you THE PASSIVE (5) 142
Unit 69 He said he was at home. REPORTED SPEECH (1) REPORTING STATEMENTS 144
Unit 70 She asked if he loved her REPORTED SPEECH (2) REPORTING QUESTIONS 146
Unit 71 He told me to listen REPORTED SPEECH (3) REPORTING REQUESTS/COMMANDS 148
Unit 72 Could you tell me EMBEDDED QUESTIONS 150
Unit 73 You're free, aren't you? QUESTION TAGS 152
Unit 74 I'm hungry. Are you? ECHO QUESTIONS 154
Unit 75 CONSOLIDATION 156

ĆWICZENIA UTRWALAJĄCE

1 **Czasy teraźniejsze** PRESENT SIMPLE i PRESENT CONTINUOUS (PRESENT PROGRESSIVE) 159
2 **Czasy przeszłe, prosty** (PAST SIMPLE) **i ciągły** (PAST CONTINUOUS) 163
3 **Czasy** PAST SIMPLE i PRESENT PERFECT 168
4 **Czas** PAST PERFECT 172
5 **Formy czasu przyszłego** 174
6 **Strona bierna** 180
7 **GERUND a bezokolicznik** 185
8 **Imiesłów** 189
9 **Zadania z IF** 192
10 **Czasowniki pomocnicze** 197
11 **Mowa zależna** 202

KLUCZ DO ĆWICZEŃ 207

zadania typu maturalnego – poziom podstawowy 220

zadania typu maturalnego – poziom rozszerzony 233

PHRASAL VERBS – a selection 247

IRREGULAR VERBS – a selection 251

UNIT 1 three books/two women REGULAR AND IRREGULAR NOUNS

Jane has two cats. Jane ma dwa koty.
Have you got any matches in the house? Czy masz w domu zapałki?
We must buy some tomatoes. Musimy kupić trochę pomidorów.
Peter and John are talking to their wives. Peter i John rozmawiają ze swymi żonami.

JAK TWORZYSZ LICZBĘ MNOGĄ RZECZOWNIKÓW?

Do większości rzeczowników dodajesz końcówkę –**s** lub –**es**, np. **book – books, match – matches.** Są to tzw. **rzeczowniki regularne**.

JAK TO SIĘ PISZE?

4 sposoby na tworzenie liczby mnogiej rzeczowników regularnych w zależności od końcówki.

ch, sh, s, x → **-es**
church – churches, bush – bushes, bus – buses, box – boxes

o → **-es**
tomato –tomatoes, potato – potatoes, ale np. tuxedo – tuxedos

-y po spółgłosce → **-i+es**
family – families, university – universities, party – parties, dolly – dollies

-f (e) → **-ves**
wife – wives, wolf – wolves, ale np. roof-roofs, chef – chefs

Most children like sweets. Większość dzieci lubi słodycze.
Men usually earn more than women. Mężczyźni zwykle zarabiają więcej niż kobiety.
Wild geese don't fly away for winter. Dzikie gęsi nie odlatują na zimę.

→ Rzeczowniki nieregularne tworzą liczbę mnogą w odrębny sposób:
man – men, woman – women, child – children, foot – feet, tooth – teeth, goose – geese, mouse – mice.
→ Niektóre rzeczowniki, jak np. sheep, deer, fish, salmon mają identyczną formę w liczbie pojedynczej i mnogiej.
→ Niektóre rzeczowniki występują, podobnie jak w języku polskim, tylko w liczbie mnogiej, np. scissors, trousers, jeans, pants, knickers.

TYPOWE BŁĘDY UWAŻAJ!

Źle: There are many ~~childrens~~ in my school.
PODPOWIEDŹ: Nie dodawaj końcówki –**s** do rzeczowników nieregularnych, które już są w liczbie mnogiej.
Dobrze: There are many children in my school.

some horses

some dogs

some sheep

some fish

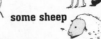

Old Macdonald has a farm.

YOUR TURN NOW! TERAZ KOLEJ NA CIEBIE!

I. Znajdź 19 ukrytych rzeczowników w liczbie mnogiej.

H	O	U	S	E	S	A	G	A	B
D	O	G	S	W	B	T	E	B	R
C	A	B	M	O	F	E	E	T	O
F	A	M	I	L	I	E	S	B	T
O	U	O	C	V	L	T	E	U	H
R	N	N	E	E	M	H	F	S	E
K	T	T	D	S	S	D	O	H	R
S	S	H	E	E	B	O	X	E	S
F	F	S	T	O	R	I	E	S	F
T	O	M	A	T	O	E	S	G	G

II. Wstaw podany rzeczownik w liczbie mnogiej.

1. We need more ______________ to make the soup. (*potato*)
2. Be careful, these ______________ are very sharp. (*knife*)
3. Do you know the song about blind ______________? (*mouse*)
4. Do you use Snow White toothpaste to brush your ______________? (*tooth*)
5. Please don't feed the ______________ (*monkey*)
6. Are these ______________ really made of gold? (*watch*)

III. Znajdź w każdej z linijek jeden rzeczownik, który nie pasuje do pozostałych.

1. cows	tables	bags	news
2. scissors	shorts	doors	jeans
3. roof	leaf	wife	knife
4. advice	information	sheep	furniture
5. potato	avocado	tomato	tuxedo
6. salmon	geese	deer	trout
7. play	family	dictionary	university

IV. Przetłumacz.

1. Cicho bądź, ci mężczyźni łowią ryby.
2. Czy to twój ojciec zrobił te półki na książki?
3. Trzy kobiety rozmawiają na przystanku.
4. Lubię ryby.
5. Susan boi się myszy.

KLUCZ

I. 1. families 2. feet 3. wolves 4. mice 5. months 6. teeth 7. geese 8. brothers 9. boxes 10. stories 11. bushes 12. forks 13. tomatoes 14. houses 15. dogs 16. films 17. aunts 18. foxes 19. months **II.** 1. potatoes 2. knives 3. mice 4. teeth 5. monkeys 6. watches **III.** 1. news 2. doors 3. roof 4. sheep 5. tuxedo 6. geese 7. play **IV.** 1. Be quiet, these men are fishing. 2. Has your father made these beautiful bookshelves. 3 Three women are talking at the bus stop. 4. I like fish. 5. Susan is afraid of mice.

UNIT 2 an apple/some advice COUNTABLE AND UNCOUNTABLE NOUNS

We need some apples to make an apple pie. Potrzebujemy trochę jabłek, aby zrobić szarlotkę.
I can give you an apple if you want. Mogę dać ci jabłko, jeśli chcesz.
I can give you some good advice. Mogę dać ci dobrą radę.
We must have a lot of apples to make a pie. Musimy mieć wiele jabłek by zrobić szarlotkę.

Rzeczowniki policzalne są to nazwy osób lub rzeczy, które można bezpośrednio policzyć.

Rzeczowniki niepoliczalne są to najczęściej nazwy materiałów (**cotton**), substancji (**water**), lub uczuć (**love**).

JAK ODRÓŻNISZ, CZY RZECZOWNIK JEST POLICZALNY, CZY NIEPOLICZALNY?

→ Rzeczowniki policzalne tworzą liczbę mnogą. W liczbie pojedynczej są często poprzedzone przedimkiem nieokreślonym **a/an**. Mogą być poprzedzone określeniami ilości, takimi jak **some, many, any, (a) few, a lot of, lots of, plenty of.**

→ Rzeczowniki niepoliczalne występują tylko w liczbie pojedynczej i łączą się z czasownikiem w liczbie pojedynczej. Nie występują z przedimkiem nieokreślonym **a/an** ani z liczebnikami. Mogą być poprzedzone przedimkiem określonym **the** lub określeniami ilości **much, (a) little, a lot of, lots of.** Często nie są poprzedzone ani przedimkiem, ani określeniem ilości.

→ Uważaj na rzeczowniki **advice, news, information, homework, money** i **furniture** – są niepoliczalne! Jeśli chcesz wyrazić określoną ilość (np. jedną wiadomość lub dwa meble), użyj wyrażenia **a piece of**. Dla innych rzeczowników niepoliczalnych musisz też użyć określenia ilości, np. **some money**, lub jakiejś innej miary, np. **a bottle of water**.

TYPOWE BŁĘDY UWAŻAJ!

Źle: This is ~~a~~ good advice.
PODPOWIEDŹ: Nie traktuj rzeczowników niepoliczalnych jako policzalne, mimo iż po polsku są one „policzalne".
Dobrze: This is good advice.

Źle: I have ~~two advices~~ for you.
PODPOWIEDŹ: Nie używaj liczebników przed rzeczownikiem niepoliczalnym traktując go tak, jakby był policzalny.
Dobrze: I have two pieces of advice for you.

Źle: He never has ~~many~~ money.
PODPOWIEDŹ: Nie używaj błędnego określenia ilości. **Many** wystepuje tylko z rzeczownikiem policzalnym w liczbie mnogiej
Dobrze: He never has much money.

YOUR TURN NOW! TERAZ KOLEJ NA CIEBIE!

I. Zakreśl rzeczowniki niepoliczalne.

advice driver city news money apple tractor water
happiness classroom luck furniture newspaper bed information
woman dollar attraction holiday love night sugar milk

II. Wstaw podane rzeczowniki w odpowiedniej formie.

1. I've got some good ____________ for you: we're going to France for two ____________! (*news, week*)
2. There are a lot of lovely ____________ in this ____________. (*house, street*)
3. She married for ____________, not for ____________. (*love, money*)
4. We must have three ____________ for the ____________. (*bowl, soup*)
5. How much ____________ do we need to get to the ____________? (*time, mountain*)
6. Can I give you some ____________ about some good ____________ in my town? (*advice, pub*)
7. How many ____________ of ____________ do you want to have in your room? (*piece, furniture*)

III. Przetłumacz na język angielski fragmenty zdań podane w nawiasach.

1. I have [*nowe meble*] in my room.
2. [*Ulice w twoim mieście*] are very clean.
3. I must buy [*trochę ryżu*].
4. Yesterday I heard [*dwie ważne informacje*].
5. [*Pieniądze nie są*] so important.

IV. A teraz popraw błędy! (Uwaga! Jedno zdanie jest poprawne.)

1. There are much cars in this street.
2. I haven't many moneys in my wallet.
3. What are the news?
4. When in the love, trust your heart.
5. We haven't got any new informations about Mary.
6. I must buy some cornflakes for breakfast.
7. The advices she gave us were all wrong.

KLUCZ

I. advice news money water happiness luck furniture information love sugar milk **II.** 1. news, weeks 2. houses, street 3. love, money 4. bowls, soup 5. time, mountains 6. advice, pubs 7. pieces, furniture **III.** 1. I have some new furniture in my room. 2. (The) streets in your town are very clean. 3. I must buy some rice. 4. Yesterday I heard two pieces of important information. 5. Money isn't so important. **IV.** 1. There are many cars in this street. 2. I haven't much money in my wallet. 3. What is the news? 4. When in love, trust your heart. 5. We haven't got any new information about Mary. 6. OK 7. The advice she gave us was all wrong.

UNIT 3 Jenny's book/my sister's jacket SAXON GENITIVE

This is my parents' flat. To jest mieszkanie moich rodziców.
I bought these flowers at the florist's. Kupiłam te kwiaty w kwiaciarni.
I like this car's design. Podoba mi się linia tego samochodu.
We're studying at Ann's for the test. Uczymy się do testu u Anny.

KIEDY UŻYWASZ SAXON GENITIVE?

1. Gdy mówisz o tym, że coś lub ktoś należy do kogoś lub czegoś.
2. Gdy mówisz o miejscach takich jak sklepy, zakłady usługowe.
3. Gdy mówisz o tym, że u kogoś jesteś lub idziesz do kogoś, np. **I went to my aunt's**.

TYPOWE BŁĘDY **UWAŻAJ!**

Zabawki chłopców są na tej półce.

Źle: The ~~boy's~~ toys are on this shelf.

PODPOWIEDŹ: Gdy coś należy do więcej niż jednej osoby, dodajesz sam apostrof do rzeczownika w liczbie mnogiej.

Dobrze: The boys' toys are on this shelf.

Źle: ~~Ann's~~ and Peter's children are very naughty.

PODPOWIEDŹ: Jeśli wymieniasz kilku właścicieli, dodajesz **'s** tylko do ostatniego rzeczownika.

Dobrze: Ann and Peter's children are very naughty.

Źle: I met Mary at the ~~greengrocer.~~

PODPOWIEDŹ: Gdy mówisz o miejscach takich jak np. sklep – opuszczasz słowo **shop**.
Zostaje samo określenie w formie **Saxon Genitive**,
at the butcher's –w sklepie mięsnym
at the newsagent's –w kiosku
at the florist's –w kwiaciarni.

Dobrze: I met Mary at the greengrocer's.

Daisy works at a florist's.
FLORIST'S

YOUR TURN NOW! TERAZ KOLEJ NA CIEBIE!

I. Przekształć odpowiedzi wg wzoru.

WZÓR A: Is this your pen? B: No, it belongs to Jenny. It's Jenny's.

1. A: Is this your money?
   B: No, I think it belongs to Bill. It's ____________________.
2. A: Is this Ben's mobile?
   B: No, it belongs to his brother. It's his ____________________.
3. A: Are these John's books?
   B: No, they belong to Peter and Jean. They are____________________.
4. A: Is this Max's house?
   B: No, it belongs to the Thompsons. It's ____________________.

II. Dopasuj połówki zdań.

1. My sister works at greengrocer's	A. go to the doctor's.
2. You are ill,	B. and she sells vegetables.
3. I'm going to London and I'll stay	C. so he must take it to the watchmaker's.
4. Tom's alarm clock doesn't work	D. so she must go to the newsagent's.
5. Mary wants to buy a new magazine	E. at my aunt's.

III. Przetłumacz podane zdania na język angielski.

1. Wczoraj spotkałem Susan w sklepie spożywczym.
2. To jest słownik Jacka i Tomka.
3. Kupiłam te spodnie u Marksa i Spencera.
4. To jest kościół św. Jakuba.
5. Impreza u Mary była bardzo udana.
6. Szkoła chłopców jest na Starym Mieście.

IV. A teraz popraw błędy!

1. We usually spend our holidays at our grandmother.
2. This is Tom's and John's room.
3. We practise football at Legia pitch twice a week.
4. My mother buys fresh salmon at the fishmonger.
5. The Browns's dog is barking.

KLUCZ

I. 1. It's Bill's. 2. It's his brother's. 3. They are Peter and Jean's. 4. It's the Thompsons'. **II.** 1B, 2A, 3E, 4C, 5D; **III.** 1. Yesterday I met Susan at the grocer's. / I met Susan at the grocer's yesterday. 2. This is Jack and Tom's dictionary. 3. I've bought these trousers at Marks and Spencer's. 4. This is St. James's church. 5. The party at Mary's/ Mary's party was very good. 6. The boys' school is in the Old Town. **IV.** 1 We usually spend our holidays at our grandmother's. 2. This is Tom and John's room. 3. We practise football at Legia's pitch twice week. 4. My mother buys fresh salmon at the fishmonger's. 5. The Browns' dog is barking.

UNIT 4

an apple/the apple/apples
ARTICLES A/AN/THE/ZERO ARTICLE

An apple is a kind of fruit. Jabłko to rodzaj owocu.
Apples are cheap. Jabłka są tanie.
The apple I have in my hand is rotten.
Jabłko, które mam w ręce, jest zgniłe.
Give me a sour apple. Daj mi kwaśne jabłko.

JAK STOSUJESZ PRZEDIMKI?

→ Przedimek nieokreślony **a/an** używany jest z rzeczownikami policzalnymi w liczbie pojedynczej, gdy:

1. mówisz o kimś lub o czymś po raz pierwszy **(John has a dog.)**
2. podajesz ogólną charakterystykę (definicję) osoby lub rzeczy **(An apple is a kind of fruit.)**
3. przed przymiotnikiem poprzedzającym rzeczownik policzalny w liczbie pojedynczej **(She is a nice girl.)**

→ **A** stosujesz przed wyrazem zaczynającym się na spółgłoskę, **an** – gdy wyraz zaczyna się na samogłoskę. Jeśli rzeczownik zaczyna się na niemą spółgłoskę, stosuj **an (an hour)**. Jeśli rzeczownik zaczyna się na **e** lub **u** wymawiane z **j** na początku, stosuj przedimek **a (a unit, a eucalyptus)**.

→ Przedimek określony **the** używany jest z rzeczownikami policzalnymi i niepoliczalnymi, gdy:

1. mówisz o kimś lub o czymś, co jest znane albo o czym już była mowa
2. wspominasz o czymś, co jest jedyne/unikalne **(Most people in Europe use the Internet.)**

→ **Przedimek tzw. zerowy**, czyli opuszczenie przedimka, ma miejsce

1. przed rzeczownikami policzalnymi w liczbie mnogiej, gdy mówisz o kimś lub o czymś po raz pierwszy, lub stwierdzasz prawdę ogólnie znaną **(Apples are good to eat.)**
2. przed rzeczownikami niepoliczalnymi **(Happiness is not for sale.)**

TYPOWE BŁĘDY **UWAŻAJ!**

Źle: You have ~~nice house~~.
PODPOWIEDŹ: Jeśli przymiotnik poprzedza rzeczownik policzalny w liczbie pojedynczej, musisz użyć przedimka.
Dobrze: You have a nice house.

Źle: Every policeman wears ~~an~~ uniform.
PODPOWIEDŹ: Wybór przedimka **a/an** zależy od wymowy następującego po nim słowa.
Dobrze: Every policeman wears a uniform.

YOUR TURN NOW! TERAZ KOLEJ NA CIEBIE!

I. Wybierz właściwy przedimek. Pamiętaj o przedimku zerowym!

1. Bob is *a/the/-/* teacher. He teaches *a/the/-/* geography.
2. Is *a/the/-/* basketball *a/the/-/* team game?
3. I must buy *a/ the/-/* new computer. *A/the/-/* old one is out of order.
4. You know that Philip works in *a/the/-/* Volvo garage. It's *a/ the/-/* best Volvo garage in our town.
5. Susanna never has *a/the/-/* time for work. She prefers to go to lots of *a/ the/-/* parties.
6. Peter is looking for *a/the/-/* new job. He's bored with *a/the/-/* old one.

II. Wstaw odpowiedni przedimek. Pamiętaj o przedimku zerowym!

Mary: ______(1) apples are expensive this year.
John: These apples are ______ (2) nice. Where did you buy them? At ______ (3) small shop in Nicolson Square?
Mary: No, I went to ______ (4) supermarket in Church Road.
John: That was ______ (5) mistake. ______ (6) supermarkets sell ______ (7) imported apples, not home-grown ones. They are always more expensive.
Mary: OK. Next time I'll go to ______ (8) small shop in Nicolson Square.

III. Przetłumacz na język angielski. Pamiętaj o przedimkach!

1. Ścisz radio, proszę. Muzyka jest badzo głośna i sąsiedzi są źli.
2. Egzamin trwał godzinę i zadania były trudne.
3. Spóźniliśmy się na autobus i nie pojechaliśmy na wycieczkę.
4. To jest koniec autostrady. Musimy teraz zjechać na lewo na dwupasmówkę. (*dual carriageway*)
5. Joanna jest wegetarianką i nie je mięsa.
6. Jedz marchewkę. Warzywa mają masę witamin.

'We missed the bus...'

IV. A teraz popraw błędy!

1. I never eat the chocolate.
2. Is there underground station near here?
3. Beckham is a best player in his team.
4. Kate works as the hairdresser.
5. Ildiko comes from Hungary so she's an European.
6. A my boyfriend likes the action films.
7. Susan is a tall.

KLUCZ

I. 1 a, - 2-, a 3 a, the 4 a/the, the 5 -, - 6 a, the **II.** 1- 2 - 3 the 4 the 5 a 6 - 7- 8 the **III.** 1. Turn down the radio, please. The music is very loud and the neighbours are angry. 2. The exam lasted an hour and the tasks were difficult. 3. We missed the bus and didn't go for the trip/excursion. 4. This is the end of the motorway. We must turn left into a/the dual carriageway. 5. Joan is a vegetarian and she doesn't eat meat. 6. Eat the carrot. Vegetables have a lot of vitamins. **IV.** 1. I never eat chocolate. 2. Is there an underground station near here? 3. Beckham is the best player in his team. 4. Kate works as a hairdresser. 5. Ildiko comes from Hungary so she's a European. 6. My boyfriend likes action films. 7. Susan is tall.

UNIT 5 I/me/my/mine PERSONAL PRONOUNS POSSESSIVES

Tell me about them. Opowiedz mi o nich.
It's my dog. To mój pies.
This book is mine. Ta książka jest moja.

FORMY ZAIMKÓW OSOBOWYCH I OKREŚLNIKÓW DZIERŻAWCZYCH

who/what (kto/co)	**I, you, he, she, it, we, they**
whose (czyje)	**my, your, his, her, its, our, their** te formy występują przed rzeczownikiem **mine, yours, his, hers, its, ours, theirs** te formy nie poprzedzają rzeczownika
who(m) (komu/kogo)	**me, you, him, her, it, us, them**

→ Zaimki **he/she** odnoszą się tylko do osób oraz do zwierząt, których płeć znamy. W stosunku do rzeczy i zwierząt ogólnie używamy zaimków **it/they**.

TYPOWE BŁĘDY **UWAŻAJ!**

Źle: ~~Yours~~ dogs are very noisy.
PODPOWIEDŹ: Formy dzierżawcze **yours, hers, ours, theirs** nie są liczbą mnogą form **your, her, our, their**.
Dobrze: Your dogs are very noisy.

Źle: This room is ~~my/your/her/our/their~~.
PODPOWIEDŹ: Form **my, your, our, their** nie stosuje się na końcu zdania.
Dobrze: This room is mine/yours/hers/ours/theirs.

Źle: This is a dog and ~~it's~~ bone.
PODPOWIEDŹ: Określnik dzierżawczy **its** piszemy bez apostrofu. Forma **it's = it is / it has**.
Dobrze: This is a dog and its bone.

Źle: This is Susan with ~~she's~~ dog.
PODPOWIEDŹ: Nie myl formy **she's** i **her**. **She's = she is/she has**.
Dobrze: This is Susan with her dog.

Źle: I like your dress. ~~She's~~ lovely.
PODPOWIEDŹ: Nie stosuj zaimków **he**, **she** w odniesieniu do przedmiotów.
Dobrze: I like your dress. It's lovely.

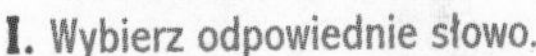

YOUR TURN NOW! TERAZ KOLEJ NA CIEBIE!

I. Wybierz odpowiednie słowo.

1. These are *your/yours* toys.
2. *My/mine* cats are cute.
3. Those shoes are *my/mine*.
4. This is *their/theirs* car.
5. This is your room and that one is *her/hers*.

II. Dokończ zdania odpowiednim zaimkiem.

WZÓR I don't know these people. Do you know them? (*they*)

1. I don't know this man. Do you know _____? (*he*)
2. This book is mine and that one is _____ (*she*)
3. I'm talking to you. Listen to _____ (*I*)
4. Our school is bigger than _____ (*they*)
5. Your room is nicer than _____ (*I*)
6. Their car is faster than _____(*we*)

III. Przetłumacz na język angielski.

1. Te walizki są nasze.
2. Znasz ją?
3. To mój chłopak.
4. Opowiedz mi o tym.
5. Daj mu ten klucz.
6. To jest ich nowy samochód.

IV. A teraz popraw błędy!

1. This is a my computer.
2. Yours friends are very talkative.
3. The baby is playing with it's toy.
4. Sorry, but this umbrella is my.
5. This doll is her.
6. Give me theirs books.
7. I don't like this blouse. She's ugly.

Proverb:
Every bird loves its nest.

Przysłowie:
Każdy ptak kocha swoje gniazdo.

KLUCZ

I. 1. your 2. my 3. mine 4. their 5. hers **II.** 1. him 2. hers 3. me 4. theirs 5. mine 6. ours **III.** 1. These suitcases are ours. 2. Do you know her? 3. This is my boyfriend. 4. Tell me about it. 5. Give him this key/Give this key to him. 6. This is their new car. **IV.** 1. This is my computer. 2. Your friends are very talkative. 3. The baby is playing with its toy. 4. Sorry, but this umbrella is mine. 5. This doll is hers. 6. Give me their books. 7. I don't like this blouse. It's ugly.

UNIT 6

long/longer/the longest beautiful/more beautiful/the most beautiful
COMPARISON OF ADJECTIVES

Tim is strong but John is stronger and Jack is the strongest.
Tim jest silny, ale John jest silniejszy, a Jack (jest) najsilniejszy.
David is the most intelligent man I know.
David jest najinteligentniejszym człowiekiem, jakiego znam.

Przymiotnik w języku angielskim ma taką samą formę niezależnie od rodzaju (męski, żeński, nijaki) i liczby.

JAK STOPNIUJESZ PRZYMIOTNIKI?

→ Dodajesz końcówkę **–(e)r** w stopniu wyższym i **–(e)st** w stopniu najwyższym.
nice – nicer – the nicest

→ Przymiotniki zakończone na spółgłoskę po jednej samogłosce podwajają spółgłoskę.
hot – hotter – the hottest

→ W przypadku przymiotników zakończonych na **–y** następuje zamiana **y** na **i** oraz dodanie **-er/-est.**
friendly – friendlier – the friendliest

→ Przymiotniki dłuższe oraz zakończone na **-ful, -less, -ing, -ed** stopniujemy opisowo **(more, the most)**
beautiful – more beautiful – the most beautiful

PRZYMIOTNIKI NIEREGULARNE

bad – worse – the worst; good – better – the best; far – further/farther – the furthest/farthest

JAK PORÓWNUJESZ DWIE RZECZY LUB OSOBY?

Susan is **taller** than Jenny. She is **more intelligent** than her friend.

TYPOWE BŁĘDY UWAŻAJ!

Źle: Anne is ~~more nice~~ than her sister.
PODPOWIEDŹ: Przymiotniki jednosylabowe stopniujesz dodając odpowiednią końcówkę.
Dobrze: Anne is nicer than her sister.

Źle: Adam is fatter ~~then~~ Matthew.
PODPOWIEDŹ: Istnieją dwa słowa o podobnej pisowni, ale różnym znaczeniu: than i then.
Than = niż, **Then** = potem
Dobrze: Adam is fatter than Matthew.

Źle: She is ~~beautifull.~~
PODPOWIEDŹ: Tylko przymiotnik **full = pełny** pisze się przez dwa **l.**
Końcówka przymiotnika **-ful** ma zawsze jedno **l**!
Dobrze: She is beautiful.

YOUR TURN NOW! TERAZ KOLEJ NA CIEBIE!

I. Połącz przeciwstawne przymiotniki

1. good
2. pretty
3. careful
4. safe
5. warm
6. healthy
7. interesting
8. bored

A. ugly
B. cold
C. dangerous
D. ill
E. bad
F. careless
G. interested
H. boring

II. Wybierz odpowiednią formę przymiotnika

1. Which is *heavier/heaviest*: 1 kg of fluff or 1 kg of stones?
2. Susan is *fatter/the fattest* girl I've ever met.
3. I think Glasgow is *farther/farthest* than Edinburgh.
4. Hannah is *proud/the proudest* woman I know.
5. This book is *expensive/more expensive* than that one.

III. Przetłumacz na język angielski.

1. Mój tata jest silniejszy niż twój!
2. Babcia Alicja jest najstarsza w naszej rodzinie.
3. To jest najmłodsze dziecko Thomsonów.
4. Mój komputer jest szybszy od twojego (niż twój).
5. Tom jest mądrzejszy od Billa.

IV. A teraz popraw błędy!

1. U2 is more popular Irish band.
2. My room is bigger then yours.
3. Clive isn't very tallest.
4. Barbara is prettiest in our class.
5. Be carefull! It's hotter than you think.
6. These flowers are more nicer than those ones.

DID YOU KNOW?

According to 38 % of women asked in a poll carried out in Britain in August 2003, Prince William has the sexiest eyes in Britain!

KLUCZ

I. 1E 2A 3F 4C 5B 6D 7H 8G **II.** 1. heavier 2. the fattest 3. farther 4. the proudest 5. more expensive **III.** 1. My dad is stronger than yours. 2. Grandma Alice is the oldest/eldest in our family. 3. This is the Thomsons' youngest child. 4. My computer is faster than yours. 5. Tom is cleverer/more clever than Bill. **IV.** 1. U2 is the most popular Irish band. 2. My room is bigger than yours. 3. Clive isn't very tall. 4. Barbara is the prettiest in our class. 5. Be careful! It's hotter than you think. 6. These flowers are nicer than those ones.

quickly/easily ADVERB

She writes quickly. Ona szybko pisze.
Walk carefully. Idź ostrożnie.
He won the race easily. Wygrał wyścig z łatwością (łatwo).

Przysłówek odpowiada na pytanie **How?** (Jak?), określa więc czasownik i często jest na końcu zdania.

She has a beautiful voice. She sings beautifully.

JAK TWORZYSZ PRZYSŁÓWKI?

Oto sposoby tworzenia przysłówków w zależności od końcówki przymiotnika:

1. Do przymiotnika dodajesz końcówkę **–ly (slow – slowly)**
2. Jeśli przymiotnik kończy się na **–le**, opuszczasz **–e** i dodajesz **–ly (terrible – terribly)**
3. Jeśli przymiotnik kończy się na **–y**, zamieniasz **–y** na **–i** oraz dodajesz końcówkę **–ly**. **(easy – easily)**
4. Niektóre przymiotniki i przysłówki mają taką samą formę, np. **far, fast, hard, high, low, near.**
5. Istnieje przysłówek **hardly**, lecz jego znaczenie jest zupełnie inne: **He works hard.** On ciężko pracuje. **He hardly works.** On prawie wcale nie pracuje.

JAK STOPNIUJESZ PRZYSŁÓWKI?

Jednosylabowe przysłówki **–er, the –est.**
fast – faster – fastest

Dłuższe przysłówki **more, the most**.
beautifully – more beautifully – most beautifully

Przysłówki nieregularne
well – better – the best
badly – worse – the worst
little – less – the least
far – farther – the farthest

TYPOWE BŁĘDY UWAŻAJ!

Źle: She speaks English ~~good/fluent.~~
PODPOWIEDŹ: Nie stosuj przymiotnika zamiast przysłówka, gdy jest mowa **jak** daną czynność wykonano.
Dobrze: She speaks English well/fluently.

Źle: He laughed ~~happyly.~~
PODPOWIEDŹ: Pamiętaj o zamianie **–y** na **–i** przy tworzeniu przysłówków od przymiotników zakończonych na **–y**.
Dobrze: He laughed happily.

HOTSPOT

W mowie potocznej, szczególnie młodzieżowej, zdarza się, że przysłówek zostaje zastąpiony przymiotnikiem. Można więc usłyszeć taki dialog: **How are you? I am good** zamiast **I am well.** Pamiętaj, że nie jest to jednak forma w pełni poprawna i nie użyj jej np. na egzaminie!

YOUR TURN NOW! TERAZ KOLEJ NA CIEBIE!

I. Które z wyrazów w ramce na pewno nie są przysłówkami?

hard lucky friendly nicely quickly heavy far noisy better bad quietly fast well small

II. Dokończ zdania wg wzoru.

WZÓR Helen is a good student. She learns well.

1. Greg is a fast runner. He runs ________.
2. My boyfriend is a secret smoker. He smokes ________.
3. Sabrina is a wonderful singer. She sings ________.
4. The children are very noisy. They play ________.
5. Martha is a hard worker. She works ________.

III. Wybierz odpowiedni wyraz.

1. Your homework is very good.
   You wrote it *good/well*.
2. Finish it *quick/quickly*!
3. Be *quiet/quietly*, I'm studying.
4. Be *good/well* and help me, please.
5. My little brother is very *careful/carefully*.
6. I understand you *perfect/perfectly*.

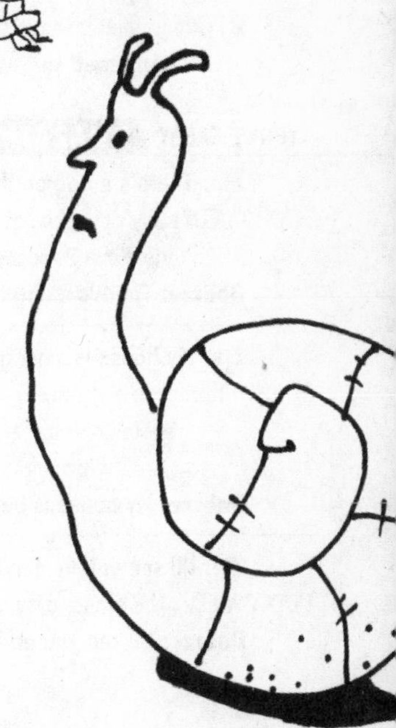
Hurry up!
Don't walk so slowly!

IV. Przetłumacz na język angielski.

1. Ona pięknie maluje.
2. Pani Brown jest złą nauczycielką i źle nas uczy.
3. Wczoraj mocno padało.
4. Mówię dobrze po angielsku.
5. Dzieciaki głośno krzyczą.

V. A teraz popraw błędy!

1. I'm sorry I'm lately.
2. I always drive careful.
3. Martin can do this exercise easy.
4. Susan is running more fast than Jenny.
5. Tom pushed the door hardly.

KLUCZ **I.** lucky, friendly, heavy, noisy, bad, small są przymiotnikami; **II.** 1. fast 2. secretly 3. wonderfully 4. noisily 5. hard **III.** 1. well, 2. quickly, 3. quiet, 4. good, 5. careful, 6. perfectly **IV.** 1. She paints beautifully. 2. Mrs Brown is a bad teacher and teaches us badly. 3. Yesterday it rained heavily. 4. I speak English well. 5. The kids are shouting loudly. **V.** 1. I'm sorry I'm late. 2. I always drive carefully. 3. Martin can do this exercise easily. 4. Susan is running faster than Jenny. 5. Tom pushed the door hard.

UNIT 8 in/on/at/between/among
PREPOSITIONS OF TIME AND PLACE

WHERE? PREPOSITIONS OF PLACE

You can see my boyfriend in this picture. Możesz zobaczyć mojego chłopaka na tym zdjęciu.
He is sitting between Anne and Tom. On siedzi między Anną i Tomkiem.
He is the tallest among the boys in my class. On jest najwyższy spośród chłopaków w mojej klasie.

WHEN? PREPOSITIONS OF TIME

The test is on Monday. Klasówka jest w poniedziałek.
I usually go on holiday in July. Zwykle wyjeżdżam na wakacje w lipcu.
The party starts at 9.00. Impreza zaczyna się o 9.00.
I always watch TV in the evening. Zawsze wieczorem oglądam telewizję.
The party is on Friday evening. Impreza jest w piątek wieczorem.

JAK PODAJESZ DATĘ?

1. Gdy podajesz datę (łącznie z dniem), zawsze stosujesz **on**.
   (It happened on 11th September 2001.)
2. Gdy wymieniasz tylko miesiąc lub rok, stosujesz **in**.
   (It happened in September 2001.)

TYPOWE BŁĘDY UWAŻAJ!

Źle: There's a dog ~~on~~ the picture.
PODPOWIEDŹ: Gdy opisujesz obrazek, używaj przyimka **in**. To samo dotyczy wyrażenia **na drzewie**, np. **Fizia Pończoszanka siedzi na drzewie. Pippi Langstrumpf is sitting in the tree.**
Dobrze: There's a dog in the picture.

Źle: My house is ~~among~~ the park and the post office.
PODPOWIEDŹ: Nie myl **among** i **between**. Przyimek **between** (pomiędzy) odnosi się do dwóch obiektów, rzeczy lub osób. Przyimek **among** (wśród, spośrod) odnosi się do wielu rzeczy lub osób.
Dobrze: My house is between the park and the post office.

Źle: I'll see you ~~in~~ Monday.
PODPOWIEDŹ: Nie stosuj przyimka **in** gdy podajesz dzień, w którym coś się odbywa.
Dobrze: I'll see you on Monday.

HOTSPOT

W mowie potocznej, przy umawianiu się na spotkanie, można przy wymienianiu dnia opuścić przyimek **on** i powiedzieć np. **See you Monday!**
Nie należy jednak tego robić na teście, bo nie jest to forma w pełni poprawna!

I. Uzupełnij zdania odpowiednim przyimkiem.

1. The film starts ____ 19.30.
2. The school year in Australia starts _____ January and finishes ____ November.
3. Christmas is always _____ 25th December.
4. The shops open _____ 9 o'clock.
5. See you ______ Saturday!
6. The bank is ______ the hotel and the Polish Embassy.
7. ______ all pop singers, Pink is my favourite.
8. I met Jeff ____ Friday, 13th November.
9. Yesterday I saw a strange bird sitting ____ the tree.

II. Połącz połówki zdań. W niektórych zdaniach może być więcej niż jedna poprawna odpowiedź.

1. I have a math test
2. There's a big difference
3. Phone me
4. Susan looks great
5. I'll see you

A. between you and your brother.
B. in this photo.
C. on Wednesday.
D. at six o'clock.
E. in the afternoon.

III. Przetłumacz na język angielski.

1. Mam urodziny w środę.
2. Wpadnij do mnie o siódmej.
3. Nowy semestr zaczyna się w lutym.
4. Parking jest pomiędzy szkołą a basenem.
5. Ich pałac stał wśród wysokich drzew.

IV. A teraz popraw błędy!

1. I saw Matthew in Saturday.
2. My first lesson starts on 8 o'clock.
3. Ralph's room is among the bathroom and the kitchen.
4. We don't go to school in 1st January.
5. Between all school subjects, I like English the best.

KLUCZ

I. 1. at 2. in, in 3. on 4. at 5. on 6. between 7. among 8. on 9. in **II.** 1C, E 2A, 3C, D, E 4B, 5C, D, E **III.** 1. My birthday is on Wednesday. 2. Come round at seven. 3. The new term starts in February. 4. The car park is between the school and the swimming pool. 5. Their palace stood among tall trees. **IV.** 1. I saw Matthew on Saturday. 2. My first lessom starts at 8 o'clock. 3. Ralph's room is between the bathroom and the kitchen. 4. We don't go to school on 1st of January. 6. Among all school subjects, I like English (the) best.

UNIT 9 I am/you are BE PRESENT SIMPLE

I am a student. Jestem uczniem/studentem.
We are the champions. Jesteśmy mistrzami (zwycięzcami).
Are they Polish? Czy oni są Polakami?
She is not at home. Nie ma jej w domu.

Czasownik **be** (być) przybiera różne formy w zależności od osoby.
Pełny bezokolicznik ma formę **to be.**

TWIERDZENIA		PYTANIA	PRZECZENIA	
I am	I'm	am I?	I am not	I'm not
you are	you're	are you?	you are not	you're not / you aren't
he is	he's	is he?	he is not	he's not / he isn't
she is	she's	is she?	she is not	she's not / she isn't
it is	it's	is it?	it is not	it's not / it isn't
we are	we're	are we?	we are not	we're not / we aren't
they are	they're	are they?	they are not	they're not / they aren't

→ Pełnych form **I am, you are not** itp. używasz tylko w tekstach formalnych, takich jak np. listy motywacyjne.

→ Form skróconych np. **you're not, she's not** używasz tylko, gdy chcesz położyć nacisk na **not**. W pozostałych wypadkach używasz form o skróconej pisowni i wymowie, np. **They aren't British.** Na pytania wymagające odpowiedzi **Yes/No** np. **Are you happy?** odpowiadasz **Yes, I am** lub **No, I'm not.** Nie powtarzasz reszty zdania, jednak sama odpowiedź **Yes** lub **No** to za mało.

→ Mówiąc o pogodzie lub podając datę czy godzinę używasz wyrażenia **It's**, np. **It's sunny today, it's Monday, it's ten o'clock.**

TYPOWE BŁĘDY UWAŻAJ!

Źle: ~~Shes'nt~~ American.
PODPOWIEDŹ: Apostrof skraca tylko partykułę **not** na **n't.**
Dobrze: She isn't American.

Źle: ~~Do they be~~ at home now? No, they ~~don't be~~ at home.
PODPOWIEDŹ: Pytania z czasownikiem **be** tworzymy przez inwersję, czyli przestawienie szyku wyrazów. Przeczenia tworzymy dodając partykułę **not** bezpośrednio po **am, is, are.** Nie używaj operatora **do/does** z czasownikiem **be**
Dobrze: Are they at home? No, they aren't.

YOUR TURN NOW! TERAZ KOLEJ NA CIEBIE!

I. Uporządkuj rozsypane wyrazy tak, aby powstały pytania do podanych odpowiedzi.

1. *Poland/you/from/are/?* ______________________
   Yes, I am.
2. *Robert/name/your/is/?* ______________________
   No, it isn't.
3. *Tuesday/is/today/it/?* ______________________
   Yes, it is.
4. *where/your/is/brother/?* ______________________
   He is at school.
5. *time/it/what/is/?* ______________________
   It's twelve o'clock.
6. *Sunday/it/today/is?* ______________________
   No, it's Monday.

II. Z podanych wyrazów ułóż zdania twierdzące. Wstaw czasownik **be** w odpowiedniej formie.

WZÓR: *very/your/dog/noisy/be* Your dog is very noisy.

1. *cupboard/the/in/shoes/your/be/* ______________________
2. *cloudy/today/it/be/* ______________________
3. *I/hungry/cold/and/be/* ______________________
4. *mother/doctor/a/be/my/* ______________________
5. *Russia/country/big/very/be/a/* ______________________
6. *American/cheerful/people/very/be* ______________________

III. Dopasuj pytania do odpowiedzi.

1. Where are your parents?
2. Are you bored?
3. Is your name Beckham?
4. What time is it?
5. Are you from Australia?
6. Am I clever?

A. No, I'm not. I'm from Poland.
B. No, it isn't. My name is Jankowski.
C. Of course not. This is very interesting.
D. They are at home.
E. Of course you are.
F. It's ten past eleven.

IV. A teraz popraw błędy!

1. We isn't at school, we is at home.
2. Do you be German?
3. Shes'nt a student, she's a teacher.

KLUCZ

I. 1. Are you from Poland? 2. Is your name Robert? 3. Is it Tuesday today? 4. Where is your brother? 5. What time is it? 6. Is it Sunday today? **II.** 1. Your shoes are in the cupboard. 2. It is cloudy today. 3. I am cold and I am hungry./I am hungry and I am cold. 4. My mother is a doctor. 5. Russia is a very big country. 6. American people are very cheerful. **III.** 1.D 2.C 3.B 4.F 5.A 6.E **IV.** 1. We are not (aren't) at school, we are (we're) at home. 2. Are you German? 3. She isn't a student, she is (she's) a teacher. / She's not a student, she is (she's) a teacher.

THERE IS/THERE ARE

Is there air-conditioning in Bob's flat? Czy w mieszkaniu Boba jest klimatyzacja?
In my bedroom there aren't any pot plants. W mojej sypialni nie ma roślin doniczkowych.
There is no single clean plate in the house! W domu nie ma ani jednego czystego talerza!
There is a huge dining table in my grandmother's dining room. U mojej babci w jadalni jest ogromny stół.

KIEDY STOSUJESZ THERE IS/THERE ARE?

→ Gdy mówisz o kimś lub o czymś co jest/znajduje się (lub czego nie ma!) w danym miejscu. W orzeczeniu stosujesz liczbę pojedynczą lub mnogą w zależności od ilości osób/przedmiotów, o których mówisz.

→ **There is/there are** często występuje w formie skróconej **there's/there're**.

→ **There is/there are** nie ma dosłownego odpowiednika w języku polskim.

TYPOWE BŁĘDY UWAŻAJ!

W naszej klasie są cztery okna.

Źle: ~~In our classrooom are four windows.~~

PODPOWIEDŹ: Mówiąc o rzeczach znajdujących się w danym miejscu użyj **there is/there are**.

Dobrze: There are four windows in our classroom.
lub In our classroom there are four windows.

W moim pokoju jest wiele książek.

Źle: ~~In my room is a lot of books.~~

PODPOWIEDŹ: Takie zdanie to kalka z języka polskiego. Nie stosuj polskiego szyku wyrazów w zdaniu ani liczby pojedynczej w orzeczeniu, gdy mowa o wielu rzeczach.

Dobrze: There are a lot of books in my room.
lub In my room there are a lot of books.

Czy w twojej szkole jest pracownia komputerowa?

Źle: ~~Is in your school a computer lab?~~

PODPOWIEDŹ: Pamiętaj, że w pytaniu nie wolno pominąć **there**, a okolicznik miejsca jest przeważnie na końcu zdania.

Dobrze: Is there a computer lab in your school?

Źle: There is ~~my~~ book on the table./There is ~~the~~ book on my desk.

PODPOWIEDŹ: Po wyrażeniu **there is** nie używaj określnika dzierżawczego ani przedimka określonego **the**.

Dobrze: There is a book on the table.

YOUR TURN NOW! TERAZ KOLEJ NA CIEBIE!

I. Uzupełnij opis pokoju Susan wyrazami z ramki. Dla ułatwienia masz podane pierwsze litery wyrazów.

bed lamp wardrobe plants chairs desk carpet armchairs computer

my room

My room is not very big, but it's quite nice. It has a big window, so it's very sunny. Opposite the window there is a (1) **w**__________. There are also a (2) **b**________, a (3) **d**_________ and two (4) **a**____________ in my room, but there are no (5) **c**________.
On the desk there is a (6) **c**_________.
Next to it there is a (7) **l**__________.
On the window sill there are many pot (8) **p**______________. A portable radio and a CD player stand on the shelf over my bed. On the floor there is a thick (9) **c**___________.
I like my room a lot.

II. Przetłumacz na język angielski.

1. Czy w twoim mieście jest basen?
2. Naprzeciwko kina jest park.
3. W mojej klasie nie ma plakatów na ścianach.
4. W lodówce nie ma mleka.

III. A teraz popraw błędy! (Uważaj! Jedno zdanie jest poprawne!)

1. There hasn't many good teachers in my school.
2. There isn't much sugar in the house.
3. In my town is no cable television.
4. There is the pencil on the table.
5. Is there two cats in the garden?

KLUCZ **I.** 1. wardrobe 2. bed 3. desk 4. armchairs 5. chairs 6. computer 7. lamp 8. plants 9. carpet **II.** 1. Is there a swimming pool in your town? 2. Opposite the cinema there is a park./There is a park opposite the cinema. 3. There are no posters on the walls in my classroom./In my classroom there are no posters on the walls./There aren't any posters on the walls in my classroom./In my classroom there aren't any posters on the walls. 4. There is no milk in the fridge./ There isn't any milk in the fridge. **III.** 1. There aren't many good teachers in my school. 2. OK 3. In my town there is no cable television./There is no cable television in my town. 4. There is a pencil on the table. 5. Are there two cats in the garden?

UNIT 11 I have/I have got PRESENT SIMPLE

I have a dog. Mam psa.
Do you have a cat? Czy masz kota?
I don't have a pet. Nie mam zwierzątka.
Susan has got an interesting job. Susan ma ciekawą pracę.
Have you got a sister? Czy masz siostrę?
I haven't got a balcony. Nie mam balkonu.

→ Czasowników **have/have got** używasz, gdy chcesz powiedzieć, że ktoś/coś ma (posiada) jakąś osobę, rzecz lub cechę. Gdy piszesz tekst oficjalny, zastosuj czasownik **have.** Czasownik **have got** jest używany w języku potocznym, najczęściej w formie skróconej (np. **I've got**)

→ Czasownik **have/have got** zmienia swoją formę w zależności od osoby. Zwróć uwagę, że inaczej formułuje się pytania i przeczenia dla **have**, a inaczej dla **have got**. Gdy używasz czasownika **have**, w pytaniach i przeczeniach stosujesz operator **do/does**. Jeśli używasz **have got**, w pytaniach stosujesz inwersję, a w przeczeniach po prostu dodajesz **not** bezpośrednio po **have/has**.

TWIERDZENIA	PYTANIA	PRZECZENIA
I/you/we/they **have**	**Do** I/you/we/they **have**?	I/you/we/they **do not have (don't have)**
He/she/it **has**	**Does** he/she/it **have**?	He/she/it **does not have (doesn't have)**
I/you/we/they **have got ('ve got)**	**Have** I/you/we/they **got**?	I/you/we/they **have not got (haven't got)**
He/she/it **has got ('s got)**	**Has** he/she/it **got**?	He/she/it **has not got (hasn't got)**

TYPOWE BŁĘDY **UWAŻAJ!**

Źle: I ~~don't have~~ got a car.
~~Does he have got~~ a motorbike?
PODPOWIEDŹ: Operatora **do/does** nie można używać z czasownikiem **have got**.
Dobrze: I don't have a car./ I haven't got a car.
Does he have a motorbike?/Has he got a motorbike?

Źle: He ~~dosen't~~ have a motorbike.
PODPOWIEDŹ: Zwróć uwagę na pisownię formy skróconej **does not = doesn't**.
Skracasz tylko partykułę **not**.
Dobrze: He doesn't have a motorbike.

Źle: ~~Have you~~ a cigarette?
PODPOWIEDŹ: Tworzenie pytań przez inwersję czasownika **have** (bez **got**) jest formą przestarzałą.
Dobrze: Have you got a cigarette?

Proverb:
Every country has its customs.

Przysłowie:
Co kraj to obyczaj.

YOUR TURN NOW! TERAZ KOLEJ NA CIEBIE!

I. Uzupełnij zdania odpowiednią formą czasownika **have**. W niektórych zdaniach, w zależności od sytuacji, możliwa jest więcej niż jedna dobra odpowiedź.

1. Mary ___________ got a lot of homework.
2. She doesn't ___________ time to go out.
3. ___________ she got a cat?
4. Mrs Thomson ___________ got a big house.
5. My parents don't ___________ a computer.

II. Ułóż pytania.

WZÓR (*you/an umbrella?*) Have you got an umbrella?

1. (*your brother/a bike?*) ___________
2. (*Jim/a golf club?*) ___________
3. (*Jeff and Jenny/a garden*) ___________
4. (*you/any English books?*) ___________
5. (*they/three children?*) ___________
6. (*I/my keys?*) ___________

III. Napisz, co ma, a czego nie ma Anna, oraz co mają, a czego nie mają państwo Brown.

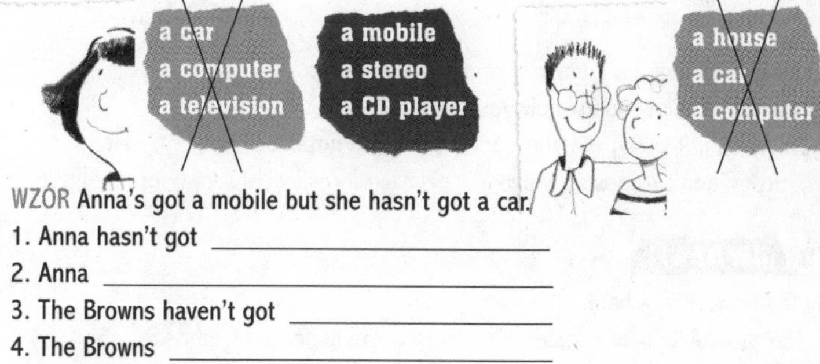

WZÓR Anna's got a mobile but she hasn't got a car.

1. Anna hasn't got ___________
2. Anna ___________
3. The Browns haven't got ___________
4. The Browns ___________
5. The Browns ___________

V. A teraz popraw zdania!

1. I don't have got a garden.
2. My brother don't have a car.
3. Do they have got a dog?
4. Have you my keys?

KLUCZ **I.** 1. has/hasn't 2. have 3. Has 4. has/hasn't 5. have **II.** 1. Has your brother got a bike? 2. Has Jim got a golf club? 3. Have Jeff and Jenny got a garden? 4. Have you got any English books? 5. Have they got three children? 6. Have I got my keys? **III.** 1. Anna hasn't got a television but she's got a stereo. 2. Anna hasn't got a computer but she's got a CD player. 3. The Browns haven't got a house but they've got a child. 4. The Browns haven't got a computer but they've got a mobile. 5. The Browns haven't got a car but they've got two bikes. **IV.** I haven't got a garden./I don't have a garden. 2. My brother doesn't have a car. 3. Do they have a dog? /Have they got a dog? 4. Have you got my keys?/Do you have my keys?

UNIT 12 I do/I work PRESENT SIMPLE

We play tennis on Saturdays. Grywamy w tenisa w soboty.
Sheila doesn't know John. Sheila nie zna Johna.
Do they work in a bank? Czy oni pracują w banku?

KIEDY STOSUJESZ PRESENT SIMPLE?

→ Do wyrażania czynności i stanów powtarzających się, rutynowych, zwyczajowych, stałych.
Forma czasownika jest taka sama dla wszystkich osób, z wyjątkiem trzeciej osoby liczby pojedynczej.

JAK TWORZYSZ TRZECIĄ OSOBĘ LICZBY POJEDYNCZEJ?

3 sposoby w zależności od końcówki czasownika.

-ch, -s, -sh, -o → **-es**
to watch – he watches
to do – he does

-y po spółgłosce -i → **-es**
to study – he studies
to tidy – he tidies

-e → **-s**
to write – he writes
to smile – he smiles

Pytania i przeczenia tworzymy przy pomocy operatora **do/does.**
Do you know John Brown? Does John know you?
He doesn't know (does not know) me and I don't know (do not know) him.
Stosuj formy skrócone don't / doesn't; jedynie w pismach formalnych używaj form pełnych.

TYPOWE BŁĘDY UWAŻAJ!

Źle: My father ~~work~~ in a bank.
PODPOWIEDŹ: Nie zapominaj o końcówce **–s** w trzeciej osobie liczby pojedynczej.
Dobrze: My father works in a bank.

Źle: ~~Know you~~ John Brown? ~~I not know~~ John Brown.
PODPOWIEDŹ: Przy tworzeniu pytań i przeczeń nie pomijaj operatora **do/does**.
Dobrze: Do you know John Brown? I don't know John Brown.

Źle: ~~I'm~~ work on a farm.
PODPOWIEDŹ: Nie stosuj **I'm** zamiast **I**.
I'm jest skróconą formą **I am**, czyli **ja jestem**.
Dobrze: I work on a farm.

Źle: Grażyna ~~dosen't~~ speak English.
PODPOWIEDŹ: Apostrof skraca tylko partykułę **not**. **Doesn't** jest skróconą formą **does not**.
Dobrze: Grażyna doesn't speak English.

YOUR TURN NOW! TERAZ KOLEJ NA CIEBIE!

I. Wybierz odpowiednią formę czasownika.

1. John and his sister ____________ tennis.
   a) play b) playing c) plays
2. A lot of teenagers ____________ dogs or cats.
   a) has b) to have c) have
3. A lot of pupils ____________ their homework every day.
   a) do b) doing c) does
4. Not many women ____________ in the police.
   a) work b) not work c) works
5. My father never ____________ football matches.
   a) doesn't watch b) watches c) watch

II. Uzupełnij zdania właściwą formą czasownika.

1. We ____________ (not/speak) French.
2. My brother and I never ____________ (get up) before seven.
3. A lot of students ____________ (play) computer games.
4. ____________ (you/study) English every day?
5. He ____________ (visit) his grandmother twice a year.

III. Przetłumacz na język angielski.

1. Grywam w szachy.
2. Mieszkam w Polsce.
3. Wielu ludzi ma samochody.
4. Niewielu Polaków zna chiński.
5. Nigdy nie pijam mleka.

IV. A teraz popraw błędy!

1. Many people is fat.
2. I never don't go to school on Sunday.
3. My brother and my sister is at home.
4. Not many people plays tennis.
5. Susan watchs television every day.

KLUCZ

I. 1a 2c 3a 4a 5b **II.** 1. don't speak 2. get up 3. play 4. Do you study 5. visits **III.** 1. I play chess. 2. I live in Poland. 3. A lot of people have cars. 4. Not many Poles know Chinese. 5. I never drink milk. **IV.** 1. A lot of people are fat. 2. I never go to school on Sunday. 3. My brother and my sister are at home. 4. Not many people play tennis. 5. Susan watches television every day.

UNIT 13 I am doing/I am working PRESENT CONTINUOUS

I am reading a book now. Czytam teraz książkę.
Is she playing a computer game at the moment? Czy ona teraz gra w grę komputerową?
They aren't watching TV now. Oni teraz nie oglądają telewizji.

KIEDY STOSUJESZ PRESENT CONTINUOUS?

→ Do wyrażania czynności odbywającej się w trakcie mówienia o niej. Jest to czynność jeszcze niezakończona.

→ Niektóre czasowniki nie występują w czasie **present continuous**, np. **agree, believe, hate, know, like, love, understand, want.**

JAK TWORZYSZ FORMY W CZASIE PRESENT CONTINUOUS?

1. Twierdzenia
Podmiot + am/are/is + czasownik + -ing

2. Pytania
Am/are/is + podmiot + czasownik + -ing

3. Przeczenia
Podmiot + am/are/is + not + czasownik + -ing

→ W czasach **continuous** czasownik **be** w odpowiedniej formie pełni funkcję pomocniczą i jest niezbędny. Czasownik główny przybiera formę **-ing (present participle)**. Jeśli czasownik kończy się na **-e**, to tworząc formę **-ing** opuszczasz **-e,** np. to **smile – she's smiling**. Jeśli czasownik kończy się na jedną spółgłoskę, to spółgłoskę tę podwajasz, np. **to sit – I'm sitting**.

→ Zazwyczaj stosujesz formy skrócone, np. **I'm writing, you're drawing, she isn't listening.**

TYPOWE BŁĘDY **UWAŻAJ!**

Źle: ~~I doing~~ my homework now.
PODPOWIEDŹ: Nie zapominaj o użyciu odpowiedniej formy czasownika **be (być)**.
Dobrze: I am doing my homework now./I'm doing my homework now

---

Mieszkam w Polsce. (stan trwały)
Źle: ~~I'm living~~ in Poland.
PODPOWIEDŹ: Nie używaj **present continuous** do wyrażania czynności/stanów stałych, powtarzających się. Użycie czasu **present continuous** zmienia znaczenie zdania. **I'm living in Poland** oznacza, że jestem w Polsce chwilowo, a na stałe mieszkam w innym kraju.
Dobrze: I live in Poland.

Źle: ~~writeing, studing, plaing~~
PODPOWIEDŹ: Uważaj na pisownię czasownika z końcówką **-ing**.
Dobrze: writing, studying, playing

YOUR TURN NOW! TERAZ KOLEJ NA CIEBIE!

I. Wybierz odpowiednią formę czasownika.

1. Sam ____________ a book at the moment.
   a) is reading b) are reading c) reads
2. Jim and Ann ____________ their homework now.
   a) is doing b) are doing c) does
3. Many people ____________ for the bus at the moment.
   a) is waiting b) are waiting c) waits
4. My brother and I ____________ a match on TV at the moment.
   a) is watching b) am watching c) are watching
5. My friend ____________ a computer game at the moment.
   a) is playing b) are playing c) plays

II. Uzupełnij tekst właściwą formą czasownika.

1. Ben: What _________ (you/do) now?
   Kate: Can't you see? (I/talk) _________ on the phone.
2. Kate: Are you using the computer at the moment?
   Ben: No, I'm not. (I/make)_________ a sandwich for you.
3. Ben: (Joan/tidy) _________ her room?
   Kate: No, I think (she/have) _________ breakfast.
4. Ben: Somebody _________ (knock) at the door.
   Kate: OK., I _________ (come).

III. Przetłumacz na język angielski.

1. Myślę o wakacjach.
2. Agnes pisze list do babci.
3. Jestem teraz zajęta, odrabiam lekcje.
4. Popatrz, Tom jedzie na rowerze!
5. Gotuję kalafior, otwórz okno, proszę!

IV. A teraz popraw błędy!

1. Mary cooking lunch at the moment.
2. Simon is smileing.
3. My father is liking football.
4. We live in Brighton at the moment.
5. I'm loving you.

KLUCZ

I. 1a 2b 3b 4c 5a **II.** 1. What are you doing now? I'm talking on the phone. 2. I'm making a sandwich for you. 3. Is Joan tidying her room? No, I think she's having breakfast. 4. Somebody is knocking at the door. OK., I'm coming. **III.** 1. I'm thinking about holidays. 2. Agnes is writing a letter to her granny. 3. I'm busy now, I'm doing my homework. 4. Look, Tom is riding his bike. 5. I'm cooking cauliflower, open the window please. **IV.** Mary is cooking lunch at the moment. 2. Simon is smiling. 3. My father likes football. 4. I'm living in Brighton at the moment. 5. I love you.

UNIT 14 now/always/often TIME EXPRESSIONS PRESENT SIMPLE & PRESENT CONTINUOUS

W języku angielskim określników czasu nie można dobierać dowolnie.
Są określniki typowe dla czasu **present simple**, inne natomiast występują z **present continuous**.

→ **Present simple** występuje z następującymi określnikami czasu:
always, usually, often, sometimes, seldom, never

She never drinks hot milk. Ona nigdy nie pije gorącego mleka.
I always listen to music in the evening. Zawsze wieczorem słucham muzyki.

→ **Present continuous** występuje z **now, at the moment, at present.**

Mary is drinking juice at the moment. Mary pije właśnie sok.
We're doing our homework now. Odrabiamy teraz lekcje (pracę domową).

Always może występować w połączeniu z **present continuous**, ale wtedy wyrażamy naszą dezaprobatę wobec faktu przedstawionego w zdaniu. Jeśli powiesz **She's always leaving her dirty shoes in the middle of the room** (Ona zawsze zostawia swoje brudne buty na środku pokoju) to znaczy to, że ten jej zwyczaj uważasz za denerwujący.

TYPOWE BŁĘDY **UWAŻAJ!**

Źle: ~~I'm sometimes going~~ to bed after midnight.
PODPOWIEDŹ: Nie stosuj określnika czasu typowego dla **present simple** w połączeniu z **present continuous.**
Dobrze: I sometimes go to bed after midnight.

Źle: I ~~read~~ a book now.
PODPOWIEDŹ: Nie stosuj określnika czasu typowego dla **present continuous** w połączeniu **z present simple**.
Dobrze: I'm reading a book now.

Źle: He ~~takes~~ a shower ~~usually~~ before breakfast.
PODPOWIEDŹ: Jeśli orzeczenie jest w **present simple**, to określnik czasu występuje między podmiotem a orzeczeniem.
Dobrze: He usually takes a shower before breakfast.

YOUR TURN NOW! TERAZ KOLEJ NA CIEBIE!

I. Wybierz właściwą formę czasownika

1. I often ______________ to the disco with my friends.
   a) go b) am going
2. Rebecca ______________ on the phone at the moment.
   a) talks b) is talking
3. Jeff never ______________ his homework on time.
   a) does b) is doing
4. Jenny ______________ her bike now.
   a) rides b) is riding
5. Bill seldom ______________ his grandparents.
   a) visits b) is visiting

II. Wstaw czasownik w odpowiedniej formie.

1. Ralph, what (you/do) ______________ now?
2. Where (you/stay) ______________ now while they are painting your flat?
3. We (seldom/go) ______________ abroad for holidays.
4. My parents (always/nag) ______________, I'm fed up with it.
5. He is a liar. (I/never/believe) ______________ him.

III. Przetłumacz na język angielski.

1. Czasami śpię do południa.
2. Ty zawsze gubisz klucze!
3. Tu zawsze pada latem.
4. Co teraz czytasz?
5. Często wysyłam SMS-y do kolegów.

IV. A teraz popraw błędy! Uważaj, jedno zdanie jest poprawne.

1. Look! The dog chases a cat!
2. The Earth goes round the Sun.
3. Steve is often shopping at the supermarket.
4. I'm never ironing my clothes.
5. Sorry, I'm not understanding you!

KLUCZ

I. 1a 2b 3a 4b 5a **II.** 1. Ralph, what are you doing now? 2. Where are you staying now while they are painting your flat? 3. We seldom go abroad for holidays. 4. My parents are always nagging. 5. I never believe him. **III.** I sometimes sleep until/till noon. 2. You are always losing your keys! 3. It always rains here in the summer. 4. What are you reading now? 5. I often send text messages to my friends. **IV.** 1. The dog is chasing a cat. 2. OK. 3. Steve often shops at the supermarket. 4. I never iron my clothes. 5. Sorry, I don't understand you!

UNIT 15 I was/they were PAST SIMPLE

I was at the cinema yesterday. Wczoraj byłam w kinie.
It was hot and sunny last Sunday. W ostatnią niedzielę było gorąco i słonecznie.
You were late again! Znowu się spóźniłeś/spóźniliście!
Were they at home in the afternoon? Czy oni byli w domu po południu?
We weren't very hungry. Nie byliśmy bardzo głodni.

JAK TWORZYSZ FORMY CZASOWNIKA TO BE W CZASIE PAST SIMPLE?

TWIERDZENIA		PYTANIA		PRZECZENIA	
I He She It	**was**	**Was**	I? he? she? it?	I He She It	**was not (wasn't)**
We You They	**were**	**Were**	we? you? they?	We You They	**were not (weren't)**

→ Stosuj formy skrócone **wasn't** i **weren't**; jedynie w pismach oficjalnych używaj form pełnych.

TYPOWE BŁĘDY **UWAŻAJ!**

Wczoraj nie byłeś/nie byliście w szkole.

Źle: You ~~wasn't~~ at school yesterday.

PODPOWIEDŹ: Forma **was/wasn't** odnosi się tylko do pierwszej i trzeciej osoby liczby pojedynczej.

Dobrze: You weren't at school yesterday.

Źle: ~~Did you be~~ tired? They ~~didn't be~~ late.

PODPOWIEDŹ: Nie używaj operatora **did** w połączeniu z czasownikiem **be**. Czasownik **be** tworzy pytania przez inwersję, czyli przestawienie orzeczenia przed podmiot. W przeczeniach dodajesz **not** bezpośrednio po **was/were**.

Dobrze: Were you tired? They weren't late.

How was your holiday in Holland?
It was fantastic in Poland.
Awful.
It was rainy and cold.

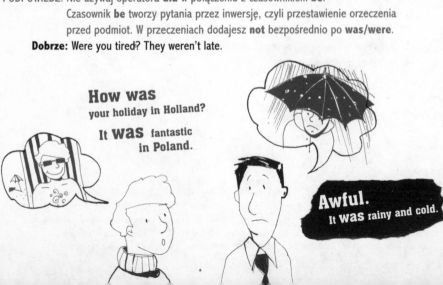

YOUR TURN NOW! TERAZ KOLEJ NA CIEBIE!

I. Uzupełnij zdania odpowiednią formą czasownika **be** w czasie **past simple**.

1. I __________ at school yesterday because I was sick.
2. We __________ very tired last Monday.
3. Susan and Ted __________ at home in the evening. They went to the cinema.
4. Bob __________ so happy that he invited some friends for a party.
5. I __________ in Cardiff last month, I was in Edinburgh.

II. Z rozsypanych wyrazów ułóż wg wzoru pytania do podanych odpowiedzi. Użyj czasownika **be** w odpowiedniej formie.

WZÓR *you/where/at two o'clock?*

Question: Where were you at two o'clock?

Answer: I was in the park with my dog.

1. what time/the meeting/yesterday?
   Q: ________________________________?
   A: At nine.
2. you/at home/in the morning?
   Q: ________________________________?
   A: No, I wasn't. I was at work.
3. the film/interesting?
   Q: ________________________________?
   A: No, it wasn't. Actually, it was quite boring.
4. Jack/at school/last week?
   Q: ________________________________?
   A: Yes, he was.
5. why/Chris/in hospital/last month?
   Q: ________________________________?
   A: Because he had an operation.

III. A teraz popraw błędy!

1. I didn't be in London, I was in Brighton.
2. Did you be at home all day?
3. They wasn't hungry.
4. I weren't busy, I were asleep.

KLUCZ

I. 1. wasn't 2. were 3. weren't 4. was 5. wasn't **II.** 1. What time was the meeting yesterday? 2. Were you at home in the morning? 3. Was the film interesting? 4. Was Jack at school last week? 5. Why was Chris in hospital last month? **III.** 1. I wasn't in London, I was in Brighton. 2. Were you at home all day? 3. They weren't hungry. 4. I wasn't busy, I was asleep.

UNIT 16 I had/I didn't have PAST SIMPLE

I had a dog when I was a child. Miałem psa gdy byłem dzieckiem.
Jenny didn't have time to cook lunch yesterday. Jenny nie miała wczoraj czasu ugotować obiadu.
Did you have a chance to speak to the manager? Czy miałeś okazję porozmawiać z szefem?

Czasownik **have** ma w czasie **past simple** jedną formę dla wszystkich osób: **had**.
Pytania i przeczenia tworzymy przy pomocy operatora **did**.

→ Forma **have got** występuje tylko w czasie **present simple.** W **past simple**, w twierdzeniach przybiera formę **had** (bez **got**), a w pytaniach i przeczeniach wymaga użycia operatora **did**.

TYPOWE BŁĘDY **UWAŻAJ!**

Źle: I ~~had got~~ a really big lunch yesterday.
PODPOWIEDŹ: Konstrukcja **have got** nie ma form czasu przeszłego.
Dobrze: I had a really big lunch yesterday.

Źle: ~~Had you~~ a tricycle when you were a child?
PODPOWIEDŹ: Czasownik **have** nie tworzy pytań przez inwersję w czasie **past simple**. Musisz użyć operatora **did** oraz **have**.
Dobrze: Did you have a tricycle when you were a child?

Źle: Sorry, but I ~~hadn't got~~ time to do my homework.
PODPOWIEDŹ: Forma **hadn't** występuje tylko jako czasownik pomocniczy w czasie **past perfect**. Przeczenia w czasie przeszłym od **have/have got** tworzymy przy pomocy operatora **did + not (didn't)** oraz **have**.
Dobrze: Sorry, but I didn't have time to do my homework.

I had a tiny bedroom in my old flat, but in my new flat I have much more space.

YOUR TURN NOW! TERAZ KOLEJ NA CIEBIE!

I. Napisz wg wzoru krótkie odpowiedzi do podanych pytań.

WZÓR Did you have time to visit the National Museum on Sunday? No, I didn't.

1. Did she have lunch yesterday? Yes, ______________.
2. Have you got a dictionary? Yes, ______________.
3. Do you have a computer? No, ______________.
4. Did Jack have many friends when he lived in London? Yes, ______________.
5. Have we got enough eggs to make an omelette? No, ______________.

II. Ułóż wg wzoru pytania do podanych odpowiedzi, dodając **have/have got** w odpowiedniej formie i czasie.

WZÓR *you/a good time at Mary's yesterday?*
Question: Did you have a good time at Mary's yesterday?
Answer: Oh, yes, I did. We had a great time.

1. you/any matches?
Q: ______________________________
A: Sorry, I haven't.
2. he/time to do the shopping yesterday?
Q: ______________________________
A: No, he didn't.
3. your parents/a car?
Q: ______________________________
A: No, they haven't.
4. you/many toys when you were a child?
Q: ______________________________
A: Yes, I did.
5. your daughter/piano lessons last year?
Q: ______________________________
A: No, she didn't. She was too busy.

III. A teraz popraw błędy!

1. I hadn't got a bike last year.
2. Had you time to finish this exercise yesterday?
3. I hadn't an English dictionary when I was in primary school.
4. Had you got a passport when you were 10 years old?

KLUCZ

I. 1. Yes, she did. 2. Yes, I have. 3. No, I don't. 4. Yes, he did. 5. No, we haven't. **II.** 1. Have you got any matches? 2. Did he have time to do the shopping yesterday? 3. Have your parents got a car? 4. Did you have many toys when you were a child? 5. Did your daughter have piano lessons last year? **III.** 1. I didn't have a bike last year. 2. Did you have time to finish this exercise yesterday? 3. I didn't have an English dictionary when I was in primary school. 4. Did you have a passport when you were 10 years old?

UNIT 17 I did/I worked PAST SIMPLE

I watched TV yesterday. Wczoraj oglądałam telewizję.
Did you go to school on Thursday? Czy poszedłeś w czwartek do szkoły?
They didn't do their math homework. Oni nie odrobili zadania domowego z matematyki.

KIEDY STOSUJESZ PAST SIMPLE?

Do wyrażania czynności już zakończonych, które działy się w określonym czasie w przeszłości.

JAK TWORZYSZ FORMY CZASOWNIKÓW REGULARNYCH W PAST SIMPLE?

Czasowniki regularne przybierają formę identyczną dla wszystkich osób.

1. Do większości czasowników regularnych dodajesz końcówkę **-ed** lub **-d** w formie podstawowej.
   work – worked
   smile – smiled
2. Jeśli czasownik kończy się na jedną spółgłoskę po jednej samogłosce, podwajasz spółgłoskę i dodajesz **-ed**.
   beg – begged
   snap – snapped
3. Jeśli czasownik kończy się na –**y** po spółgłosce, wymieniasz **-y** na **-i** oraz dodajesz **-ed**.
   study – studied
   tidy – tidied

→ Czasowniki nieregularne (lista na str 000) tworzą formy **past simple** odrębnie.
Form czasowników nieregularnych trzeba się nauczyć na pamięć!

→ Pytania i przeczenia tworzymy przy pomocy operatora **did** (dla wszystkich osób). W zdaniach z operatorem czasownik właściwy występuje w swojej podstawowej formie (tj. w bezokoliczniku bez **to**), np. **Did they finish their project? They didn't start it yet.**

TYPOWE BŁĘDY UWAŻAJ!

Źle: Did you ~~watched~~ TV yesterday?
PODPOWIEDŹ: W pytaniach używaj operatora **did** oraz czasownika w formie podstawowej.
Dobrze: Did you watch TV yesterday?

Źle: I didn't ~~watched~~ TV yesterday.
PODPOWIEDŹ: W przeczeniach obowiązuje ta sama zasada, co w pytaniach.
Dobrze: I didn't watch TV yesterday.

Źle I ~~did'nt~~ play computer games last week.
PODPOWIEDŹ: Apostrof skraca wyraz **not**, a więc **not=n't.**
Dobrze: I didn't play computer games last week.

YOUR TURN NOW! TERAZ KOLEJ NA CIEBIE!

I. Wstaw czasownik w formie **past simple**. Uważaj na czasowniki nieregularne!

WZÓR Tom ____________ (*break*) a vase last night. Tom broke a vase last night.
1. Mary ____________ (*go*) to school yesterday.
2. We ____________ (*buy*) a new computer in May.
3. My father ____________ (*lose*) his wallet on Friday.
4. Mr Brown ____________ (*study*) medicine when he was young.
5. Ann and Ben ____________ (*fly*) to New York in September.
6. Somebody ____________ (*steal*) my car two days ago.
7. Columbus ____________ (*sail*) west to discover the fastest route to India.

II. Ułóż pytania w czasie **past simple**.

WZÓR ____________ (*you/finish*) your homework? Did you finish your homework?
1. ____________ (*you/go*) to the cinema on Sunday?
2. ____________ (*he/pass*) his exam last week?
3. ____________ (*she/see*) him at school yesterday?
4. ____________ (*they/dance*) together?
5. ____________ (*you/walk*) the dog?

III. A teraz popraw błędy!

1. Did you bought milk yesterday?
2. Eve breaked her leg last month.
3. Mary didn't wanted to go to the disco.
4. We did'nt go to France last year.

CROSSWORD

IV. Rozwiąż krzyżówkę – wszędzie wstaw czasownik w czasie **past simple**.

Poziomo – **Across**
1. watch, 6. dream, 7. build,
10. eat, 11 keep, 12. read

Pionowo – **Down**
1. wear, 2. take, 3. have
4. dent, 5. write, 7. break
8. lose, 9. make

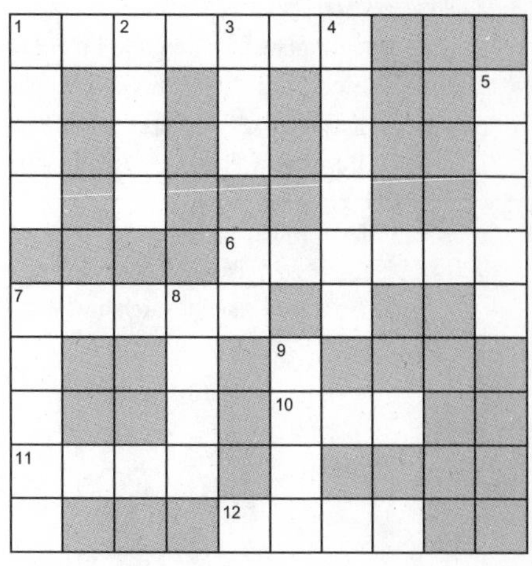

KLUCZ

I. 1. went 2. bought 3. lost 4. studied 5. flew 6. stole 7. sailed **II.** 1. Did you go to the cinema on Sunday? 2. Did he pass his exam last week? 3. Did she see him at school yesterday? 4. Did they dance together? 5. Did you walk the dog?/Did you take the dog for a walk? **III.** 1. Did you buy milk yesterday? 2. Eva broke her leg last month. 3. Mary didn't want to go to the disco. 4. We didn't go to France last year. **IV. Poziomo:** 1. watched 6. dreamt 7. built 10. ate 11. kept 12. read **Pionowo:** 1. wore 2. took 3. had 4. dented 5. wrote 7. broke 8. lost 9. made

UNIT 18 I was doing/I was working PAST CONTINUOUS

Yesterday at two o'clock I was walking my dog. Wczoraj o drugiej wyprowadzałam psa.
While I was peeling potatoes, Jim was making tea. Gdy ja obierałam ziemniaki, Jim robił herbatę.
While I was drinking tea, somebody knocked at the door. Gdy piłam herbatę, ktoś zapukał do drzwi.

KIEDY STOSUJESZ PAST CONTINUOUS?

Do wyrażania

1. czynności, które odbywały się w określonym momencie w przeszłości.
2. dwóch jednocześnie odbywających się czynności w przeszłości.
3. czynności, które stanowiły tło dla innych czynności lub wydarzeń.

→ Tworzenie formy **-ing** w czasie **past continuous** jest takie samo, jak w **present continuous.** Niektóre czasowniki nie występują w czasie **past continuous**, np. **agree, believe, hate, know, like, love, want**.

→ Czasowi **past continuous** często towarzyszy spójnik **while = podczas**, który sugeruje, że czynność trwała dość długo.

TYPOWE BŁĘDY **UWAŻAJ!**

Poszedłem wczoraj do sklepu.

Źle: I ~~was going~~ to the shop yesterday.

PODPOWIEDŹ: Do opisania pojedynczego wydarzenia z przeszłości używaj czasu **past simple**.

Dobrze: I went to the shop yesterday.

Kiedy spacerowałem po parku, zgubiłem komórkę.

Źle: ~~When I walked in the park, I was losing my mobile.~~

PODPOWIEDŹ: Stosuj **past continuous** gdy mówisz o czymś, co stanowiło tło dla innych czynności lub wydarzeń. Do opisania krótszego wydarzenia użyj czasu **past simple.**

Dobrze: While I was walking in the park, I lost my mobile.

Źle: I ~~was'nt~~ watching TV.

PODPOWIEDŹ: Skracasz tylko partykułę **not**; **wasn't = was not**.

Dobrze: I wasn't watching TV. = I was not watching TV.

While Little Red Riding Hood was walking in the forest, she met a big bad wolf.

YOUR TURN NOW! TERAZ KOLEJ NA CIEBIE!

I. Wybierz odpowiednią formę czasownika.

1. I broke my fingernail while I __________ my plants.
   a) *was watering* b) *were watering* b) *watered* d) *water*
2. While Susan __________ her bike, she bumped into a tree.
   a) *was riding* b) *were riding* c) *rode* d) *ride*
3. While Little Red Riding Hood was walking in the forest, she __________ a wolf.
   a) *was seeing* b) *were seeing* c) *saw* d) *see*
4. While Tom and Jerry __________ a mouse, they found a piece of sausage.
   a) *was chasing* b) *were chasing* c) *chased* d) *chase*
5. Yesterday at two o'clock I __________ lunch with my family.
   a) *was having* b) *were having* c) *had* d) *have*
6. While Mary was reading a newspaper, Jim and Tom __________ a match on TV.
   a) *watched* b) *watch* c) *was watching* d) *were watching*

II. Wstaw czasownik w czasie **past continuous**.

1. I __________ (*listen*) to music while I __________ (*do*) my English homework.
2. While the children __________ (*play*) ball in the garden, their parents __________ (*play*) bridge in the sitting room.
3. I __________ (*live*) in Japan in 2003.
4. What __________ (*you/do*) on Monday evening?
5. While I __________ (*bake a cake*), my husband __________ (*clean*) windows in the hall.
6. It was a nice day yesterday, the sun __________ (*shine*) and it was very warm.

III. Przetłumacz na język angielski.

1. Gdy ja surfowałam po internecie, Ralph oglądał mecz w TV.
2. James zgubił komórkę gdy jeździł na rolkach.
3. Rozładowała mi się bateria gdy wysyłałam SMS.
4. Oni pili piwo, podczas gdy my graliśmy w karty.

IV. A teraz popraw błędy! Uważaj, jedno zdanie jest poprawne.

1. Tim was wanting to buy a new computer but his father refused to pay for it.
2. You were'nt listening to me.
3. While I was doing my homework, the telephone rang.
4. Ben was finding 10 euros while he was walking in the park.

KLUCZ

I. 1.a 2.a 3.c 4.b 5.a 6.d **II.** 1 I was listening to music while I was doing my English homework. 2. While the children were playing ball in the garden, their parents were playing bridge in the sitting room. 3. I was living in Japan in 2003. 4. What were you doing on Monday evening? 5. While I was baking a cake, my husband was cleaning windows in the hall. 6. It was a nice day yesterday, the sun was shining and it was very warm. **III.** 1. While I was surfing the Internet, Ralph was watching a match on TV. 2. James lost his mobile when he was rollerblading. 3. The battery went flat while I was sending a text message. 4. They were drinking beer while we were playing cards. **IV.** Tim wanted to buy a computer but his father refused to pay for it. 2. You weren't listening to me. 3. OK 4. Ben found 10 euros while he was walking in the park.

UNIT 19 I have worked/I have done/I have been PRESENT PERFECT

I have cleaned my room. Posprzątałem mój pokój (i teraz jest czysto).
We have known him for two years. Znamy go od dwóch lat.
I haven't seen him since Christmas. Nie widziałem go od Bożego Narodzenia.

KIEDY STOSUJESZ PRESENT PERFECT?

Do wyrażania

1. czynności lub stanów, które miały miejsce w przeszłości, a ich skutki są widoczne teraz
2. czynności lub stanów, wyrażających doświadczenia życiowe osoby żyjącej
3. czynności lub stanów, które rozpoczęły się jakiś czas temu i trwają do tej pory (stosujesz wówczas przyimki **for** lub **since**)

→ Przyimek **for** wyraża przez jaki okres czasu trwa dana czynność lub stan, a przyimek **since** wyraża od jakiego momentu w przeszłości trwa dana czynność lub stan.

W języku polskim **present perfect** wyrażany jest w zależności od kontekstu przez czas teraźniejszy lub przeszły.

TYPOWE BŁĘDY UWAŻAJ!

Odwiedziłem Irlandię pięć razy (*ale być może znów tam kiedyś pojadę*).

Źle: ~~I visited~~ Ireland five times.

PODPOWIEDŹ: Gdy mówisz oczynnościach/stanach będących doświadczeniem życiowym osoby żyjącej, używaj **present perfect**

Dobrze: I have visited Ireland five times.

Źle: I ~~have broken~~ my leg three weeks ago.

PODPOWIEDŹ: Jeśli wiadomo, kiedy zdarzenie nastąpiło, zastosuj **past simple**.

Dobrze: I broke my leg three weeks ago.

Źle: Agatha Christie ~~has written~~ a lot of detective stories.

PODPOWIEDŹ: Gdy mówisz o wydarzeniach z przeszłości, dotyczących osób już nieżyjących, używaj **past simple**.

Dobrze: Agatha Christie wrote a lot of detective stories.

(Agatha Christie już nie żyje i nic więcej nie napisze.)

Źle: ~~I live~~ in this flat for two years.

PODPOWIEDŹ: W stosunku do czynności/stanów trwających do chwili obecnej używaj **present perfect**.

Dobrze: I have lived in this flat for two years.

Źle: We have lived here ~~since~~ three years.

PODPOWIEDŹ: Gdy mówisz, przez jaki okres czasu trwa dana czynność lub stan, używaj **for**.

Dobrze: We have lived here for three years.

YOUR TURN NOW! TERAZ KOLEJ NA CIEBIE!

I. Wstaw czasownik w formie **present perfect**.

She is cleaning her shoes.

1. She ____________ her shoes.

He is tidying his room.

2. He ____________ his room.

II. Uzupełnij zdania odpowiednim czasownikiem z ramki w formie **present perfect**.

do eat find take write

1. My dog ______________ my lunch!
2. Susan ______________ her homework.
3. I ______________ a letter.
4. My brother ______________ a wallet.
5. Tom ______________ my umbrella.

III. Uzupełnij zdania przyimkami **since**, **for**.

1. I have worked in this company __________ three years.
2. Helen has known Paul ___________ 2001.
3. We have lived in this flat __________ January 2002.
4. Mary hasn't been to the cinema __________ six months.

IV. Przetłumacz na język angielski.

1. Mam tego psa od ośmiu lat.
2. John nie widział Mary od dwóch miesiecy.
3. Bob przeczytał gazetę.
4. Matthew nie dzwonił do mnie od Bożego Narodzenia.

V. A teraz popraw błędy!

1. She knows Susan for two years.
2. They hasn't written to me since New Year.
3. I haven't seen uncle Matthew since two months.
4. My parents have teached me a lot of things.

KLUCZ

I 1. She has cleaned her shoes. 2. He has tidied his room. **II** 1. My dog has eaten my lunch! 2. Susan has done her homework. 3. I have written a letter. 4. My brother has found a wallet. 5. Tom has taken my umbrella. **III** 1. for 2. since 3. since 4. for **IV** 1. I've had this dog for eight years. 2. John hasn't seen Mary for two months. 3. Bob has read the newspaper. 4. Matthew hasn't phoned me since Christmas. **V** 1. She has known Susan for two years. 2. They haven't written to me since New Year. 3. I haven't seen uncle Matthew for two months. 4. My parents have taught me a lot of things.

UNIT 20 I did & I have done PAST SIMPLE & PRESENT PERFECT

→ **Past simple** łączy się z takimi wyrażeniami jak **ago, in 1998, last week,** gdy mówisz, kiedy coś się zdarzyło.

PAST SIMPLE **two years ago, in 2000, in March, last year, last Friday**

I went to England three years ago. Pojechałam do Anglii trzy lata temu.
I finished primary school in 1998. Ukończyłem szkołę podstawową w 1998.
I bought this book last week. Kupiłem tę książkę w zeszłym tygodniu.

→ **Present perfect** łączy się z **for, since, yet, already, just, ever, never,** gdy mówisz, jak długo coś trwa, albo że właśnie się zaczęło lub skończyło.

PRESENT PERFECT **for two months, since Monday, yet, already, just, ever, never**

I have known Mary for six months. Znam Mary od sześciu miesięcy.
John has known Mary since 2001. John zna Mary od 2001 r.
Have they finished their test yet? Czy już skończyli klasówkę?
She has already washed the dishes. Ona już umyła naczynia.
The film has just started. Film właśnie się rozpoczął.
Have you ever been to London? Czy byłaś kiedyś w Londynie?

TYPOWE BŁĘDY **UWAŻAJ!**

Źle: ~~I have been~~ to England two years ago.
PODPOWIEDŹ: Gdy podany jest czas (moment) wydarzenia, używaj **past simple**.
Dobrze: I was in England two years ago.

Źle: ~~I know Jim since 1995.~~
PODPOWIEDŹ: Gdy mówisz jak długo lub od jakiego momentu coś trwa, używaj **present perfect**.
Dobrze: I have known Jim since 1995.

Where's Bill?
He's gone to Greece. He was there last year too.

YOUR TURN NOW! TERAZ KOLEJ NA CIEBIE!

I. Wybierz odpowiednią formę czasownika.

1. Mary __________ her exams last week. a) *passed* b) *has passed*
2. My neighbours __________ all countries in Europe. a) *visited* b) *have visited*
3. Shakespeare __________ 'Hamlet' and many other plays. a) *wrote* b) *has written*
4. I __________ to London three times. a) *was* b) *have been*
5. My mother __________ her work yet. a) *didn't finish* b) *hasn't finished*

II. Wstaw czasownik w odpowiedniej formie.

1. I (*be*) __________ in Berlin two years ago.
2. We (*see*) __________ this film already.
3. Janek (*never/eat*) __________ Chinese food.
4. He (*not water*)__________ the plants today.
5. (*you/ever/ride*) __________ a horse?

III. Wybierz **for** lub **since**.

1. My father has worked in this shop ________ (*for/since*) ten years.
2. Julia has lived in Bishopton __________ (*for/since*) May 2000.
3. I've known Ted __________ (*since/for*) three weeks.
4. I haven't eaten anything __________ (*since/for*) yesterday.
5. They haven't phoned __________ (*since/for*) Wednesday.

IV. Przetłumacz na język angielski

1. Jeszcze nie zjedliśmy obiadu.
2. Posprzątałam mój pokój.
3. W poniedziałek Adam nie poszedł do szkoły.
4. Mark był w Grecji w 2001r.
5. Właśnie skończyłam to ćwiczenie.

V. A teraz popraw błędy!

1. The Thomsons didn't visit Poland yet.
2. Sarah lives with her aunt for two months.
3. Adam Mickiewicz has lived in Paris.
4. They haven't been to Cracow since three years.
5. Hooray! We just finished this job!

KLUCZ

I 1.a 2.b 3.a 4.b 5.b **II** 1. was 2. have seen 3. has never eaten 4. hasn't watered 5. Have you ever ridden **III** 1. for, 2. since, 3. for, 4. since, 5. since **IV** 1. We haven't had lunch yet. 2. I've tidied my room. 3. Adam didn't go to school on Monday. 4. Mark was in Greece in 2001. 5. I've just finished this exercise. **V**. 1. The Thomsons haven't visited Poland yet. 2. Sarah has lived with her aunt for two months. 3. Adam Mickiewicz lived in Paris. 4. They haven't been to Cracow for three years. 5. Hooray! We've just finished this job!

UNIT 21 I will do/I will be FUTURE SIMPLE

I will give up smoking. Rzucę palenie.
They will buy a new computer. Oni kupią nowy komputer.
The summer will be hot this year. Lato będzie upalne w tym roku.

KIEDY STOSUJESZ FUTURE SIMPLE?

Do wyrażania

1. spontanicznej decyzji podjętej przed chwilą
   (You look tired, I'll help you.)
2. obietnicy
   (Of course I'll lend you my camera.)
3. odmowy
   (I won't play tomorrow.)
4. opinii
   (I think Hannah won't pass her driving test.)
5. przewidywania przyszłości
   (In the future people will spend their holidays on the Moon.)
6. prośby
   (Will you shut the window, please?)

TYPOWE BŁĘDY UWAŻAJ!

Źle: I have already decided, ~~I will throw~~ a party on Saturday.
PODPOWIEDŹ: Jeśli czynność jest zaplanowana wcześniej, używaj konstrukcji **be going to** (> unit 22)
Dobrze: I have already decided, I'm going to throw a party on Saturday.

Źle: Someone's knocking, ~~I open the door.~~
PODPOWIEDŹ : Do wyrażania spontanicznych decyzji podjętych przed chwilą użyj **future simple** a nie **present simple**.
Dobrze: Someone's knocking, I'll open the door.

Źle: ~~I want~~ go out tonight, I'm too tired.
PODPOWIEDŹ: Nie myl **I want** = chcę z **I won't** = nie będę (czegoś robić);
won't = will not,
I want to help you. = Chcę ci pomóc. **I won't help you.** = Nie pomogę ci.
Dobrze: I won't go out tonight, I'm too tired.

YOUR TURN NOW! TERAZ KOLEJ NA CIEBIE!

I. Postanawiasz zmienić swoje życie od poniedziałku.
Uzupełnij zdania formą **will ('ll)** lub **will not (won't)**.

1. I ________ be late for school again.
2. I ________ gossip about my friends.
3. I ________ help my parents.
4. I ________ forget to do my homework.
5. I ________ cheat on tests.

II. Połącz połówki zdań.

1. Don't worry
2. I'm sorry
3. You look tired
4. We don't have any money
5. I have a test tomorrow

A. I'll clean up the kitchen.
B. so we won't go on holiday this year.
C. I'll lend you some money.
D. so I'll study tonight.
E. I'll never be late again.

III. Przetłumacz na język angielski.

1. Pożyczysz mi swój rower?
2. Ja wezmę psa na spacer!
3. Napiszę do ciebie list, nie martw się.
4. Gdzie zostawisz klucze?
5. Ta torba jest dość ciężka, pomogę ci nieść.

IV. A teraz popraw błędy!

1. I want eat it, it's awful.
2. I know, I buy this CD for my boyfriend.
3. Do you bring me this book tonight?
4. I leave the message on your desk, OK.?
5. She want come, she's ill.

KLUCZ

I 1. won't 2. won't 3. 'll 4. won't 5. won't **II** 1.C 2.E 3.A 4.B 5.D **III** 1. Will you lend me your bike? 2. I'll take the dog for a walk. 3. I'll write you a letter, don't worry. 4. Where will you leave the keys? 5. This bag is quite heavy, I'll help you carry it. **IV** 1. I won't eat it, it's awful. 2. I know, I'll buy this CD for my boyfriend. 3. Will you bring me this book tonight? 4. I'll leave the message on your desk, OK? 5. She won't come, she's ill.

UNIT 22 be going to

We're going to save money this year. W tym roku mamy zamiar oszczędzać pieniądze.
Be careful! You're going to fall down the stairs! Uważaj! Spadniesz ze schodów!
I'm going to give up smoking next Monday. Mam zamiar (zamierzam) rzucić palenie w przyszły poniedziałek.

KIEDY STOSUJESZ KONSTRUKCJĘ BE GOING TO?

Do wyrażania

1. planów i zamiarów podjętych wcześniej
   (I'm going to visit my grandma this weekend.)
2. przewidywania na podstawie ewidentnych przesłanek.
   (Look at the sky! It's going to rain.)

TYPOWE BŁĘDY UWAŻAJ!

Źle: ~~We will buy~~ a digital camera. I've discussed it with my family.
PODPOWIEDŹ: Czynności zaplanowane wcześniej wyrażamy przy pomocy konstrukcji **be going to**.
Dobrze: We're going to buy a digital camera. I've discussed it with my family.

Źle: ~~She going~~ to move house.
PODPOWIEDŹ: Konstrukcja **be going to** musi zawierać czasownik **be** w odpowiedniej formie.
Dobrze: She's going to move house.

YOUR TURN NOW! TERAZ KOLEJ NA CIEBIE!

I. Dopasuj podpis do obrazka.

1 2 3 4

A. I'm going to buy this car.
B. I'm going to watch the news.
C. I'm going to have lunch.
D. I'm going to make a call.

II. Wybierz odpowiednią formę czasownika.

1. I have no idea what to cook today. Oh, I know.
   I_______(*am going to cook/will cook*) spaghetti!
2. I've decided to repaint this bedroom.
   Really? What colour ________ (*are you going to paint/will you paint*) it?
3. Have you decided what to buy for Tom?
   Not yet. I think I _________ (*am going to buy/will buy*) him a CD.
4. I _________ (*will finish/am going to finish*) this composition today, I promise.
5. Dave phoned while you were away.
   I know, I _________ (*will phone/am going to phone*) him later.

III. Przetłumacz na język angielski.

1. Kiedy masz zamiar skończyć ten projekt?
2. Chodź, pokażę ci twój pokój.
3. Czy będzie jutro padało?
4. W 2100 roku każdy będzie miał swój prywatny samolot.
5. Susan jest w ciąży, będzie miała bliźnięta.

IV. A teraz popraw błędy! (Jedno zdanie jest poprawne).

1. I'm going to lend you my CD player, I promise.
2. I love you. Are you going to marry me, please?
3. Why are you taking your swimsuit? Will you swim?
4. Have you forgotten your pen? Don't worry, I'll lend you mine.
5. Are you going to help me, please?

KLUCZ I. 1B 2C 3D 4A **II** 1. will cook 2. are you going to paint 3. will buy 4. will finish 5. am going to phone **III.** 1. When are you going to finish this project? 2. Come, I'll show you your room. 3. Will it rain tomorrow? 4. In 2100 everybody will have a personal plane. 5. Susan is pregnant, she's going to have twins. **IV** 1. I'll lend you my CD player, I promise. 2. I love you. Will you marry me, please? 3. Why are you taking your swimsuit? Are you going to swim? 4. OK 5. Will you help me, please?

UNIT 23 I can do CAN

Peter can play the guitar. Peter umie grać na gitarze.
Jonathan can swim a mile in record time. Jonathan potrafi przepłynąć milę w rekordowym czasie.
Chris cannot cook. Chris nie umie gotować.
He can't even make scrambled eggs. On nie potrafi nawet zrobić jajecznicy.
Can you open the window please? Czy możesz otworzyć okno?
OK, you can stay up late tonight. OK, możesz dziś nie kłaść się spać wcześnie.
You can't go to the disco tonight. Dziś wieczorem nie możesz (nie wolno ci) pójść na dyskotekę.

KIEDY STOSUJESZ CZASOWNIK CAN?

Do wskazania umiejętności, pozwolenia lub braku pozwolenia.
Przeczenie **cannot (can't)** wyraża brak umiejętności, pozwolenia lub możliwości.

Can tworzy pytania przez inwersję, a przeczenia przez dodanie **not** bezpośrednio po **can**; **cannot** to jeden wyraz.

TYPOWE BŁĘDY UWAŻAJ!

Źle: She can ~~to~~ sing.
PODPOWIEDŹ: Przed czasownikiem następującym po **can** nie używaj przyimka **to**.
Dobrze: She can sing.

Źle: ~~Do you can swim?~~
PODPOWIEDŹ: W pytaniach lub przeczeniach z **can** nie używaj operatora **do**.
Dobrze: Can you swim?

Źle: We ~~cannot~~ speak Chinese.
PODPOWIEDŹ: Używaj skróconej formy przeczenia **can't**. Formę pełną **cannot** stosuj tylko w oficjalnych wypowiedziach pisemnych.
Dobrze: We can't speak Chinese.

HOTSPOT

Zapamiętaj, że samogłoska w wyrazie **can't** to długie *[a:]*,
tak jak w wyrazach **car** lub **park**.
Nie skracaj jej do krótkiej samogłoski, takiej jak w **bus**,
gdyż niechcący wypowiesz inne słowo, które brzmi wulgarnie.

Can you walk on your hands backwards?

YOUR TURN NOW! TERAZ KOLEJ NA CIEBIE!

I. Przepisz zdania wg wzoru, używając **can/can't**. Nie zmieniaj znaczenia zdań.

WZÓR I don't know how to drive. I can't drive.

1. Do you know how to knit?
2. Francesca doesn't know how to use a computer.
3. Angela knows very well how to speak French.
4. Does he know how to make a cake?
5. I don't know how to do this exercise.

II. Uzupełnij dialogi poprawną formą **can/can't** oraz odpowiednimi czasownikami z ramki.

cook use type help drive watch

1. A: ________ you ________ spaghetti?
   B: Of course, you idiot. Everybody ________ ________ spaghetti.
2. A: John is a bad driver, you know. In fact, I think he ________ ________ at all.
   B: So how come he's got a driving licence?
3. A: What! You ________ ________! So how ________ you ________ a computer?
   B: Well, I ________.
4. A: ________ you ________ me please? This bag is very heavy.
   B: I'm sorry, I ________. I've got two heavy bags and a backpack to carry.
5. A: Mum, ________ I ________ the film on TV tonight, please?
   B: Yes, you ________, but make sure you do your homework first.

III. Przetłumacz na język angielski.

1. Czy mogę użyć twojej komórki?
2. James na pewno potrafi naprawić twój samochód.
3. Pat umie bardzo dobrze robić na drutach.
4. Czy mogę dziś wieczór zostać dłużej u Betty?

IV. A teraz popraw błędy!

1. I don't can sew.
2. They can not assess his progress.
3. We can't to go there.
4. Do you can swim?

KLUCZ

I. 1. Can you knit? 2. Francesca can't use a computer. 3. Angela can speak French very well. 4. Can he make a cake? 5. I can't do this exercise. **II.** 1. A: Can – cook, B: can – cook, 2. A: can't – drive, 3. A: can't – type, can – use, B: can't, 4. A: Can – help, B: can't, 5. A: can – watch, B: can **III.** 1. Can I use your mobile (please)? 2. James can surely mend your car. 3. Pat can knit very well. 4. Can I stay longer at Betty's tonight (please)? **IV.** 1. I can't sew. 2. They cannot assess his progress. 3. We can't go there. 4. Can you swim?

UNIT 24 must/have to/have got to do

I must learn English because my boyfriend is English. Muszę uczyć się angielskiego, bo mój chłopak jest Anglikiem.
Piotr has to stay in bed because he is ill. Piotr musi zostać w łóżku, bo jest chory.
You must declare these cigarettes. Musisz zgłosić te papierosy (przy kontroli celnej).
She's got to practise the violin every day. Ona musi codziennie ćwiczyć grę na skrzypcach.

KIEDY STOSUJESZ CZASOWNIK MUST?

1. Do wyrażenia nakazu i zakazu, tj. przymusu, zwykle „wewnętrznego", wynikającego z własnej woli dokonania czegoś, np. **I must phone my mother.**
2. Do wyrażenia przymusu stanowiącego ogólnie przyjęte prawo, np. **Soldiers must wear military uniforms**.
3. Gdy wydajesz komu polecenie, np. **You must finish this project before Monday**.

→ **Must** tworzy pytania przez inwersję, a przeczenia przez dodanie **not** bezpośrednio po **must**. **(Must you go now? You must not/mustn't use your dictionary during tests.)**

→ Czasownik **must** ma tę samą formę dla wszystkich osób.

→ Zwróć uwagę, że **must not (mustn't)** nie oznacza **nie muszę**, lecz kategoryczny zakaz. **(You mustn't touch it! = Nie wolno ci tego dotykać!)**

KIEDY STOSUJESZ KONSTRUKCJĘ HAVE TO/HAVE GOT TO?

Do wyrażenia przymusu, zwykle pochodzącego od czynników zewnętrznych, znajdujących się poza naszą kontrolą.

→ Do tworzenia pytań i przeczeń w konstrukcji **have to** używa się operatora **do** w odpowiedniej formie. Pytania i przeczenia w konstrukcji **have got to** tworzysz jak w **present perfect**.

TYPOWE BŁĘDY UWAŻAJ!

Źle: I must ~~to~~ go there.
PODPOWIEDŹ: **Must** łączy się z czasownikiem bezpośrednio, bez przyimka **to**.
Dobrze: I must go there.

Źle: ~~Do I really must get up now?~~
PODPOWIEDŹ: Tworząc pytania i przeczenia z **must** nie dodawaj operatora **do/does.**
Dobrze: Must I really get up now?

Źle: ~~I mustn't go to school tomorrow, it's a holiday.~~
PODPOWIEDŹ: **Mustn't** oznacza zakaz, a nie brak konieczności. Jeśli nie musisz czegoś robić, użyj **I don't have to...**
Dobrze: I don't have to go to school tomorrow, it's a holiday.

HOTSPOT!

W mowie potocznej używaj struktury **have got to** w formie skróconej (**I've got to do it**). Wyraz **got** nie ma tu własnego znaczenia, podkreśla jedynie przymus.

YOUR TURN NOW! TERAZ KOLEJ NA CIEBIE!

I. Dopasuj części zdań z kolumn **A** i **B**.

A

1. I have a toothache. I've
2. We're entering a mosque. You
3. Must you make
4. This bag is heavy. Can you please
5. Kate's good at maths. She can
6. Do I have
7. John missed a lot of school this month. He

B

a. to visit my grandparents every Sunday?
b. so much noise? I'm trying to learn.
c. got to see a dentist.
d. must take your shoes off.
e. now has to catch up with the new material
f. carry it for me?
g. do the sums in no time.

II. Wybierz poprawną formę.

1. Look! This sweater has a hole in it. You *had to/have to* change before you go out.
2. My sister has a flu so she *has to/have to* stay in bed.
3. John wants to study astronomy, so he will *have to/have to* work on maths really hard this year.
4. Last year our history teacher was very demanding. We *have to/had to* learn all the dates by heart.
5. My computer is very old. I *has to/will have to* buy a new one soon.
6. Peter spends a fortune on his mobile. He *has to/had to* learn how to save on his calls.
7. I think it's going to rain. We *have to/has to* take an umbrella.

III. Przetłumacz na język angielski.

1. Musisz zrobić to ćwiczenie jeszcze raz.
2. Muszę teraz skończyć wypracowanie.
3. Musimy jutro wstać wcześnie, bo nasz pociąg odjeżdża o 6: 30 rano.
4. Co? Nie kupiliście jeszcze prezentu dla Mamy! Musicie zrobić to jutro z samego rana!
5. Czy musisz właśnie teraz słuchać muzyki?

IV. A teraz popraw błędy! (Uważaj! Niektóre zdania są poprawne.)

1. He must to study harder.
2. Do I really must clean my shoes?
3. She doesn't have to go to bed just now.
4. Do I really have tidy my room?
5. Have you to write this composition tonight?
6. We must hurry; it's getting late.

KLUCZ

I. 1c 2d 3b 4f 5g 6a 7e. **II.** 1. have to; 2. has to; 3. will have to; 4. had to; 5. will have to; 6. has to; 7. have to **III.** 1. You have to/You've got to/ do this exercise again. 2. I must/I have to/ I've got to finish my composition now. 3. We have to/We've got to get up early tomorrow because our train leaves at 6: 30 a. m. 4. What? You haven't bought a present for Mum yet! You have to/ You've got to do it first thing tomorrow morning. 5. Must you listen to music just now? **IV.** 1. He must study harder. 2. Must I really clean my shoes? 3. OK. 4. Do I really have to tidy my room? 5. Do you have to write this composition tonight? 6. OK.

UNIT 25 CONSOLIDATION

Po przerobieniu części BASIC pora na trochę relaksu i podsumowanie.

I. Przeczytaj historyjkę i wstaw czasownik w odpowiedniej formie.

The other day Steve Clinton ______ (*come*) home from the pub. Suddenly he saw a young boy looking for something next to the lamp post.

'What ______ (*you/do*) here, my boy?' he asked.
'I ______ (*look*) for my key', answered the boy.
'______ (*you/lose*) it here?'
'No, over there, round the corner', said the boy.
'So why _____ (*you/look*) for it here?', Steve was surprised.
'Because it's dark over there', was the answer.

II. Które z tych zdań są niepoprawne? Czy umiesz je poprawić?

1. Mother went to the market and she bought a meat.
2. I'm thinking Susan will pass her exam. She knows everything.
3. I didn't never ride a camel.
4. I seldom do crosswords.
5. The news are horrible.

III. A oto garść przysłów angielskich. Czy potrafisz połączyć rozsypane połówki?

1. A new broom ...
6. Think today...
4. Beggars ...
3. Bad news ...
2. Actions speak louder...
7. An apple a day ...
5. There is no smoke...

B. ..... than words.
A. ... has wings.
C. ...sweeps well.
G. ...and speak tomorrow.
E. ... keeps the doctor away.
D. ...without fire.
F. ...cannot be choosers.

Interpretacja wyników testu

Jeśli uzyskałeś co najmniej 30 punktów – gratulacje! Możesz przejść do części INTERMEDIATE. Jeśli masz mniej niż 30 punktów, powinieneś przeczytać wybrane partie materiału jeszcze raz. Jeśli nieprawidłowo odpowiedziałeś na któreś z pytań 1-10, przeanalizuj ponownie rozdziały 1-4. Jeśli masz problemy z udzieleniem prawidłowych odpowiedzi do pytań 11-18, wróć do rozdziałów 5-9. Jeśli sprawiły Ci kłopot odpowiedzi na pytania 19-23, wróć do rozdziałów 10-14. Jeśli nie udzieliłeś poprawnej odpowiedzi na pytania 24-27, przeanalizuj ponownie rozdziały 15-16. Jeśli pytania 28-29 sprawiły Ci trudność, wróć do rozdziałów 17 i 18. Jeśli pytania 30-35 wydały Ci się niejasne, przeczytaj ponownie rozdziały 19-24. Wykonaj ten sam test dopiero po kilku dniach, aby sprawdzić, ile naprawdę pamiętasz. POWODZENIA!

KLUCZ

I. was coming – are you doing – am looking – have you lost – are you looking. **II.** 1. Mother went to the market and she bought some meat. 2. I think Susan will pass her exam. She knows everything. 3. I have never ridden a camel. 4. OK. 5. The news is horrible. **III.** 1.C 2.B 3.A 4.F 5.D 6.G 7.E

SPRAWDŹ SIĘ!

Wykonaj poniższy test, a następnie sprawdź, czy musisz coś powtórzyć, czy możesz przejść do następnej części INTERMEDIATE.

1. These ________________ (*watch/watches*) are very expensive, I can't buy them.
2. Nowadays a lot of people ______________ (*have/has*) personal computers at home.
3. I have two ______________ (*pieces of advice/advises*) for you: go to sleep early and don't eat sweets after supper.
4. I've heard ____________ (*a/an/the/some*) interesting information on the radio today.
5. Go to the ______________ (*newsagent/newsagent's*) and buy a newspaper.
6. We spent two weeks at my ______________ (*grandparents/grandparents'*).
7. Joan is a teenager and she wears __________ (*a/an/the/-*) uniform for school.
8. My husband is ________ (*a/an/the/-*) engineer and he enjoys his job a lot.
9. __________ (*a/an/the/-*) potatoes are not expensive and many people eat them every day.
10. There are some apples on (*a/ the/-*) table in my kitchen.
11. Sorry, but this bag is __________ (*my/mine*).
12. (*Her/hers*) ________ children are very naughty, they are always fighting.
13. This is ___________ (*good/better/the best*) cinema in our town, all others are worse.
14. Tom is ______________ (*intelligent/more intelligent/the most intelligent*) than Jerry.
15. Theresa is an excellent singer, she sings _______________ (*beautiful/beautifully*).
16. David has his driving test ______________ (*in/on*) Friday.
17. Lucy is sitting ______________ (*among/between*) Elizabeth and Mary.
18. ______________ (*Do you/are you*) happy?
19. ______________ (*Are there/Are*) any computers in your school?
20. ______________ (*Do you have got/Have you got*) many friends at school?
21. Mr Smith ______________ (*teaches/is teaching*) math in a primary school.
22. Fausto is Italian and he ______________ (*lives/is living*) in Rome.
23. ________________ (*Was you/were you*) tired after the party?
24. ________________ (*Did you have/Had you*) a math test yesterday?
25. Did you ______________ (*visited/visit*) Mary on Sunday?
26. My mother ______________ (*was buying/bought*) me a pair of shoes yesterday.
27. I ______________ (*live/have lived*) in Piaseczno all my life.
28. J. K. Rowling ______________ (*wrote/has written*) a series of books about Harry Potter.
29. I haven't seen George ______________ (*since/for*) two months.
30. Susan hasn't been to London ____________ (*since/for*) 2001.
31. 'I have a headache.' 'I ______________ (*'m going to/'ll*) give you a pill'.
32. Ralph ________________ (*is going to/will*) study law, he has already decided.
33. You __________ (*don't have to/mustn't*) do the shopping. I've already bought some food.
34. Helen doesn't know how to play the piano. She ____________ (*can't/mustn't*) play it.
35. ______________ (*Do you can/Can you*) speak English?

1. watches, 2. have, 3. pieces of advice, 4. some, 5. newsagent's, 6. grandparents', 7. a, 8. an, 9. -, 10. the, 11. mine, 12. her, 13. the best, 14. more intelligent, 15. beautifully 16.on, 17. between, 18. Are you, 19. Are there, 20. Have you got, 21. teaches, 22. lives, 23. Were you, 24. Did you have, 25. visit, 26. bought, 27. have lived, 28. has written, 29. for, 30. since. 31. 'll, 32. is going, 33. don't have, 34. can't, 35. Can you;

UNIT 26 two coffees/coffee NOUNS: COUNTABLE OR UNCOUNTABLE?

Iron Bridge is the first bridge in Britain made completely of iron.
Iron Bridge to pierwszy most w Wielkiej Brytanii wykonany całkowicie z żelaza.
I must buy a new iron. Muszę kupić nowe żelazko.
Many houses in Scotland are built of stone, not brick.
Wiele domów w Szkocji zbudowanych jest z kamienia, nie z cegły.
Look at this jewellery and all these precious stones. Spójrz na tę biżuterię i te wszystkie drogie kamienie.
Books have been made of paper for ages. Od wieków książki robi się z papieru.
Where are today's papers? Gdzie są dzisiejsze gazety?
You mustn't drink so much coffee. Nie wolno ci pić tyle kawy.
Two coffees, please. Dwie kawy proszę.
An apple is a kind of fruit. Jabłko to rodzaj owocu.
Look, this sign reads 'Fruits'. Patrz, tu jest napisane „Owoce" (= stoisko z owocami).

POLICZALNE CZY NIEPOLICZALNE?

→ Niektóre rzeczowniki w języku angielskim występują, w zależności od kontekstu, zarówno jako policzalne jak i niepoliczalne. Do tej kategorii należą przede wszystkim nazwy rodzajów materiałów (niepoliczalne) i przedmioty (policzalne) wykonane z tych materiałów, a także niektóre produkty spożywcze. Czasem, choć nie zawsze, w takim wypadku następuje również pewna zmiana znaczenia (np. **iron** – żelazo, **an iron** – żelazko; **glass** – szkło, **a glass** – szklanka, **glasses** – okulary).

→ Rzeczownik w liczbie pojedynczej, który jest nazwą przedmiotu, a nie materiału, z którego ten przedmiot został sporządzony, jest policzalny, a więc wymaga poprzedzenia określnikiem.

→ Rzeczownik, który jest nazwą materiału, jest niepoliczalny, a więc gdy mówisz o tym materiale po raz pierwszy nie poprzedzasz go określnikiem, lub poprzedzasz wyrazem **some** (np. **I must buy some silk to make a blouse.**)

TYPOWE BŁĘDY UWAŻAJ!

Podaj mi gazetę.
Źle: ~~Please give me paper.~~
PODPOWIEDŹ: Gdy mówisz o pojedynczym przedmiocie, a nie o materiale, z którego ten przedmiot został sporządzony, nie opuszczaj określników.
Dobrze: Please give me the paper.

Źle: This dress is made of ~~the~~ cotton.
PODPOWIEDŹ: Niepotrzebne jest dodawanie określników przed rzeczownikiem, który jest nazwą materiału.
Dobrze: This dress is made of cotton.

YOUR TURN NOW!

I. Choose the correct form of the noun. Be careful: in one sentence both forms may be correct!

1. The Chinese invented *paper/papers* a long time ago.
2. Look out! There's broken *glasses/glass* on the floor.
3. Have you got *tea/teas* on your shopping list?
4. The stained *glass/glasses* in the Rheims Cathedral is breathtaking!
5. Is it true that *irons/iron* are made of *irons/iron*?
6. We put *paper/papers* for recycling in this box.
7. These *glasses/glass* are very old and Grandpa can't use them any longer.

II. Decide if the nouns in italics are used in the text as countable or uncountable.

EXAMPLE *linen* U *property* C

Linen has very desirable *properties* which make it very comfortable to wear. It looks good, and it washes best of all textile *fibres.* With each *wash* the *surface* comes up new without affecting its *durability.* It is, in fact, the strongest natural *fibre.* It is sensitive to *moisture* and can absorb up to one fifth of its dry *weight* of *water* without feeling damp on the *surface.* It also gives up its *moisture* into the surrounding *atmosphere* more rapidly than any other *textile.* That is why it is so comfortable to wear in warm or humid *weather.*

Now check in a dictionary if they are always used like that.

III. Translate into English.

1. Czy twoje nowe okulary są naprawdę ze szkła?
2. – Dwa piwa proszę – powiedział James Bond.
3. Spójrz! Te szklanki są z plastiku.
4. Żelazka używamy do prasowania ubrań.
5. Uważaj! Na tych kamieniach łatwo jest skręcić kostkę.

IV. Now correct the mistakes.

1. This blouse is made of linens.
2. Look out! Iron is hot!
3. A tea, anyone?
4. Coffee are sold over there.
5. Rosslyn Chapel is built of stones.

KEY

I. 1. paper 2. glass 3. tea 4. glass 5. irons, iron 6. both forms are correct but there is a change in meaning: Papier/gazety na makulaturę składamy do tego pudła. 7. glasses **II.** U: linen, durability, moisture, weight, water, atmosphere, weather; C: property, fibre, wash, surface, textile. In some specific contexts the nouns weight, water and weather are countable. **III.** 1. Are your new glasses really made of glass? 2. 'Two beers please', said James Bond. 3. Look! These glasses are made of plastic. 4. We use an iron to iron/to press clothes. 5. Look out! It's easy to twist your ankle on these stones. **IV** 1. This blouse is made of linen. 2. Look out! This/The iron is hot. 3. Tea, anyone? 4. Coffee is sold over there. 5. Rosslyn Chapel is built of stone.

UNIT 27 scissors/door/family/police SINGULAR OR PLURAL

Could you hand me the scissors, please? Czy możesz mi podać nożyczki?
We always wear light clothes in the summer. W lecie zawsze nosimy lekkie ubrania.
Why is this door always open? Dlaczego te drzwi są zawsze otwarte?
Immigrants' lives are never easy. Życie imigrantów nigdy nie jest łatwe.
My family are coming for Easter. Moja rodzina przyjeżdża na Wielkanoc.
My family consists of four people. Moja rodzina składa się z czterech osób.
The police are looking for the four men responsible for stealing a famous painting by Leonardo da Vinci. Policja szuka czterech mężczyzn odpowiedzialnych za kradzież słynnego obrazu Leonarda da Vinci.

Niektóre rzeczowniki (tzw. **pair nouns**, np. **scissors, trousers**) występują tylko w liczbie mnogiej, podobnie jak w języku polskim. Nie poprzedzasz ich przedimkiem **a/an**, lecz np. wyrażeniem **a pair of** (trousers). Inne rzeczowniki zmieniają znaczenie, gdy dodamy końcówkę **–s** (np. **people** – ludzie, **peoples** – ludy).

→ Użycie form liczby pojedynczej i mnogiej rzeczowników nie zawsze jest identyczne w języku polskim i angielskim. Rzeczownik „drzwi" w języku polskim przybiera wyłącznie formę liczby mnogiej, natomiast w języku angielskim tworzy zarówno formę liczby pojedynczej **(a door)** jak i mnogiej **(doors)**. Czasem w języku polskim używasz rzeczownika w liczbie pojedynczej np. „życie" (jakiejś grupy ludzi), natomiast w języku angielskim musisz użyć liczby mnogiej (np. **farmers' lives**).

Niektóre rzeczowniki zbiorowe, tzw. **collective nouns,** występują w liczbie pojedynczej, gdy odnoszą się do całej grupy, a jako rzeczowniki w liczbie mnogiej, gdy dotyczą poszczególnych jej członków. Są to: **army, band, board, class, club, committee, community, company, crew, family, the majority, management, orchestra, public, staff, team, union.**

Niektóre **collective nouns** (np. **police, cattle, vermin**) występują tylko w liczbie mnogiej i łączą się z czasownikiem w liczbie mnogiej.

TYPOWE BŁĘDY **UWAŻAJ!**

Źle: During the war many refugees' ~~life was~~ in great danger.
PODPOWIEDŹ: Nie stosuj w języku angielskim automatycznie tej samej liczby, w której dany rzeczownik występuje w języku polskim.
Dobrze: During the war many refugees' lives were in great danger.

Źle: The police ~~is~~ looking for the murderer.
PODPOWIEDŹ: Zapamiętaj, jakie collective nouns wystepują w języku angielskim tylko w liczbie mnogiej.
Dobrze: The police are looking for the murderer.

YOUR TURN NOW!

I. Use the nouns from the box to complete mini-dialogues.

stairs trousers scissors shorts contents glasses jeans pliers

1. A. Have you seen my ________________? I can't cut out the pattern without them.
   B. Here they are. What are you going to make?
   A. A pair of ________________ for Jim.
   B. Don't you think he'd prefer a pair of Levi's ________________?
2. A. Where are you going for you holidays this year?
   B. To the Bermudas.
   A. So you're surely taking your Bermuda ________________?
   B. You bet! I've already packed them.
3. A. Will this book help me in my project, do you think?
   B. I don't know. You better look through the table of ________________ before you buy it.
4. A. Have you seen my ________________? I'm as blind as a bat without them.
   B. Yes, look, they're on the mantelpiece. Here you are.
5. A. Gosh, what a climb! Will it ever end?
   B. What did you expect? You've got to climb a lot of steep ________________ to reach the top of the Mariacka Tower.
6. A. I have no idea how to cut this wire.
   B. Neither have I. Here, use the ________________. Maybe they'll help.

II. Compare the two headlines. Decide why each of them uses a different verb form though they have the same subject.

1. THE GOVERNMENT have decided to introduce a new tax

2. **THE GOVERNMENT IS LYING TO THE NATION ABOUT THE CAUSES OF THE WAR**

III. Choose the correct form of the verb.

1. The British Royal family *has/have* many members.
2. The main door of Coventry Cathedral *are/is* beautifully ornamented.
3. The police *is/are going* to punish severely people who drink and drive.
4. John's family *are/is* all very talented musically.

IV. And now correct the mistakes! In each sentence 1-6 there is one word which should not be there. Find it and cross it out.

(1) My family are very many artistic. (2) My eldest sister makes the paper cut-outs; she can do wonders with her scissors. (3) My middle old sister sings in a folk music band. (4) She has a much beautiful voice. (5) My youngest sister works in a wood. (6) She carves characters from a folk stories. Recently, our local government have decided to give my talented sisters special grants.

KEY **I.** 1. scissors, trousers/jeans, jeans 2. shorts 3. contents 4. glasses 5. stairs 6. pliers **II.** The first sentence stresses that the decision has been made jointly, by all government members; in the second sentence the government is treated as one body. **III.** 1. has 2. is 3. are 4. are **IV.** 1. ~~many~~ 2. ~~the~~ 3. ~~old~~ 4. ~~much~~ 5. ~~a~~ 6. ~~a~~

Don't go near the Ibrox stadium today; gangs of the Rangers' fans can be rowdy.
Nie chodź dziś w okolice stadionu Ibrox; grupy fanów Rangersów mogą rozrabiać.
The flock of sheep grazing in this valley belongs to the Gąsienica family.
Stado owiec pasące się w tej dolinie należy do rodziny Gąsieniców.
On their wedding anniversary Andrzej always brings Klaudyna a big bunch of roses.
W rocznicę ślubu Andrzej zawsze przynosi Klaudynie wielki bukiet róż.

Podobnie jak w języku polskim, niektóre rzeczowniki, tzw. **group nouns**, określają zbiorczo grupę osób, zwierząt lub rzeczy należących do jednego gatunku lub do siebie podobnych (np. **a herd of cows, a gang of football fans, a set of tools**). W zależności od potrzeby, **group nouns** występują albo w liczbie pojedynczej **(a swarm)**, albo mnogiej **(swarms)**. Rzeczownik, który określają, jest zawsze w liczbie mnogiej **(a swarm of bees/swarms of bees)**.

WYJĄTEK: nazwy niektórych ryb występują tylko w liczbie pojedynczej, nawet gdy ich ławica składa się z wielu osobników (np. **a shoal of herring/salmon**, ale **a shoal of sardines**).

TYPOWE BŁĘDY **UWAŻAJ!**

Źle: In autumn, big ~~herds~~ of birds are flying south.

PODPOWIEDŹ: Zapamiętaj, jaki rzeczownik łączy się z jaką grupą osób, zwierząt lub rzeczy. (> ćwicz.1 str. 57)

Dobrze: In autumn, big flocks of birds are flying south.

Źle: John gave Mary ~~bunch of flowers.~~

PODPOWIEDŹ: Nie zapominaj o przedimku przed rzeczownikiem policzalnym w liczbie pojedynczej.

Dobrze: John gave Mary a bunch of flowers.

It is a duty of every society to help the poor, the old and the infirm.
Obowiązkiem każdego społeczeństwa jest pomagać biednym, starym i chorym.
Every animal takes care of its young. Każde zwierzę troszczy się o swoje młode (=młode osobniki).

→ Osobną kategorię stanowią rzeczowniki tworzone od przymiotników poprzedzonych przedimkiem określonym **the**, np. **the homeless** (bezdomni), **the unemployed** (bezrobotni), lub określnikiem dzierżawczym np. **its young** (swoje młode).

TYPOWE BŁĘDY **UWAŻAJ!**

Źle: The best policy to help ~~poor~~ is to teach them to help themselves.

PODPOWIEDŹ: Pamiętaj o dodaniu **the** przed przymiotnikiem w funkcji rzeczownika.

Dobrze: The best policy to help the poor is to teach them to help themselves.

YOUR TURN NOW!

I. Match the words in columns A and B.

1. a pack of	a. cows
2. a bunch of	b. geese
3. a crowd of	c. wolves
4. a herd of	d. cowboys
5. a gang of	e. schoolkids
6. a flock of	f. passers-by
7. a swarm of	g. mosquitos
8. a group of	h. carnations

II. Fill the gaps with a suitable noun from the box.

pile clump set row

We set out in the early afternoon, leaving behind the dull city with its (1) ______ of identical houses stretching from street to street, for miles on end. We must have driven for quite a few hours when John suddenly cried out: 'Look there, beyond this (2) ______ of trees! Can you see them?' Peter and I looked in the direction John's dirty finger was pointing to. Michael, always a serious scholar, reached for his (3) ______ of binoculars. Even Suzy, our youngest, who had been sleeping peacefully on a (4) ______ of clothes we had thrown pell-mell into the back of the car, sat up and stared into the distance. Yes, there they were, glowing warmly in the setting sun. The mountains. Our home.

III. Find the 'odd man' in each line and cross it out.

1. Swarm is used for bees, starlings, midges.
2. Flock is used for geese, sheep, cows.
3. Set is used for tools, appliances, commodities.
4. Gang is used for wolves, schoolboys, football fans.
5. Pack is used for wolves, pigs, dogs.
6. Herd is used for deer, herring, goats.

IV. Substitute each phrase in the brackets by a suitable group noun.

1. Ageism is defined as contempt for (people who are not young).
2. Unfortunately, there is now a growing number of (people who have nowhere to live) in Poland.
3. Marek Kotański founded MONAR to help (who took drugs).
4. (People who have a lot of money) will never understand (people who have very little money).
5. Do you think that (people who have no jobs) should get some extra social benefits?

KEY

I. 1.c 2.h 3.f 4.a 5.d. 6.b 7.g 8.e **II.** 1. rows 2. clump 3. set 4. pile **III.** 1. ~~starlings~~ 2. ~~cows~~ 3. ~~commodities~~ 4. ~~wolves~~ 5. ~~pigs~~ 6. ~~herring~~ **IV.** 1. the old 2. the homeless 3. the addicted 4. the rich; the poor 5. the unemployed

UNIT 29 a film star/a T-shirt/sunglasses COMPOUND NOUNS

Is there a telephone booth near here? Czy w pobliżu jest budka telefoniczna?
Science fiction has many fans all over the world.
Literatura science fiction ma wielu wielbicieli na całym świecie.
With ever-growing popularity of credit cards, having a cheque book is no longer very necessary.
Wraz z wzrastającą popularnością kart kredytowych posiadanie książeczki czekowej nie jest już bardzo potrzebne.
Jacek's mother-in-law loves looking after his children.
Teściowa Jacka uwielbia opiekować się jego dziećmi.
All kids love ice cream. Wszystkie dzieci uwielbiają lody.

Rzeczowniki złożone (tzw. **compound nouns**) to najczęściej dwa, czasem trzy, rzeczowniki tworzące razem jedno pojęcie (np. **alarm clock, first aid kit**).

JAK TO SIĘ PISZE?

W przeszłości człony rzeczownika złożonego często oddzielano myślnikiem (np. **drawing-room**). Obecnie ta tendencja zanika, a człony pisane są albo oddzielnie (np. **washing machine, dining room, credit card**), albo razem, jako jeden wyraz (np. **earrings, sunglasses, toothpaste, boyfriend, headache**).

TYPOWE BŁĘDY UWAŻAJ!

Źle: Have you got a first aid ~~box~~ in your car?
PODPOWIEDŹ: Nie zmieniaj członów **compound nouns**; musisz je zapamiętać w całości.
Dobrze: Have you got a first aid kit in your car?

Źle: Frances is not very friendly towards her ~~mother in law~~.
PODPOWIEDŹ: W pisowni złożeń dotyczących rodziny męża/żony (tj. **in-laws**) nie opuszcza się myślnika.
Dobrze: Frances is not very friendly towards her mother-in-law.

Źle: These ~~ear rings~~ are made of gold.
PODPOWIEDŹ: Zapamiętaj, które z rzeczowników złożonych piszemy razem. W razie wątpliwości posłuż się słownikiem.
Dobrze: These earrings are made of gold.

DID YOU KNOW?

ICE PRICE
(based on a note found in a Scottish paper in the extremely hot summer of 2003)
A small cone of ice cream which 'tasted of frozen, watered-down washing up liquid' and which even the dog didn't want to lick, cost the writer £ 1.50 in Edinburgh's Princes Street Gardens. The task he set for the readers: to write in and say who sells the cheapest and best ice cream. How about recommending *Zielona Budka*, folks?

YOUR TURN NOW!

I. Label the pictures. The first letters of the words are given.

1. t__ o_____ 2. h___d_____ 3. w______ m________ 4. s_g________ 5. T-______

II. Complete the definitions.

1. A person who looks after your children when you go out for the evening is called a ________.
2. A place you take your mail to in order to be sent is called a __________.
3. A school activity which involves writing and which you hate most is called a __________.
4. A sum of money which is deduced from your salary by a special office is called _______.
5. A person who plays leading roles in box office hits shown in cinemas is called a ________.

III. Add the missing part of each compound noun in the story.

place room school dryer mistress clock

The (1) alarm ________ went off, as usual, at 6 a.m. sharp. Miss Henley, the (2) head________, woke up with a sigh. Only she knew how she hated that noise which woke her up from sweetest dreams – even on Sundays. 'And this is Monday, the inspection day', she thought, quickly getting out of bed. All days started early at her (3) boarding ________, but Mondays were the worst, especially in this dark winter weather. She showered and dressed quickly, hurriedly running the (4) hair________ over her wet hair. She wanted to be downstairs before everybody else, for though she had absolute trust in Mrs Brown, the cook, and Emma, the maid, she thought it best to supervise all preparations herself. She ran down the stairs and looked into the kitchen where morning porridge was already steaming; then went to the big (5) dining ________, still dark on this winter morning. The long table was set, a huge log fire was burning in the (6) fire ________. But where were Emma and Mrs Brown?

IV. Below are some words to do with city traffic. Match each word with right 'partners' to make **compound nouns**.

warden stop driver jam ticket crossing lights station lot permit tunnel bridge mall

Traffic	Bus	Parking	Underground	Pedestrian

KEY **I.** 1. tin opener 2. hairdryer 3. washing machine 4. sunglasses 5. T-shirt **II.** 1. babysitter 2. post office 3. classtest 4. income tax 5. film star **III.** 1. alarm clock 2. headmistress 3. boarding school 4. hairdryer 5.dining room/ dining hall 6. fireplace **IV.** Traffic – traffic warden, traffic jam, traffic lights. Bus – bus driver, bus stop, bus ticket. Parking – parking lot, parking permit, parking ticket. Underground – underground station, underground ticket. Pedestrian – pedestrian crossing, pedestrian bridge, pedestrian mall.

UNIT 30 going/doing/swimming GERUND

Jogging will make you fit. Jogging uczyni cię sprawnym.
My friend has taken up swimming. Mój przyjaciel zaczął uprawiać pływanie.
Taking afternoon classes gives you a chance of meeting new people. Chodzenie na kursy popołudniowe daje ci szansę poznania nowych ludzi.
Not getting a promotion is depressing. Nieotrzymanie awansu jest przygnębiające.
Window shopping is her favourite pastime. Oglądanie wystaw sklepowych jest jej ulubionym sposobem spędzania wolnego czasu.
No parking! Parkowanie wzbronione!
The giving of presents is an important part of Christmas celebration.
Dawanie prezentów jest istotną częścią świąt Bożego Narodzenia.

→ **Gerund**, czyli tzw. rzeczownik odsłowny, tworzysz identycznie jak **present participle (verb + -ing)**. Odpowiada to polskiemu np. skakać – skakanie, śpiewać – śpiewanie. Formę przeczącą tworzysz dodając **not + verb -ing.**

→ **Gerund** może być poprzedzony przedimkiem **the**, określnikami **this/that**, zaimkami **me, you, him, her, us, them (object pronouns)**, określnikami dzierżawczymi **my, your, Peter's** itp. W mowie potocznej można używać (**object pronouns**) np. **Corruption led to his/him resigning from the post.** W wypowiedzi oficjalnej należy powiedzieć **Corruption led to his resigning from the post**.

KIEDY STOSUJESZ GERUND?

1. Jako podmiot w zdaniu. Gerund może występować samodzielnie, np. **Skiing is fun** lub być częścią rzeczownika **compound noun**, (> unit 29), np. **Diving boards are made of plastic.**
2. Jako dopełnienie w zdaniu, np. **They escaped by jumping through the window.**
3. Do wyrażania zakazu, np. **No smoking.**
4. Z niektórymi czasownikami, np. **enjoy, try, stop** (> unit 97)

TYPOWE BŁĘDY **UWAŻAJ!**

Źle: There ~~isn't~~ smoking in the library.
PODPOWIEDŹ: Aby powiedzieć, że coś jest niedozwolone, musisz użyć partykuły **no + gerund.**
Dobrze: There's no smoking in the library.

Źle: The ~~dancing samba~~ needs some skills.
PODPOWIEDŹ: Jeśli używasz przedimka **the**, musisz zastosować przyimek **of**.
Dobrze: The dancing of samba needs some skills.

YOUR TURN NOW!

I. Complete the sentences by putting the right verb in the gerund form.

start meet speak go wash shave have ride write be throw give smoke

1. __________ new people is a major advantage of __________ on holiday.
2. Chris and Mary consider __________ a family and __________ children.
3. __________ this woolen sweater in hot water can ruin it!
4. Mark hates __________. He thinks that some girls find stubble attractive.
5. __________ French is easier than __________ it.
6. __________ is forbidden in the office, sorry.
7. __________ parties every weekend makes me tired.
8. __________ presents to children on their birthdays is so pleasant.
9. I like __________ my new bike.
10. Are you afraid of __________ alone in a dark room?

II. Do the crossword.

1. Frank Sinatra loved ______ in the rain.
2. __________ television is sometimes a waste of time.
3. Sitting all day and doing nothing __________ so boring!
4. This is a private property. You are no allowed to cross it. The sign reads: No __________ !
5. Sorry, but __________ in the waiting room is strictly prohibited.
6. Is kissing __________ public approved in your country?
7. __________ and disagreeing is essential in human communication.
8. __________ a bike is both pleasure and fun.
9. What do you think of the Chicago Bulls? Have you seen __________ playing basketball?
10. Reading a __________ is my daily routine.

CROSSWORD

III. Correct the mistakes where necessary.

1. The washing silk clothes in a washing machine can spoil their texture.
2. The whole family has taken up rollerblading.
3. Constant dieting can be hazardous for your health.
4. No eating any fruit isn't good for you.

KEY

I. 1. Meeting, going 2. starting, having 3. Washing 4. shaving 5. Speaking, writing 6. Smoking 7. Throwing 8. giving 9. riding 10. being **II.** 1. singing 2. watching 3. is 4.trespassing 5.smoking 6. in 7. agreeing 8. Riding 9. them 10. newspaper **III.** 1. Washing silk clothes in a washing machine can spoil their texture./The washing of silk clothes in a washing machine can spoil their texture. 2. OK. 3. OK. 4. Not eating any fruit isn't good for you.

UNIT 31 the Pacific/the British Isles/the USA
THE ARTICLE PRECEDING GEOGRAPHICAL NAMES

Is the Caspian Sea a sea or a big lake? Czy Morze Kaspijskie to morze, czy duże jezioro?
Have you ever been to the Sahara? Czy kiedykolwiek byłeś na Saharze?
I always spend my holidays in the Tatras. Zawsze spędzam wakacje w Tatrach.
Bill Gates lives in the States (= the United States of America). Bill Gates mieszka w USA.

KIEDY STOSUJESZ PRZEDIMEK OKREŚLONY THE PRZED NAZWAMI GEOGRAFICZNYMI?

→ Przed nazwami geograficznymi oceanów, mórz, rzek, pustyni, pasm górskich i archipelagów wysp (np. **the Atlantic, the Caspian Sea, the Vistula, the Sahara, the Tatras, the British Isles**) oraz krajów, których nazwy sugerują liczbę mnogą (**the Netherlands, the Philippines**), a także przed nazwami odnoszącymi się do geografii politycznej, nie fizycznej, tj. takimi, które mają w nazwie **Republic** (np. **the Republic of China**), **Kingdom** (**the United Kingom**), **Union** (**the Soviet Union**), **States** (**the USA**) or **Emirates** (**the United Arab Emirates**).

→ Nazwy geograficzne dotyczące wody i piasku zwykle wymagają użycia **the**. WYJĄTEK: jeziora! Pasma górskie wymagają **the**, ale przed nazwami poszczególnych szczytów nie stosujesz przedimka.

My aunt lives in Tours, in France. Moja ciocia mieszka w Tours, we Francji.
Does Nessie the Monster live in Loch Ness? Czy potwór Nessie mieszka w Loch Ness?
Jonathan was in Warsaw last year. Jonathan był w Warszawie w zeszłym roku.

→ Opuszczasz **the** przed nazwami geograficznymi krajów, regionów, stanów, miast, jezior, szczytów górskich i poszczególnych wysp (**Poland, Northern Italy, Texas, Warsaw, Loch Ness, Giewont, Crete**). Nazwy regionów zawierające **of** poprzedzasz przedimkiem **the** (**the South of England**) WYJĄTKI: **the Hague** = Haga, **the Vatican City**.

TYPOWE BŁĘDY **UWAŻAJ!**

Źle: I spent my last holidays in ~~the~~ northern Italy.
PODPOWIEDŹ: Pamiętaj, że wiele nazw geograficznych nie wymaga przedimka **the**; nie dodawaj go niepotrzebnie.
Dobrze: I spent my last holidays in northern Italy.

Źle: He crossed ~~Gobi~~ on his motorbike.
PODPOWIEDŹ: Zapamiętaj, które nazwy geograficzne wymagają przedimka. Przed takimi nazwami nie opuszczaj **the**.
Dobrze: He crossed the Gobi on his motorbike.

HOTSPOT!

We are heading **north**. Zmierzamy na północ. (= w kierunku północnym)
Reindeer live in **the North**. Renifery żyją na Północy.

Gdy mówisz o kierunku, opuszczasz przedimek. Gdy mówisz o stronie świata, używasz **the.**

YOUR TURN NOW!

I. Find the correct sentences.

1. There is a story in the Bible about the Jews crossing Red Sea.
2. The Vistula is the largest river in Poland.
3. Carol was born in the North Carolina.
4. The south of England is the warmest part of Britain.
5. Crete is my favourite holiday destination.

II. **The** or the **'zero' article**?

1. Crossing *the/-* Atlantic was not easy before the invention of steam ships.
2. Varna is a well-known holiday resort on the Bulgarian coast of *the/-* Black Sea.
3. Have you ever taken part in the run up *the/-* Ben Nevis, the highest mountain in Scotland?
4. In the 19th century *the/-* Glasgow was famous for its shipbuilding industry.
5. Do you know that Jeff went climbing in *the/-* Himalayas last year?
6. Andrew and his family have lived in *the/-* Netherlands for the last ten years.
7. I must take Bob to *the/-* Mazury when he comes to Poland next time.
8. She doesn't live in Canada, she lives in *the/-* USA.
9. It's difficult to climb *the/-* Giewont wearing high-heeled shoes.
10. Carol and Pat have been to Africa many times, but they've never seen *the/-* Sahara.

III. Choose the correct article.

Edinburgh, (1) *a/the/-* capital of Scotland, is one of (2) *a/the/-* most interesting towns in (3) *a/the/-* British Isles. People often call it the Athens of (4) *a/the/-* North. There are (5) *a/the/-* few reasons for that. First, (6) *a/the/-* whole district of Edinburgh, called (7) *a/the/-* New Town, dates back to (8) *a/the/-* 18th century and is (9) *a/the/-* fine example of (10) *a/the/-* neoclassical architecture. Secondly, Edinburgh was also (11) *a/the/-* very important place intellectually at (12) *a/the/-* time of (13) *a/the/-* Enlightenment. It was (14) *a/the/-* home of David Hume, the philosopher, and many other leading thinkers of (15) *a/the/-* Age of Reason. There is, however, one crucial difference between Edinburgh and Athens – (16) *a/the/-* climate!

PLEASE NOTE: 'The Athens of the North' (sentence 2) is not a geographical term.
It's a metaphor which suggests that in the 18th century Edinburgh was unique, 'the only one'.
That's why in this sentence there is the definite article in front of 'Athens'.
In the last sentence 'Athens' relates to the name of a real town. It is a geographical term and therefore there is no article in front of it.

KEY

I. 1. incorrect (the Red Sea) 2. correct 3. incorrect ('the' jest zbędne) 4. correct 5. correct **II.** 1. the 2. the 3. – 4. – 5. the 6. the 7. – 8. the 9. – 10. the **III.** 1. the 2. the 3. the 4. the 5. a 6. a/the 7. the 8. the 9. a 10. – 11. a 12. the 13. the 14. the 15. the 16 the

UNIT 32 in prison, in the prison ARTICLES WITH PLACES

Let's meet at Kennedy Airport. Spotkajmy się na lotnisku Kennedy'ego.
Ralph took a photo of the White House. Ralph zrobił zdjęcie Białego Domu.
Steve is in prison because he robbed a bank. Steve jest w więzieniu, gdyż obrabował bank.
Susan is going to the prison to visit Steve. Susan idzie do więzienia odwiedzić Steve'a.
Mark studies law at Warsaw University. Mark studiuje prawo na Uniwersytecie Warszawskim.

KIEDY STOSUJESZ PRZEDIMEK THE MÓWIĄC O MIEJSCACH LUB INSTYTUCJACH?

1. Większość nazw budynków i instytucji zawiera przedimek **the**, np. **the Marriott Hotel, the National Theatre, the British Council, the Tate Gallery, the Odeon** (kino).
2. Nazwy, w skład których wchodzi przyimek **of**, zwykle są poprzedzone przedimkiem **the**, np. **the Houses of Parliament, the Great Wall of China, the Museum of Modern Art, the University of Warsaw.**

KIEDY NIE STOSUJESZ PRZEDIMKA THE MÓWIĄC O MIEJSCACH, ULICACH, INSTYTUCJACH?

1. Gdy mówisz o ulicach, placach, np. **There's a good restaurant in Oxford Street.** (wyjątek: **the High Street**).
2. Gdy mówisz o miejscach/instytucjach składających się z dwóch wyrazów, z których pierwszy jest nazwą miasta lub nazwiskiem, np. **Warsaw University, London Zoo, Chopin Airport.**
3. Gdy mówisz o sklepach, restauracjach, hotelach, bankach, których nazwy zawierają nazwisko właściciela lub założyciela, np. **Harrods, Jenny's Guest House, Lloyds Bank**, a także o kościołach, np. **St Paul's Church.**

STOSOWAĆ THE CZY NIE STOSOWAĆ?

PORÓWNAJ: John is sick, so he is **in hospital.**
Mary is a doctor and she works **in the hospital.**

→ Jeśli mówiąc o danym miejscu/instytucji, masz na myśli ich funkcję, nie stosujesz **the**. Odnosi się to do takich rzeczowników jak np. **church, prison, hospital, court, home, work, bed, class.**

→ Jeśli instytucję traktujesz jako czyjeś miejsce pracy lub masz na myśli budynek, musisz użyć **the**.

Niektóre nazwy instytucji, linii lotniczych itp. nie zawierają **the**, np. **British Airways, LOT, IBM, Sony,** ale np. **the British Council, the National Bank of Poland.**

TYPOWE BŁĘDY UWAŻAJ!

Źle: My brother is studying mathematics at ~~the~~ Warsaw University.
PODPOWIEDŹ: Jeśli nazwa jest dwuczłonowa i zawiera nazwę miasta lub nazwisko, nie stosujesz **the**. Jeśli nazwa zawiera **of**, trzeba użyć **the**.
Dobrze: My brother is studying mathematics at Warsaw University/the University of Warsaw.

Źle: Martin is in ~~the~~ bed because he has flu.
PODPOWIEDŹ: Forma **in bed** nie wymaga **the**.
Dobrze: Martin is in bed because he has flu.

YOUR TURN NOW!

I. Complete the sentences with **the** where necessary.

1. They're putting a new roof on _____ prison in my town.
2. My sister is a nurse and she works in _____ hospital in Płońsk.
3. _____ University of Cambridge is one of the oldest universities in Europe.
4. See you at _____ Victoria Station at 12 o'clock!
5. Have you ever been to _____ Warsaw Zoo?
6. Dr Robinson lives in _____ Dover Street.
7. There are a few theatres in _____ Palace of Culture in Warsaw.
8. I spent the whole weekend at _____ home.
9. _____ Statue of Liberty is in New York.
10. My grandma always goes to _____ church on Sunday.

II. Put the following names into two columns as in the example.

(_) University of London, (_) London Zoo, (_) University of East Anglia, (_) Baldwin Street, (_) Royal Castle, (_) Grand Hotel, (_) Oxford University, (_) British Museum, (_) Nelson's Column, (_) St. Anne's Church, (_) Victoria Park, (_) Albert's Memorial, (_) Palace of Westminster, (_) Singapore Airlines, (_) St. Jacob's Chapel, (_) Marks&Spencer's

THE	NO ARTICLE
The University of London	London Zoo

III. Complete the sentences using the word given. Remember to put **the** where necessary.

SCHOOL
1. Susan is a teenager. She goes to _______ every day.
2. Susan's father wants to speak to her English teacher. He's gone to _______ to meet her.

HOSPITAL
3. George has broken his leg and now he's in _______.
4. Let's go to _______ to visit him, he must be bored.

PRISON
5. Kevin is in _______ for robbery.
6. Jackie is a psychologist and she went to _______ to talk to Kevin.

CHURCH
7. My mother is a very religious person. Every day she goes to _______ to attend a Mass.
8. This week it's her duty to clean _______.

BED
9. I love staying in _______ till noon on Sundays.
10. I found this golden ring in _______ while I was cleaning the room, would you believe?

KEY

I. 1. the 2. the 3. The 4.- 5.- 6.- 7. the 8.- 9. The 10.- **II. Column THE:** the University of East Anglia, the Royal Castle, the Grand Hotel, the British Museum, the Palace of Westminster **Column NO ARTICLE:** Baldwin Street, Oxford University, Nelson's Column, St. Anne's Church, Victoria Park, Albert's Memorial, Singapore Airlines, St. Jacob's Chapel, Marks&Spencer's; **III.** 1. school, 2. the school, 3. hospital, 4. the hospital, 5. prison, 6. the prison, 7. church, 8. the church, 9. bed, 10. the bed

UNIT 33 the one on the right PRONOUNS ONE, ONES

I like that girl, the one on the right. Podoba mi się ta dziewczyna, ta po prawej.
Bring some new books and some old ones. Przynieś kilka nowych książek i kilka starych.
This pen is mine and that one is Jenny's. To pióro jest moje, a tamto Jenny.
One never knows what will happen. Nigdy nie wiadomo, co się wydarzy.

KIEDY UŻYWASZ ONE/ONES?

Gdy nie chcesz po raz drugi powtarzać policzalnego rzeczownika, np. **These are my new shoes and those are my old ones.**

Gdy używasz **ones,** musisz dodać dodatkowe określenie danych rzeczy lub osób, np. **I'm going to buy new trousers. This time I'll buy <u>red</u> ones.**

Gdy wymieniasz liczbę czegoś, możesz użyć **ones** tylko wtedy, gdy między liczebnikiem a **ones** znajduje się przymiotnik, np. **I have two horses and my neighbour has three young ones.**

→ Czasami **one/ones** można opuścić, np. **I don't like these shirts. What about those (ones) on that shelf?**

Nie można opuścić **one/ones** po **the, the main, the only, every** i przymiotniku, np. **Do you like these shoes? No, I prefer those black ones.**

→ **One** może też pełnić funkcję zaimka nieokreślonego w znaczeniu **any person**, co ma wydźwięk raczej oficjalny, np. **One should look after one's children.**

→ Z rzeczownikami niepoliczalnymi stosuj **some/any**, nigdy **one/ones**, np. **Don't eat this bread. Take some fresh (bread).**

TYPOWE BŁĘDY UWAŻAJ!

Źle: There was no fresh milk so I bought ~~a powdered one.~~

PODPOWIEDŹ: Nigdy nie używaj **one/ones** zamiast rzeczownika niepoliczalnego.
Powtórz rzeczownik, albo go w ogóle opuść.

Dobrze: There was no fresh milk so I bought some powdered (milk).

Źle: I've got the photos. I put ~~ones~~ in the drawer.

PODPOWIEDŹ: **One/ones** możesz użyć jeśli masz na myśli nieokreśloną rzecz lub osobę.
Jeśli masz na myśli konkretną, określoną rzecz lub osobę, użyj zaimka osobowego w odpowiedniej formie.

Dobrze: I've got the photos. I put them in the drawer.

YOUR TURN NOW!

I. Make sentences as in the example. Use **one** or **ones**.

EXAMPLE These plates are very nice. (*Each plate is nicely decorated.*)
Each one is nicely decorated.

1. This jacket is worn-out. *(I need a new jacket.)* ______________________.
2. I went to the supermarket to buy some food. (*Which supermarket did you go to?*)
   ______________________?
3. I watched some good films last week. (*Which film did you like best?*)
   ______________________?
4. I like green apples. (*I don't like red apples.*) ______________________.
5. Who is this man? (*This man in a black suit.*) ______________________.

II. Complete the dialogue. Put **one/ones/some** where necessary.

A: Here, I've bought this bottle of mineral water for you.
B: Oh, no! You've bought a small _______(1) and I asked you to buy two big _______(2).
A: Sorry, they didn't have any big _______(3), only small _______(4).
B: Which shop did you go to?
A: The _______(5) next to the bookshop.
B: Why didn't you go to the _______ (6) round the corner?
A: I met a friend of mine and he wanted to go to the bookshop.
B: Which friend? The _______ (7) with red hair?
A: Yes, John. And we've bought _______(8) strawberry biscuits.
B: Not again! You know I hate strawberry biscuits. I prefer plain _______(9).
A: There are _______ (10) plain _______ (11) in the cupboard, look!

III. Correct the mistakes in these sentences. Be careful, one sentence is correct!

1. I threw away my old jeans because I bought some new.
2. If you need a pencil, I can get some for you.
3. If you like grapes, I'll bring you ones.
4. If you need tomatoes, I'll bring you some fresh ones from the garden.
5. I'm not sure if I'll need any money but I'd better take ones.
6. I have one daughter and Mary has two ones.
7. Where are my glasses? I've put some in the drawer.

KEY

I. 1. I need a new one. 2. Which one did you go to? 3. Which one did you like best? 4. I don't like red ones. 5. The one in a black suit. **II.** 1. one 2. ones 3. ones 4. ones 5. one 6. one 7. one 8. some 9. ones 10. some 11. ones **III.** 1. I threw away my old jeans because I bought some new ones. 2. If you want a pencil, I can get one for you. 3. If you like grapes, I'll bring you some. 4. OK. 5. I'm not sure if I'll need any money but I'd better take some. 6. I have one daughter and Mary has two. 7. Where are my glasses? I've put them in the drawer.

I've cut myself on my knife! Skaleczyłam się nożem!
Joan, look at yourself! Joan, popatrz na siebie!
Lynn has made herself a sandwich. Lynne zrobiła sobie kanapkę.
Jeff lives by himself/on his own/alone. Jeff mieszka sam.
The computer has switched itself off automatically. Komputer wyłączył się automatycznie.
We've built this house ourselves. Sami zbudowaliśmy ten dom (nikt inny).
We've built this house by ourselves. Sami zbudowaliśmy ten dom (bez niczyjej pomocy).
Tom and Jerry, behave yourselves! Tom i Jerry, zachowujcie się!
They helped themselves to the cake. Poczęstowali się ciastem.

Odpowiednikiem angielskich **reflexive pronouns** są polskie zaimki **sam/a, sami/same, się, sobie, siebie**.

KIEDY STOSUJESZ REFLEXIVE PRONOUNS?

Gdy dopełnieniem zdania jest ta sama osoba lub rzecz, która stanowi podmiot.
WYJĄTEK: **His diaries are all about himself.**

→ **Reflexive pronouns** mogą wystąpić z takimi czasownikami jak: **behave, burn, cut, dry, enjoy, hurt, help, kill**.

→ **Wash, dress, shave** zazwyczaj nie występują z **reflexive pronouns**, chyba że chcesz podkreślić, że czynność wymagała pokonania jakichś trudności. (**She dressed herself although she had a broken arm.**)

→ **Reflexive pronouns** mogą występować wymiennie z konstrukcją **on my/his own** etc., która znaczy to samo, co **alone**.

TYPOWE BŁĘDY UWAŻAJ!

Źle: Children, you can dry ~~yourself~~ on these towels.
PODPOWIEDŹ: Zaimek **yourself** odnosi się do liczby pojedynczej.
Dobrze: Children, you can dry yourselves on these towels.

Źle: My sons are always fighting with ~~themselves~~.
PODPOWIEDŹ: Nie stosuj zaimka zwrotnego zamiast **each other/one another** (> unit 38).
Dobrze: My sons are always fighting with each other.

HOTSPOT!

PORÓWNAJ: Sheila looked behind **herself**.
Sheila looked behind **her**.

Oba te zdania są poprawne, ale różnią się znaczeniem. Pierwsze przetłumaczymy: Sheila popatrzyła (sobie) przez ramię (tj. na coś, co było bezpośrednio za nią). Drugie oznacza, że Sheila popatrzyła za siebie – na coś, co było za nią, blisko lub daleko.

YOUR TURN NOW!

I. Complete the sentences with a suitable reflexive pronoun.

1. Gregory hates living by __________, he likes having a company around.
2. Jenny, help __________ to the grapes, please.
3. Hey, you both, be careful or you will burn __________.
4. We enjoyed __________ at the party, it was great.
5. The Browns prefer spending their holidays by __________ to having other people's company.
6. I don't know what has happened. The light went off by __________.
7. Elizabeth cooked lunch __________, there was nobody at home to help her.

II. Choose the right verb from the box and complete the sentences with a suitable reflexive pronoun where necessary. Remember to change the verb into the right form.

help	burn	get dressed	buy	make	do	teach

1. Mary, _________ and off we go!
2. George, please, sit comfortably and _________ at home.
3. These biscuits are delicious, _________, please.
4. Jackie _________ a new dress for her prom.
5. Julie, have you _________ your homework by _________ or have you copied it?
6. He didn't have driving lessons. He _______________ how to drive.
7. Don't touch it, children, it's very hot, you can _________.

III. Join the broken sentences.

1. Tom is only three but he
2. I hope my children were nice and
3. Did you enjoy
4. It's OK., I can
5. We decided to keep

a. yourself at Wendy's party?
b. pay for myself, no problem.
c. can dress himself.
d. most of the paintings for ourselves.
e. behaved themselves.

IV. Correct the mistakes where necessary.

1. How are you feeling yourself?
2. Relax yourself, you are overworked.
3. Hurry up yourselves, we have very little time.
4. Did you really do it by yourself?
5. He has a broken arm but still he can dress alone.

KEY

I. 1. himself 2. yourself 3. yourselves 4. ourselves 5. themselves 6. itself 7. herself **II.** 1. get dressed 2. make yourself 3. help yourself/yourselves 4. bought herself 5. have you done your homework by yourself or… 6. taught himself 7. burn yourselves **III.** 1c 2e 3a 4b 5d **IV.** 1. How do you feel/How are you feeling? 2. Relax, you're overworked. 3. Hurry up, we have very little time. 4. OK. 5. He has a broken arm but still he can dress himself.

UNIT 35 another/the second/other/the other/others/the others

Can I have another cup of tea, please? Czy mogę dostać jeszcze jedną filiżankę herbaty?
I don't like this jacket. I'll buy another one. Nie podoba mi się ta kurtka. Kupię inną.
This jacket is too big for me but the other one is just right.
Ta kurtka jest na mnie za duża, ale ta druga jest w sam raz.
This shop assistant was very rude, but the other ones were polite.
Ten sprzedawca był bardzo niegrzeczny, ale inni byli uprzejmi.
There are other shopping centres in this town. I'll take you there.
W tym mieście są inne centra handlowe. Zabiorę cię tam.
The first shop was not bad, the second one was also good but the third one was the best.
Pierwszy sklep nie był zły, drugi też był dobry, ale ten trzeci był najlepszy.
Some people like jackets, others prefer long coats.
Niektórzy ludzie lubią kurtki, inni wolą długie płaszcze.

JAK STOSUJESZ ANOTHER, THE SECOND, OTHER, THE OTHER, ORAZ OTHERS, THE OTHERS?

1. **another** – przed rzeczownikiem policzalnym w liczbie pojedynczej, w znaczeniu **a different one, one more**.
2. **the second** – przed rzeczownikiem w liczbie pojedynczej, gdy wymieniasz więcej niż dwie rzeczy lub osoby. Raczej nie stosuj tego określenia jeśli masz do wyboru tylko dwie rzeczy z danego zbioru/gatunku.
3. **the other** – przed rzeczownikami policzalnymi w liczbie pojedynczej w znaczeniu **not this one, the remaining one** lub odpowiednio w liczbie mnogiej – **not these ones, the remaining ones**.
4. **other** – przed rzeczownikiem w liczbie mnogiej. Odpowiada to polskiemu **inni/inne** (ludzie, rzeczy).
5. **others/the others** – odpowiadają polskiemu **inni/inne**. Nie występują przed rzeczownikiem, lecz go zastępują. **The others** stosujesz jeśli mówiąc **inni** masz na myśli określone osoby lub rzeczy (**Let's wait for the others!**)

TYPOWE BŁĘDY **UWAŻAJ!**

Źle: I have ~~others~~ books too.
PODPOWIEDŹ: Jeśli chcesz użyć słowa **inne/inni** przed rzeczownikiem w liczbie mnogiej, użyj **other**.
Dobrze: I have other books too.

Źle: Could you show me another ~~jackets~~?
PODPOWIEDŹ: Słowo **another** poprzedza rzeczownik w liczbie pojedynczej, nie mnogiej.
Dobrze: Could you show me another jacket?

YOUR TURN NOW!

I. Complete these sentences with **another, other, the other, others, the others, the second**.

1. This tie is too bright. Could you show me __________ one?
2. In my group only Kasia speaks English fluently, __________ students are not so good.
3. Some pop singers are more popular than __________.
4. I can't wait for you all day. I have __________ things to do.
5. I don't like these sweaters. Show me some __________ ones, please.
6. The first concert was very successful, __________ one was also interesting, but the third one was a disaster.
7. I've found __________ way to solve this problem.
8. I'm sure there must be some __________ ways to solve this problem.
9. We are early so let's wait for __________ people.
10. 'Could you show me Tim in this photo?' 'Sure. Look, he's __________ on the left.'
11. We have finished this exercise. __________ are still working.

II. Correct the mistakes.

1. Show me the second book, please. I don't like this one.
2. Let's find other hotel, this one is too expensive.
3. Beckham played beautifully, but others were lazy.
4. Krysia is a very good pupil but the others children in her class don't like her very much.
5. Don't worry, I have another glasses.
6. Let's discuss others points of view as well.
7. Some people like their pizza spicy, the others prefer it mild.

HOTSPOT!

COMPARE: Give me **a second chance**, please.
Give me **another chance**, please.

These sentences have very similar meanings. The only difference is that 'a second chance' means that you've had only one chance so far. 'Another chance' could mean that you've already had one, or two, or even more chances!

'Please give me
another chance, dear.'

KEY

I. 1. another 2. the other 3. others 4. other 5. other 6. the second 7. another 8. other 9. other/the other 10. the second 11. The others **II.** 1. Show me another book, please. I don't like this one. 2. Let's find another hotel, this one is too expensive. 3. Beckham played beautifully but the others were lazy. 4. Krysia is a very good pupil but the other children in her class don't like her very much. 5. Don't worry, I have other glasses. 6. Let's discuss other points of view as well. 7. Some people like their pizza spicy, others prefer it mild.

UNIT 36 all/whole/every

All Poles are proud of their past. Wszyscy Polacy są dumni ze swojej przeszłości.
Every Pole likes a pork chop. Każdy Polak lubi schabowego.
She spent the whole day (all day) studying for her exam. Spędziła cały dzień ucząc się do egzaminu.
The hurricane destroyed the whole village. Huragan zrujnował całą wieś.

KIEDY STOSUJESZ ALL?

All występuje z rzeczownikami policzalnymi w liczbie mnogiej oraz z rzeczownikami niepoliczalnymi. Jeśli mówisz o określonej, konkretnej grupie osób lub rzeczy, musisz użyć **all the.**

All teachers complain about their salaries.
All the students in my school are smart.
All the water has been spilled.

All/all of możesz użyć wymiennie przed rzeczownikiem poprzedzonym określnikiem. Jeśli rzeczownik występuje bez określnika, nie używa się **all of**.

All (of) my friends like horse-riding.
All cigarettes are harmful.

KIEDY STOSUJESZ WHOLE?

Gdy mówisz o czymś jako o całości, np. **The whole building was burnt.**
Whole buildings were burnt.

→ **Whole** nie występuje z rzeczownikami niepoliczalnymi.

→ W wyrażeniach określających długość czasu stosujemy **all** lub **the whole (of)**, np. **Stop sitting here all day doing nothing!**
She spent the whole day doing nothing.
She spent the whole of the day doing nothing.

KIEDY STOSUJESZ EVERY?

Z rzeczownikiem w liczbie pojedynczej, gdy mówisz o osobach lub rzeczach jako o pewnej całości, np. **Every child must be vaccinated against common infectious diseases.**
(> unit 37)

TYPOWE BŁĘDY UWAŻAJ!

Źle: I've spent the ~~whole my~~ childhood in this village.
PODPOWIEDŹ: Nie opuszczaj **of** w konstrukcjach **whole** + określnik dzierżawczy + rzeczownik
Dobrze: I've spent the whole of my childhood in this village.

Źle: ~~All children~~ in the kindergarten like Mary.
PODPOWIEDŹ: Nie pomijaj **the** w kostrukcji z **all** dotyczącej ściśle określonej grupy osób lub rzeczy.
Dobrze: All the children in the kindergarten like Mary.

YOUR TURN NOW!

I. Complete the sentences. Use **all, all (of) the, every, whole, a/the whole of**.

1. She spent ________ her money on gambling.
2. George has been shopping __________ afternoon.
3. We were thirsty so we drank _______ bottle of mineral water.
4. They have finished _______ work and went home.
5. ___________ the city was damaged in the fire.
6. I have just finished reading ' ______ the President's Men' by Jeremy Archer.
7. _______ building belongs to the Thomsons, not just part of it.
8. ___________ teachers in this school are well-qualified.
9. _________ us were very tired after the trip.
10. Put ___________ the books on this shelf, please.
11. _________ American loves fast food.
12. ________ jacket was dirty.

II. Do the crossword and find the clue.

1. I can't watch the whole match on TV today, I'm too ________ right now.
2. We spent all the ___________ at the seaside, it was great!
3. All these __________ were taken in Italy. Look, here is Marion lying on the beach.
4. All the _________ in the play were excellent.
5. The bus was overcrowded and all the _________ were occupied by some young people.
6. Every _________ must take examinations at the end of the term.
7. The whole _________ was redecorated before 1st September.

CROSSWORD

III. Correct the mistakes.

1. All you know Mary Brown, don't you?
2. The whole my salary comes into my bank account.
3. Whole money was spent on charity actions.
4. All students in this group passed the exam.

KEY

I. 1. all/all of 2. the whole/all 3. a whole 4. the whole 5. All/ The whole of 6. All 7. The whole 8. All (of) the 9. All of 10. all 11. Every 12. The whole **II.** 1. busy 2. summer 3. pictures 4. actors 5. seats 6. student 7. school **Clue:** SUCCESS **III.** 1. All of you know Mary Brown, don't you?/You all know Mary Brown, don't you? 2. The whole of my salary comes into my bank account/My whole salary comes into my bank account. 3. All money was spent on charity actions. 4. All the students/All of the students passed the exam.

UNIT 37 every/each/each of

Every child (all children) should go to school. Każde dziecko powinno chodzić do szkoły. Wszystkie dzieci powinny chodzić do szkoły.
Each child got a piece of cake. Każde dziecko dostało po kawałku ciasta.
Each of my children plays the piano. Każde z moich dzieci gra na pianinie.
The tickects are £ 25 each. Bilety są po 25 funtów (każdy).

KIEDY UŻYWASZ EVERY?

1. Gdy mówisz o wielu rzeczach lub osobach jako o pewnej całości, grupie, np.
   Every student must attend classes. = All students must attend classes.
2. Gdy mówisz, że coś zdarza w regularnych odstępach czasu, np.
   I take a shower every morning. Every six months I go to the dentist's.

→ **Every other day = every second day**

KIEDY UŻYWASZ EACH/ EACH OF?

1. Gdy mówisz o rzeczy lub osobie jako o jednostce, traktując je indywidualnie, np.
   Each player shook hands with the captain of the team.
2. **Each** może także występować w zdaniu samodzielnie, np.
   These cookies cost 30 cents each.

→ Zarówno **each**, jak i **every** występują z czasownikiem w liczbie pojedynczej.

3. Gdy mówisz o rzeczy lub osobie należącej do pewnej określonej grupy używasz konstrukcji **each of. Each of** łączy się z rzeczownikiem w liczbie mnogiej, np.
   Each of my sisters has two children.

TYPOWE BŁĘDY UWAŻAJ!

Źle: Each of my cousins ~~live~~ in Warsaw.
PODPOWIEDŹ: W konstrukcji **each of** nie stosuj czasownika w liczbie mnogiej.
Dobrze: Each of my cousins lives in Warsaw.

Źle: ~~Every~~ shoe of this pair has a broken heel.
PODPOWIEDŹ: Nie używaj **every** w stosunku do pary, tj. dwóch osób lub rzeczy.
Dobrze: Each shoe of this pair has a broken heel.

HOTPOINT!

Często nie ma różnicy, czy użyjesz **each** czy **every**.
Each house/every house in this street has a red roof.

YOUR TURN NOW!

I. Complete the dialogues with **each** or **every**.

A: You have a great flat, Kate!
B: Yes, there are four bedrooms, so _________ (1) child has a separate room to sleep and study.

A: How often do you phone your grandaparents, Jeff?
B: I try to phone them _________ (2) day but sometimes I'm too busy.

A: Does it cost a lot if you have a party _________ (3) week?
B: No, if _________ (4) guest brings some food. We share the cost, you know.

A: Does _________ (5) of your friends have a computer at home?
B: That's right. _________ (6) evening we send e-mails to each other.

A: Did you enjoy the training, Mary?
B: Yes, _________ (7) minute of the training was extremely interesting. Pity that you didn't come too.

A: Did you get nice wedding presents, Jenny?
B: Not particularly. _________ (8) of my aunts gave me an iron, can you believe it?

A: Does it take you long to pack for your holiday, Mark?
B: Well, it depends, but _________ (9) time I go on holiday I try to pack up my things at least a week before I leave.

A: How much did you pay for the tickets, Bob?
B: They cost me 10 euros _________ (10).

II. Correct the mistakes.

1. Each second Monday I have to stay in the office till 7 pm.
2. Each my aunt is over 30.
3. The concert was marvellous. I enjoyed each minute of it.
4. Look at this exercise and study every sentence carefully.

III. Join the broken sentences.

1. Take these pills	a. each.
2. These roses cost one euro	b. bowl each.
3. I have two cats and they have a separate	c. second week.
4. We have an English test every	d. every six hours.
5. Jim and Martha, each of you must write the test	e. on your own, copying is prohibited.

KEY

I. 1. each/every 2. every 3. every 4. each/every 5. each 6. every 7. every 8. each 9. every/each 10. each **II.** 1. Every second Monday I have to stay in the office till 7 pm. 2. Each of my aunts is over 30. 3. The concert was marvellous. I enjoyed every minute of it. 4. OK. **III.** 1d 2a 3b 4c 5e

UNIT 38 each other/one another

They love each other/one another so much that they want to marry.
Kochają się tak bardzo, że chcą się pobrać.
We are such good friends that we can spend hours talking to each other/one another.
Jesteśmy tak dobrymi przyjaciółmi, że możemy spędzać godziny rozmawiając ze sobą.
Stop shouting at each other/one another, the baby is sleeping.
Przestańcie na siebie krzyczeć, dziecko śpi.
We often help each other/one another. Często pomagamy sobie nawzajem.

KIEDY STOSUJESZ EACH OTHER/ONE ANOTHER?

→ Gdy czynność lub uczucie skierowane są wzajemnie na drugą osobę lub inne osoby. W zasadzie nie ma różnicy, czy stosujesz **each other** czy **one another,** choć niektórzy językownawcy są zdania, że **each other** odnosi się do dwóch osób, a **one another** do większej liczby osób. Różnice te jednak zacierają się i obecnie nie ma znaczenia, której z tych form używasz.

→ Gdy czynność jest skierowana na podmiot zdania, używasz odpowiedniego zaimka zwrotnego, np. **John has built the greenhouse himself.**

PORÓWNAJ: Cats wash themselves by licking their fur.
My cats often wash each other by licking each other's fur.

TYPOWE BŁĘDY UWAŻAJ!

Źle: They are in love and every day they phone ~~themselves.~~

PODPOWIEDŹ: Gdy czynność jest wzajemna, tzn. skierowana jest na inną osobę, nie używamy zaimka zwrotnego (np. **themselves**), lecz zaimka względnego **each other** lub **one another.**

Dobrze: They are in love and every day they phone each other/one another.

They are looking at themselves.
They are looking at each other.

HOTSPOT!

Życzenie **Nawzajem!** to po angielsku **The same to you!**

YOUR TURN NOW!

I. Complete the sentences with a suitable reflexive or reciprocal pronoun.

1. We often meet __________ in the park, while we're walking our dogs.
2. Dear children, help __________ to the sweets.
3. My neighbour shouts at his wife and she shouts at him. They shout at __________.
4. We're neighbours. We live next to __________.
5. I'll miss you! Let's promise we'll be in touch with __________ as often as possible.

II. Think up a suitable word, do the crossword and find the clue.

CROSSWORD

1. Kate, you're very naughty, behave __________!
2. Green is my favourite __________. All others don't suit me, I think.
3. I have painted this room by __________, really!
4. This problem is very __________. We can't solve it by ourselves.
5. We seldom __________ letters to each other these days; we prefer to phone.
6. Can't you __________ this document yourself? The printer is over there.

III. Translate.

1. Szczęśliwego Nowego Roku! Nawzajem!
2. Usiądź i ucz się, bo jutro masz egzamin.
3. Sama upiekłaś to ciasto, czy je kupiłaś?
4. Spotkajmy się jutro wieczorem.

IV. Correct the mistakes.

1. We haven't seen ourselves recently.
2. I heard you were ill. How are you feeling yourself now?
3. We support ourselves whenever possible.
4. They had an argument and now they don't talk to themselves.

KEY

I. 1. each other/one another 2. yourselves 3. each other/one another 4. each other/one another 5. each other/one another **II.** 1. yourself 2. colour 3. myself 4. complicated 5. write 6. print **Clue:** SUMMER **III.** 1. Happy New Year! The same to you! 2. Sit down and study, because you have an exam tomorrow. 3. Did you bake this cake yourself or did you buy it? 4. Let's meet tomorrow evening. IV. 1. We haven't seen each other/one another recently. 2. I heard you were ill. How are you feeling now? 3. We support each other/one another whenever possible. 4. They had an argument and now they don't talk to each other/one another.

UNIT 39 both (of)/either (of)/neither (of)

Both (of) these language schools are good. Obydwie te szkoły językowe są dobre.
Both schools are good. Obydwie szkoły są dobre.
You can go to either school. Możesz chodzić do dowolnej szkoły (którejkolwiek z nich).
I haven't been to either of those schools. Nie byłam w żadnej z tych szkół.
Neither of these jackets was expensive. Żadna z tych dwóch kurtek nie była droga.

KIEDY UŻYWASZ BOTH?

Gdy mówisz o dwóch osobach lub rzeczach jako grupie. **Both** występuje przed rzeczownikiem w liczbie mnogiej i łączy się z czasownikami w liczbie mnogiej, np. **Both children play the violin.** **Both** może również występować na końcu zdania, np. **I love them both.**

KIEDY UŻYWAMY EITHER/NEITHER?

Gdy mówisz o dwóch osobach lub rzeczach, odnosząc się do nich indywidualnie.

Either występuje przed rzeczownikiem w liczbie pojedynczej, np. **Either explanation was good.**

Neither występuje w zdaniach przeczących przed rzeczownikiem w liczbie pojedynczej i łączy się z czasownikami w liczbie pojedynczej, np. **Neither lecture was interesting.**

KIEDY UŻYWASZ BOTH OF/EITHER OF/NEITHER OF?

Konstrukcji tych możesz używać z zaimkiem w liczbie mnogiej lub z rzeczownikiem w liczbie mnogiej, jednak przed rzeczownikiem musi znajdować się przedimek określony **the**, zaimek **these/those** lub określnik dzierżawczy.

Both of the restaurants were expensive. Both of them were expensive.
Either of these children can say this poem. Either of them can do this.
Neither of our children failed the test. Neither of them failed the test.

→ **Both**, **either** i **neither** mogą również występować samodzielnie.

Milk or sugar for you? Both, please.
Coke or orange juice? Either, I don't mind.
Is Bob English or American? Neither. He's Scottish.

TYPOWE BŁĘDY UWAŻAJ!

Źle: Neither boy ~~didn't go~~ to school yesterday.

PODPOWIEDŹ: Gdy używasz **neither/neither** of pamiętaj o zasadzie pojedynczego przeczenia. Czasownik jest w formie twierdzącej, chociaż zdanie jako całość jest przeczące.

Dobrze: Neither boy went to school yesterday.

I. Complete the sentences with **both, either, neither**. Add **of** where necessary.

1. __________ my parents lives in Warsaw. They live in Malbork.
2. I've got two computers. Unfortunately, __________ them are quite old.
3. Ralph caught the ball with __________ hands.
4. __________ these schools were recommended by Mr Smith.
5. There are two coffee machines in this bar and __________ them is working.
6. I've got two bikes, so you can borrow __________ them and we'll go cycling.
7. Jim and Mary, tidy up the mess, __________ you!
8. To tell you the truth, __________ film was worth seeing.

II. Do the crossword and find the clue.

CROSSWORD

1. __________ of the hotels was good so we looked for another place to stay.
2. There were two people in the room and both of __________ were wearing black suits.
3. Would you like __________ or lemon in your tea? Neither, thank you.
4. I couldn't phone you from my office because both __________ were broken.
5. __________ you received my two letters? Yes, both of them, thank you.
6. You can park on __________ side of the street, it's up to you.
7. Is the meeting on Monday or on __________? Neither, it's on Wednesday.
8. Which of these __________ by Picasso do you like best? Neither, I don't like his style.
9. Elizabeth and Mary, get to work, both of __________!
10. Have you got a scanner and a __________ at home? Yes, I have both.

III. Correct the mistakes.

1. Both them have passed their driving test.
2. Neither of us didn't go to work yesterday.
3. Mary couldn't see neither person in the darkness.

KEY

I. 1. Neither of 2. both of 3. both 4. Both (of) 5. neither of 6. either of 7. both of 8. neither **II.** 1. Neither 2. them 3. milk 4. telephones 5. Have 6. either 7. Tuesday 8. paintings 9. you 10. printer **CLUE:** TELEVISION **III.** 1. Both of them have passed their driving test. 2. Neither of us went to work yesterday. 3. Mary couldn't see either person in the darkness/Mary could see neither person in the darkness.

UNIT 40 IT as a subject

It took me two hours to get home yesterday. Dwie godziny zajął mi wczoraj powrót do domu.
Is it far to the shopping centre? Czy daleko jest do centrum handlowego?
It's cloudy today. Pochmurno dzisiaj/Dzisiaj jest pochmurno.
It's a pity that Susan didn't come. Szkoda, że Susan nie przyszła.
It's no use talking to Ben. He never listens. Nie ma sensu rozmawiać z Benem. On nigdy nie słucha.
It was Margaret who ate all of the cake. To Margaret zjadła całe ciasto.
It's the children I'm worrying about. To o dzieci tak się martwię.

KIEDY STOSUJESZ IT JAKO PODMIOT?

It wasn't me who broke the vase, Mum!

Do wyrażania czasu
It's two o'clock.

Do wyrażania odległości
It's 200m to the nearest bus stop.

Do opisywania pogody
It's snowing.

Do wyrażania opinii, emocji, odczuć
It's interesting to visit foreign countries.

Do podkreślenia lub identyfikacji osoby/rzeczy
It's Jim who came late.

W wyrażeniach **It's been + period of time + since**
It's been ages since we last met.

TYPOWE BŁĘDY UWAŻAJ!

Źle: ~~They're~~ the children I'm talking about.
PODPOWIEDŹ: Nie zamieniaj **it** na **they**, nawet jeśli rzeczownik jest w liczbie mnogiej. **It** + czasownik w liczbie pojedynczej stosuje się zarówno do rzeczowników w liczbie pojedynczej jak i mnogiej.
Dobrze: It's the children I'm talking about.

Źle: ~~There was~~ a sunny day yesterday.
PODPOWIEDŹ: Nie można stosować wymiennie **there** zamiast **it**. **It** jako podmiot stosujesz, gdy mówisz o doznaniach zmysłowych.
Dobrze: It was a sunny day yesterday.

HOTSPOT!

W wyrażeniu **It's been + period of time + since** można opuścić wyraz **been**.

YOUR TURN NOW!

I. Join the broken sentences.

1. Love it
2. It's a long way
3. It's been three years
4. It's Jenny who
5. It's getting late
6. I like my town

a. since I moved house.
b. fed the dog.
c. to San Francisco.
d. or leave it.
e. but it would be nicer to live in the forest.
f. so we must go home.

II. Do the crossword and find the clue.

1. It's a long ______ from here to the station.
2. What day is it ___________?
3. It's a ________ that you're too busy to come with us.
4. It's no _____ asking him for help.
5. It's three weeks _______ we last talked on the phone.
6. It ________ us ten months to finish this book.
7. It's been _________ talking to you.
8. It's ____________. Maybe it will rain later.
9. It's Jack who broke the _________. There's glass everywhere.

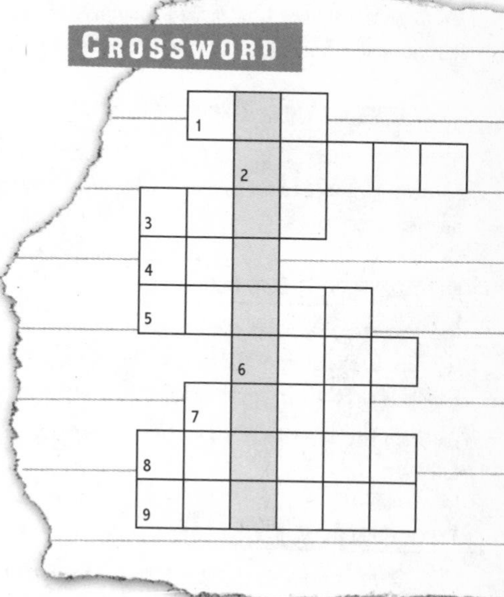

III. Correct the mistakes where necessary.

1. Who's that? They're Jim and Jenny.
2. There has already been discussed.
3. It nothing serious, don't worry.
4. It's important to start learning a foreign language as early as posssible.

HOTSPOT!

COMPARE: It's Elizabeth speaking.
This is Elizabeth speaking.

Answering the phone you can use **it** or **this**.

KEY

I. 1d 2c 3a 4b 5f 6e **II.** 1. way 2. today 3. pity 4. use 5. since 6. took 7. nice 8. cloudy 9. window **CLUE:** ATTENTION **III.** 1. Who's that? It's Jim and Jenny. 2. It's (it has) already been discussed. 3. It's (it is) nothing serious, don't worry. 4. OK.

UNIT 41 IT as a subject/THERE as a subject

They live in a big city. There's a lot of noise in their street.
Oni mieszkają w dużym mieście. Na ich ulicy jest dużo hałasu.
They live in a big city. It's very noisy in their street.
Oni mieszkają w dużym mieście. Na ich ulicy jest bardzo hałaśliwie.
There's a burglar in their flat. W ich mieszkaniu jest/znajduje się włamywacz.
It's dangerous to enter this flat now. Niebezpiecznie jest teraz wejść do tego mieszkania.
It was windy yesterday. Wczoraj było wietrznie.
There was a strong wind yesterday. Wczoraj był silny wiatr.
It's Jack and Agatha who broke the vase. To Jacek i Agata stłukli wazon.
It's three years since I last visited London. Trzy lata minęły odkąd po raz ostatni byłam w Londynie.
It's four miles from here to Bishopton. Stąd do Bishopton są cztery mile.

KIEDY UŻYWASZ THERE JAKO PODMIOTU?

Gdy mówisz o czymś po raz pierwszy, wspominasz, że ktoś lub coś jest, istnieje w danym miejscu. Konstrukcja **there+be** występuje w liczbie pojedynczej lub mnogiej zgodnie z formą następującego po niej rzeczownika.

KIEDY UŻYWASZ IT JAKO PODMIOTU?

Gdy chcesz opisać jakiś stan, pogodę, podać czas, odległość, lub podkreślić jakąś sytuację, np. **It's the Browns who are giving the party on Friday, not the Greens.**
Konstrukcja **it's** występuje zawsze w liczbie pojedynczej.

→ Zarówno **there's** jak i **it's** zazwyczaj odpowiadają polskiemu **jest**, dlatego często popełniamy tu błędy.

TYPOWE BŁĘDY UWAŻAJ!

Źle: ~~There's~~ so stuffy in this room. Let's open the window.
PODPOWIEDŹ: Nie zastępuj konstrukcji **it is** przez **there is** jeśli mówisz o odczuciach zmysłowych.
Dobrze: It's so stuffy in this room. Let's open the window.

Źle: ~~They are~~ the girls who bought the flowers.
PODPOWIEDŹ: Konstrukcja **it is** (**it's**) odnosi się zarówno do liczby pojedynczej jak i mnogiej.
Dobrze: It's the girls who bought the flowers.

Źle: ~~There are~~ two years since I saw him.
PODPOWIEDŹ: Pamiętaj, że podając czas lub odległość używasz konstrukcji **it's**, nie **there's**, nawet jeśli następujący po niej rzeczownik jest w liczbie mnogiej.
Dobrze: It's two years since I saw him.

YOUR TURN NOW!

I. Complete the sentences with a suitable form of **there is** or **it is**.

1. __________ a hole in my bucket, dear Lisa!
2. The journey took us four hours. __________ a lot of traffic jams.
3. __________ difficult to understand the lecture on the theory of relativity last Monday.
4. How far __________ from Kielce to Radom?
5. Two days ago __________ a terrible storm in our area.
6. I wanted to visit Madame Tissaud's but __________ no time for that.
7. __________ so dark in here, I can't see anything.
8. __________ Bob's birthday last Sunday and I completely forgot about it!

II. Paraphrase the sentences as in the example.

EXAMPLE: It's a sandy beach. There's a lot of sand on the beach.

1. It was a stormy day yesterday. There ______________________.
2. It's messy in your room, George. There______________________.
3. My coffee had too much sugar in it. There ______________________.
4. It's possible to go to Cracow by plane. There______________________.
5. It will be very frosty at the weekend. There______________________.

III. Join the broken sentences. There is more than one possibility.

A	**B**
1. It's	a. John, not Martin, who answered the phone.
2. There was	b. warmer outside than I thought.
3. It was	c. takes me an hour to get to work.
4. There is	d. a big demonstration in Warsaw yesterday.
5. It	e. a hole in these tights, look!

IV. Correct the mistakes where necessary.

1. The journey took two hours. It was a traffic jam.
2. It's a storm over Warsaw last night.
3. It's a strange man at the door.
4. There's no time left, sorry.
5. There is a lot of children in the playground.

KEY

I. 1. There's 2. There were 3. It was 4. is it 5. there was 6. there was 7. It's 8. It was **II.** 1. There was a storm yesterday. 2. There's a mess in your room, George. 3. There was too much sugar in my coffee. 4. There's a possibility of going to Cracow by plane. 5. There will be a lot of frost at the weekend. **III.** 1a/b 2d 3a/b 4e 5c **IV.** 1. There was a traffic jam. 2. There was a storm over Warsaw last night. 3. There's a strange man at the door. 4. OK. 5. There are a lot of children in the playground.

UNIT 42 (a) little/(a) few

I have (very) little money so I can't afford a new car.
Mam mało pieniędzy, więc nie stać mnie na nowy samochód.
I have a little money so maybe I'll buy a car. Mam trochę pieniędzy, więc może kupię samochód.
I have (very) few friends so I can't throw a party.
Mam (bardzo) niewielu przyjaciół, więc nie mogę urządzić imprezy.
I have a few friends so I don't feel lonely. Mam kilku przyjaciół, więc nie czuję się samotna.
Do you speak English? Yes, a little. Czy mówisz po angielsku? Tak, trochę.

KIEDY UŻYWASZ LITTLE/A LITTLE?

Z rzeczownikami niepoliczalnymi, gdy chcemy powiedzieć, że mamy pewną ilość czegoś.
Little time, little money oznacza **mało czasu**, **mało pieniędzy**, co ma wydźwięk negatywny.
A little time, a little money oznacza **trochę czasu**, **trochę pieniędzy**, co ma wydźwięk pozytywny.

KIEDY UŻYWASZ FEW/A FEW?

Z rzeczownikami policzalnymi, gdy chcemy powiedzieć, że mamy pewną liczbę czegoś.
Few children, few friends oznacza niewiele dzieci, niewielu przyjaciół, co ma wydźwięk negatywny.
A few children, a few friends oznacza kilkoro dzieci, kilku przyjaciół, co ma wydźwięk pozytywny.

→ Zarówno **a little** jak i **a few** można zastąpić przez określenia **some, a lot of, lots of**.
→ Określenia **little** i **few** występują zazwyczaj w połączeniu z **very** lub **too**, np.
I have very little time so I can't go to the cinema tonight.
I have too little time to go to the cinema tonight.

TYPOWE BŁĘDY UWAŻAJ!

Źle: There are ~~a~~ few good motorways in Poland so transport is poor.
PODPOWIEDŹ: Wyrażając krytyczną opinię nie dodawaj przedimka **a**, ponieważ zmienia on znaczenie określeń **little** i **few** z negatywnego na pozytywne.
Dobrze: There are few good motorways in Poland so transport is poor.

Źle: I have ~~little~~ books in English.
PODPOWIEDŹ: Z rzeczownikami policzalnymi używamy **few/a few**. Określenia **little/a little** łączą się z rzeczownikami policzalnymi tylko sporadycznie, w ściśle określonej sytuacji (> patrz HotSpot).
Dobrze: I have very few books in English.

HOTSPOT!

Zdanie **Tomek knows a little people in London** nie musi być błędem, lecz może wyrażać typowe dla języka angielskiego niedopowiedzenie i oznaczać, że Tomek zna trochę, a może nawet całkiem sporo ludzi w Londynie. Na egzaminie jednak lepiej z rzeczownikami policzalnymi używać **few/a few**.

YOUR TURN NOW!

I. Complete the sentences using **few** or **little**.

1. He has become a chairman although he has very _______ education.
2. Very _______ people in Poland can speak Japanese.
3. There are very _______ good pubs in Warsaw.
4. I have too _______ flour to make a cake.
5. Steve has too _______ money to buy a house.

II. Complete the sentences using **a few** or **a little**.

1. Can you dance the samba? Yes, _________.
2. Could you lend me ________ euros, please?
3. There was ________ ice on the lake this morning.
4. Elizabeth smokes only _______ cigarettes a day. She is trying to give up.
5. George bought ______ bottles of wine.
6. She gave the dog ________ soup. It looked so hungry.
7. I need _________ time to think over your suggestion.
8. Ralph knows __________ words in Arabic.

III. Add **a** where necessary.

1. I'm going to buy ______ few souvenirs while I am in London.
2. Could I ask you ______ few questions?
3. Susan is lucky, she has ______ few problems to solve.
4. I have ______ little time this morning so I can't take the dog for a walk.
5. There are ______ few things in this world that give me more pleasure than reading a good book.
6. ______ few houses in Poland have air-conditioning.

IV. Correct the mistakes where necessary.

1. I managed to save little money so I think I'll buy a new computer.
2. I need a few weeks to prepare for the exam.
3. Norman has very little friends in Warsaw so he spends most of his time on his own.
4. We should take few days off, we're so tired.
5. You need a little eggs to make pancakes.

KEY

I. 1. little 2. few 3. few 4. little 5. little **II.** 1. a little 2. a few 3. a little 4. a few 5. a few 6. a little 7. a little 8. a few **III.** 1. a 2. a 3. – 4. – 5. – 6. – **IV.** 1. I managed to save a little money so I think I'll buy a new computer. 2. OK 3. Norman has very few friends in Warsaw so he spends most of his time on his own. 4. We should take a few days off, we're so tired. 5. You need a few eggs to make pancakes.

UNIT 43 more/less/fewer/the most/the least/the fewest

I have less time than I thought. Mam mniej czasu niż myślałam.
I know fewer people than you do. Znam mniej ludzi niż ty.
Susan is less shy now than she was last year. Susan jest teraz mniej nieśmiała niż była w zeszłym roku.
There are more computers in this lab than in my office.
W tej pracowni jest więcej komputerów niż w moim biurze.

KIEDY STOSUJESZ MORE?

Gdy chcesz wyrazić, że czegoś jest więcej niż czegoś innego. **More** używamy zarówno z rzeczownikami niepoliczalnymi, jak i z policzalnymi w liczbie mnogiej, a także przy stopniowaniu przymiotników **more, the most** (> unit 6).

KIEDY STOSUJESZ LESS?

Gdy chcesz wyrazić, że czegoś jest mniej. **Less** występuje z rzeczownikami niepoliczalnymi, a także przy stopniowaniu przymiotników (**less, the least**).

KIEDY STOSUJESZ FEWER?

Gdy chcesz wyrazić, że pewna liczba czegoś jest mniejsza. **Fewer** łączy się tylko z rzeczownikami policzalnymi.

→ Określenia **a little** i **a few** odpowiadają polskim określeniom **trochę** i **kilka** i podobnie jak one nie stopniują się.

→ Stopniować można tylko określenia bez przedimka:

much – more – the most	**many – more – the most**
little – less – the least	**few – fewer/less – the fewest/the least.**

TYPOWE BŁĘDY UWAŻAJ!

Źle: I have ~~a~~ fewer friends than you do.
PODPOWIEDŹ: Przed określeniami ilości **more**, **less**, **fewer** nie stawia się przedimka nieokreślonego.
Dobrze: I have fewer friends than you do.

Źle: I have ~~fewer~~ luggage than you do.
PODPOWIEDŹ: Określenia **fewer** nie używa się z rzeczownikami niepoliczalnymi.
Dobrze: I have less luggage than you do.

Źle: My dog is little (small). It is ~~less~~ than yours.
PODPOWIEDŹ: Jeśli używasz **little** jako przymiotnika, stopniujesz go **smaller** – **smallest**, a nie jako **less** – **least.**
Dobrze: My dog is little. It is smaller than yours.

HOTSPOT!

W mowie potocznej coraz częściej używa się **less** zamiast **fewer** z rzeczownikami policzalnymi w liczbie mnogiej.

YOUR TURN NOW!

I. Complete the sentences with **more**, **less** or **fewer**.

1. Doctors earn __________ money than lawyers, but teachers earn the least.
2. Martin had __________ days off work than anybody in the office.
3. This car will cost you, more or __________, about 10,000 euros.
4. Ann made __________ mistakes in her test than Jerry.
5. It is __________ hot today than it was yesterday.
6. I have __________ free time these days than I used to have, I'm very busy.
7. We have __________ money in our bank account than we expected.

II. Complete the sentences with **less/the least** or **fewer/the fewest**.

1. Of all my cars, the Fiat 126 consumed ________ petrol.
2. Ralph is the student who made ________ mistakes in the English test.
3. You should eat ________ sweets.
4. Monica drives ________ carefully than she promised.
5. Kate is very impatient; she has ________ patience of all people I know.
6. ________ probable situation is that George will come over with a bunch of roses.
7. The other day we went shopping for clothes and I had ________ money to spend so I bought the fewest things.

III. Join these broken proverbs.

1. Last
2. The greatest talkers
3. Few words
4. The less said
5. Many are called
6. Many receive advice
7. Books and friends should be few

a) but good.
b) but few profit by it.
c) are best.
d) but few are chosen.
e) are the least active.
f) the better.
g) but not least.

IV. Correct these sentences where necessary.

1. Martha has got very few self-confidence, she is so shy.
2. She spoke English the least fluently last year than she does now.
3. The trip to Paris was less interesting than I expected.
4. Malden is less dangerous town I know.
5. Put fewer sugar into your cup of coffee; it'll taste better.
6. I am very proud of myself because today I've made the least mistakes in my English test than in my last week's test.

KEY

I. 1. less 2. fewer/less 3. less 4. fewer/less 5. less 6. less 7. less **II.** 1. the least 2. the fewest/the least 3. fewer/less 4. less 5. the least 6. The least 7. the least **III.** 1.g 2.e 3.c 4.f 5.d 6.b 7. a **IV.** 1. Martha has got very little self-confidence, she is so shy. 2. She spoke English less fluently last year than she does now. 3. OK 4. Malden is the least dangerous town I know. 5. Put less sugar into your cup of coffee; it'll taste better. 6. I am very proud of myself because I've made fewer/less mistakes in my English test than in my last week's test.

UNIT 44 enough/too

He had too little money to go on holiday. Miał za mało pieniędzy, aby pojechać na wakacje.
He didn't have enough money to go on holiday. Nie miał dość pieniędzy, aby pojechać na wakacje.
John is too weak to lift this suitcase. John jest za słaby, aby podnieść tę walizkę.
John isn't strong enough to lift this suitcase. John nie jest wystarczająco silny, aby podnieść tę walizkę.
She speaks English fluently enough to communicate. Ona mówi po angielsku wystarczająco płynnie, aby się porozumiewać.
Slow down, you're driving too fast. Zwolnij, jedziesz zbyt szybko.
It's much/far too cold to go for a walk. Jest dużo za zimno, aby pójść na spacer.
There were far too many people on the beach. Na plaży było zbyt wiele osób.
That's enough! Dosyć tego! Wystarczy!
That's too much, really. To za dużo, naprawdę.
Is there enough of this soup for Ben? Czy jest dość tej zupy dla Bena?/Czy wystarczy tej zupy dla Bena?

KIEDY STOSUJESZ ENOUGH?

Jeśli chcesz powiedzieć, że czegoś jest wystarczająco dużo lub dosyć; **enough** ma wydźwięk pozytywny. **Enough** występuje przed rzeczownikiem, ale po przymiotniku lub przysłówku. Może również występować samodzielnie. (**Enough is enough = Co za dużo to niezdrowo.**)

→ **Enough of** stosuje się z rzeczownikiem poprzedzonym przez **this/that**.

KIEDY STOSUJESZ TOO?

Too w znaczeniu **zbyt**, **za mało/za dużo** ma wydźwięk negatywny (**too little, too many, too quickly**).

Too występuje przed przymiotnikiem lub przysłówkiem. Nie występuje z rzeczownikiem.

TYPOWE BŁĘDY UWAŻAJ!

Źle: She is ~~enough pretty~~ to win the beauty contest.
PODPOWIEDŹ: Nie stosuj **enough** przed przymiotnikiem lub przysłówkiem, lecz po nich.
Dobrze: She is pretty enough to win the beauty contest.

Źle: He is ~~too much~~ generous.
PODPOWIEDŹ: Wzmocnienie **much** lub **far** występuje zawsze przed **too**.
Dobrze: He is much too generous./ He is far too generous.

Źle: I've got ~~enought~~ time to finish this project.
PODPOWIEDŹ: Postaraj się zapamiętać niełatwą pisownię wyrazu **enough**.
Dobrze: I've got enough time to finish this project.

YOUR TURN NOW!

I. Complete the sentences with **too** or **enough** and one of the words in the box.

busy rich short experienced gentle fresh

1. My dog is ____________ to bite anybody.
2. Sheila is ____________ to afford going on holiday in the Bahamas.
3. Is there ____________ bread for breakfast?
4. Sorry, I can't go to the cinema tonight. I'm ____________.
5. Bob is ____________ to get this job.
6. Susan ____________ to play basketball.

II. Paraphrase the sentences using **too** or **enough** as in the example.

EXAMPLE: My mother is too impatient to wait so long.
My mother isn't patient enough to wait so long.

1. It's too cold to play football outside. It ____________________.
2. I'm not strong enough to carry this suitcase. I ____________________.
3. Jeff is too young to get married. Jeff ____________________.
4. We have too little money to buy a house. We ____________________.
5. Jim isn't brave enough to ask Jenny for help. Jim ____________________.
6. These trousers are too small for me. These trousers ____________________.

III. Join the broken sentences.

1. Have we got enough
2. The weather is too bad
3. It's too late
4. The soup was
5. Is your room

a. to make it for the concert.
b. warm enough?
c. money for the tickets?
d. too salty.
e. to go climbing.

IV. Correct the mistakes.

1. Do we have enought flour to make pancakes?
2. You're driving enough fast to get a fine for speeding.
3. There's much enough time to finish this exercise.
4. The film was boring enough to watch it till the end.
5. They were too much exhausted to finish the race.

KEY

I. 1. too cute 2. rich enough 3. enough fresh bread 4. too busy 5. experienced enough 6. too short **II.** 1. It isn't warm enough to play football outside. 2. I'm too weak to carry this suitcase. 3. Jeff isn't old enough to get married. 4. We don't have enough money to buy a house. 5. Jim is too shy to ask Jenny for help. 6. These trousers aren't big enough for me. **III.** 1c 2e 3a 4d 5b **IV.** 1. Do we have enough flour to make pancakes? 2. You're driving fast enough to get a fine for speeding. 3. There's enough time to finish this exercise./There is much time to finish this exercise. 4. The film was too boring to watch it till the end. 5. They were much too exhausted to finish the race.

UNIT 45 A nice large new house ORDER OF ADJECTIVES

There is a large round wooden table in the kitchen. W kuchni jest duży okrągły drewniany stół.
Ben is a naughty little boy. Ben to niegrzeczny mały chłopczyk.
My grandma loves old Russian songs. Moja babcia lubi stare rosyjskie piosenki.

KOLEJNOŚĆ PRZYMIOTNIKÓW

Jeśli chcesz użyć kilku przymiotników, aby coś lub kogoś określić, zazwyczaj musisz zastosować się do schematu kolejności przymiotników przedstawionego w tabelce.

Opinion	How good?	General/ Specific	A lovely, comfortable room
Description	What size?	Size	A large hall
	What shape?	Shape	A round table
	How old?	Age	An old painting
	What colour?	Colour	A black and white sofa
	Where from?	Origin	A Russian song
	Made of?	Material	A wooden shelf
	What type/function?	Type/Purpose	An electric kettle A bread knife

→ Czasami w funkcji przymiotnika może występować rzeczownik lub rzeczownik odsłowny (**gerund**).

→ Nie używaj więcej niż trzech – czterech przymiotników naraz w jednym zdaniu. Jeśli chcesz użyć dwóch przymiotników tej samej kategorii, użyj spójnika **and** np. **a brown and green leaf, a chrome and steel table, a stable and long-lasting relationship**. Jeśli stosujesz kilka przymiotników różnych kategorii, nie używaj **and**, np. **a fantastic soft beige leather armchair**.

TYPOWE BŁĘDY UWAŻAJ!

Źle: It's a ~~charming small round twentieth-century English brass jewellery~~ box.
PODPOWIEDŹ: Jeśli zależy Ci, aby jednak użyć więcej niż czterech przymiotników, wyraź to jako zdanie złożone.
Dobrze: It's a charming English jewellery box, made of brass and dating from the twentieeth century. It's small and round.

Źle: It's a ~~large, black, beautiful, leather~~ sofa.
PODPOWIEDŹ: Trzymaj się ustalonego schematu kolejności przymiotników.
Dobrze: It's a beautiful large black leather sofa.

Źle: He bought a big ~~and~~ black jacket.
PODPOWIEDŹ: Nie używaj **and**, jeśli każdy przymiotnik reprezentuje inną kategorię.
Dobrze: He bought a big black jacket.

YOUR TURN NOW!

I. Put the following adjectives into the right column.

brownish stable yellowish French enormous tiny Asian spicy fresh frozen metal expensive new dirty ancient paper friendly small military horrible white noisy Japanese round ancient young black rectangular plastic electric warm woollen

1. Opinion	
2. Size	
3. Shape	
4. Age	
5. Colour	
6. Origin	
7. Material	
8. Type/purpose	

II. Make sentences as in the example.

EXAMPLE: a motorbike (Japanese, red, fast, black) This is a fast, red and black Japanese motorbike.

1. an apple (big, red, delicious) ____________________
2. spiders (African, black, huge, dangerous) ____________________
3. a coat (long, fashionable, white, leather) ____________________
4. children (young, noisy, nice) ____________________
5. a meal (Indian delicious, spicy) ____________________
6. a cup (Chinese, old, small, beautiful) ____________________
7. a handbag (Italian, leather, brown, big) ____________________
8. blocks of flats (huge, modern, concrete) ____________________
9. stamps (English, nineteenth-century, postage, valuable) ____________________

III. Correct the mistakes.

1. I went to the market and bought some big green sour apples.
2. I saw a brass old French carriage clock in the museum.
3. He had black interesting big eyes.
4. My neighbours have a German big fierce black dog.
5. There's an Egyptian stone big statue in the university hall.
6. There's a steel sharp bread knife in the drawer.

KEY **I.** 1. Opinion: expensive, friendly, horrible, stable, noisy, spicy, dirty, warm 2. Size: enormous, tiny, small 3. Shape: round, rectangular 4. Age: new, young, ancient 5. Colour: brownish, yellowish, black, white 6. Origin: French, Asian, Japanese 7. Material: metal, plastic, woollen, paper 8. Type/purpose: frozen, fresh, electric, military **II.** 1. This is a delicious big red apple. 2. These are dangerous huge black African spiders. 3. This is a fashionable long white leather coat. 4. They're nice but noisy young children. 5. It's a delicious spicy Indian meal. 6. It's a beautiful small old Chinese cup. 7. This is a big brown Italian leather handbag. 8. These are modern huge concrete blocks of flats. 9. These are valuable nineteenth-century English postage stamps. **III.** 1. I went to the market and bought some sour big green apples. 2. I saw an old French brass carriage clock in the museum. 3. He had interesting big black eyes. 4. My neighbours have a fierce big black German dog. 5. There's a big Egyptian stone statue in the university hall. 6. There's a sharp steel bread knife in the drawer.

UNIT 46 Good-looking man/high-heeled shoes
COMPOUND ADJECTIVES

I took a five-hour exam yesterday. Wczoraj zdawałam pięciogodzinny egzamin.
Bob caught a five-kilo pike and was very proud.
Bob złapał pięciokilogramowego szczupaka i był bardzo dumny.
These high-heeled shoes are quite expensive. Te buty na wysokich obcasach są dość drogie.
We went on a six-day trip to France. Pojechaliśmy na sześciodniową wycieczkę do Francji.
Dover is in south-east England. Dover leży w południowo-wschodniej Anglii.
We stayed in a four-star hotel. Zatrzymaliśmy się w czterogwiazdkowym hotelu.

CO TO JEST COMPOUND ADJECTIVE?

Jest to przymiotnik złożony z dwóch wyrazów, rzadziej z trzech, zwykle pisanych z kreską.

KIEDY STOSUJESZ COMPOUND ADJECTIVE?

Kiedy chcesz opisać coś szczegółowo, możesz posłużyć się przymiotnikiem złożonym, czyli **compound adjective**.

Distance: a five-minute walk, a three-kilometre road
Weight: a six-kilo turkey, a two-pound packet of sweets
Height: a ten-foot wooden fence, a ninety-metre tower
Length: a two-metre pole, a 200-kilometre border
Time: a three-hour exam, a 45-minute lesson
Number: a four-man crew of the boat, a seven-person lift
Appearance: a good-looking actor, a short-sleeved shirt
Character/type: an easy-going student, a second-hand Mercedes

→ **Compound adjectives with well and badly.**
Na ogół są to przymiotniki o przeciwstawnym znaczeniu.

a well-painted picture – a badly-painted picture,
a well-written book – a badly-written book
a well-directed film – a badly-directed film
a well-organised meeting – a badly-organised meeting

WYJĄTEK: **a well-known writer**

TYPOWE BŁĘDY UWAŻAJ!

Źle: This was a tiring, ~~seven-hours~~ meeting.
PODPOWIEDŹ: Rzeczownik wchodzący w skład przymiotnika złożonego jest zawsze w liczbie pojedynczej.
Dobrze: This was a tiring, seven-hour meeting.

YOUR TURN NOW!

I. Match the words from the column on the left with the words on the right to make compound adjectives. Sometimes more than one compound adjective is possible.

1. badly	A. going
2. well	B. time
3. part	C. handed
4. left	D. written
5. easy	E. known
6. second	F. east
7. brand	G. new
8. north	H. hand

II. Complete the senteces with suitable compound adjectives. Choose the words from the box.

good new minute part inch euro going well

1. I was surprised when I found a ten-__________ note on the floor.
2. My friend has just bought a brand-__________ Fiat.
3. Have you ever met a __________-known person?
4. It's a twenty-__________ walk from the station to the hotel.
5. My sister got a __________-time job in the bank.
6. Jenny was dancing with a __________-looking young man.
7. I like Bill because he is so easy-__________.
8. There is a six-__________ nail on the table.

III. Replace the underlined part of each sentence with a suitable compound adjective as in the example.

EXAMPLE: This composition is not written well.
This is a badly-written composition.

1. The walk which lasts twenty kilometres may be exhausting for some people.
2. Peter bought a completely new motorcycle.
3. Cindy Crawford is a famous model.
4. Mary, who is ten years old, is very clever.
5. The Smiths are rich yet they bought a used Nissan Micra.
6. The crew, consisting of six men, was rescued in the stormy weather

KEY

I. 1D, 2D/E, 3B, 4C, 5A, 6H, 7G, 8F **II.** 1. a ten-euro note, 2. a brand-new Fiat, 3. a well-known person, 4. a twenty-minute walk, 5. a part-time job, 6. a good-looking young man, 7. so easy-going, 8. a six-inch nail **III.** 1. The twenty-kilometre walk may be exhausting for some people. 2. Peter bought a brand-new motorcycle. 3. Cindy Crawford is a well-known model. 4. Mary, a ten-year-old girl, is very clever. 5. The Smiths are well-off yet they bought a second-hand Nissan Micra. 6. The six-man crew was rescued in the stormy weather.

UNIT 47 as...as/not so...as

Jack was running as fast as he could. Jack biegł tak szybko jak (tylko) mógł.
Susan is as beautiful as her mother. Susan jest tak piękna jak jej matka.
I'm as tall as you. Jestem tak wysoka jak ty.
You should rest as much as possible. Powinieneś odpoczywać tak dużo, jak to możliwe.
I didn't have as much money as I thought. Nie miałam tyle pieniędzy, ile myślałam, że mam.
This bag is as light as a feather, I can lift it easily. Ta torba jest lekka jak piórko, mogę ją łatwo podnieść.
Her hands were cold as ice. Jej ręce były zimne jak lód.
Tim is not as (so) strong as Tom. Tim nie jest tak silny jak Tom.

KIEDY UŻYWASZ KONSTRUKCJI AS...AS...?

Gdy chcesz powiedzieć, że dwie rzeczy lub osoby mają jedną podobną cechę. Konstrukcji **as... as...** używasz z przymiotnikiem, przysłówkiem, zaimkiem osobowym lub zdaniem podrzędnym. W mowie potocznej, a szczególnie w amerykańskiej angielszczyźnie, pierwsze **as** możesz opuścić.

KIEDY UŻYWASZ KONSTRUKCJI NOT AS.... AS... LUB NOT SO...AS...?

W zdaniach przeczących, gdy chcesz powiedzieć, że coś lub ktoś różni się od innej rzeczy lub osoby; także ze zdaniem podrzędnym. W konstrukcji **not as...as...** lub **not so... as...** nie można opuścić pierwszego członu.

TYPOWE BŁĘDY UWAŻAJ!

Źle: She is ~~so~~ tall as her brother.
PODPOWIEDŹ: W zdaniach twierdzących nie stosuje się konstrukcji **so... as...**
Dobrze: She is as tall as her brother.

Źle: Mary looked as fresh as a ~~morning~~.
PODPOWIEDŹ: Wiele wyrażeń typu **as...as...** ma charakter idiomatyczny. W tłumaczeniu z języka polskiego na angielski (i odwrotnie) trzeba zastosować odpowiednik właściwy dla danego języka; nie można tłumaczyć dosłownie.
Dobrze: Mary looked as fresh as a daisy.

HOTSPOT!

Wiele podręczników zamieszcza listę barwnych angielskich wyrażeń idiomatycznych z konstrukcją **as... as**. Czasami porównania te mogą brzmieć trochę staroświecko we współczesnej angielszczyźnie, ale nadal są przedmiotem testów i zadań egzaminacyjnych, więc dobrze jest je znać.

YOUR TURN NOW!

I. Match the parts of these idiomatic expressions.

1. as fit	a. as lead
2. as cool	b. as a mule
3. as drunk	c. as gold
4. as fresh	d. as a dog
5. as old	e. as ditchwater
6. as good	f. as a fiddle
7. as stubborn	g. as a judge
8. as different	h. as a lord
9. as strong	i. as a rake
10. as sick	j. as chalk from cheese
11. as dull	k. as a beetroot
12. as sober	l. as a cucumber
13. as large	m. as a daisy
14. as red	n. as the hills
15. as thin	o. as life
16. as heavy	p. as a horse
17. as gentle	r. as a lamb

II. Complete the sentences with a suitable expression of comparison.

1. What has happened? You look so pale.
   You are ________________.
2. Jim is so calm. Whatever happens,
   he remains ________________.
3. After the party of yours I was really sick.
   I was ________________. I drank too much.
4. Stop dieting, Susan. You're very thin. You ________________.
5. Don't be afraid of my dog. Rex is big but he's very gentle.
   He's ________________.
6. Nick never listens to me. He's very stubborn.
   He's ________________.

III. Correct the mistakes.

1. This joke is as old as the world.
2. Ann is as stubborn as a donkey.
3. I've slept well and now I feel as fresh as a morning.

KEY

I. 1f, 2l, 3h, 4m, 5n, 6c, 7b, 8j, 9p, 10d, 11e, 12g, 13o, 14k, 15i, 16a, 17r **II.** 1. You are as white as a sheet. 2. Whatever happens, he remains as cool as a cucumber. 3. After the party of yours I was as sick as a dog/as drunk as a lord. 4. You're as thin as a rake. 5. He's as gentle as a lamb. 6. He's as stubborn as a mule. **III.** 1. This joke is as old as the hills. 2. Ann is as stubborn as a mule. 3. I've slept well and now I feel as fresh as a daisy.

UNIT 48 like/as

She looks like a princess in this dress. Ona wygląda jak księżniczka w tej sukni.
Your house is beautiful! It's like a palace. Twój dom jest piękny. Jest jak pałac.
Nobody tells jokes as uncle Mark does. Nikt tak nie opowiada dowcipów jak wujek Marek.
Mary worked as a waitress for a year. Mary pracowała przez rok jako kelnerka.
You're late as usual. Jak zwykle spóźniłaś się.
As you know, we're visiting grandma on Friday. Jak wiesz, w piątek idziemy do babci.

KIEDY UŻYWASZ LIKE?

Like jako przyimek występuje przed rzeczownikiem lub zaimkiem i wyraża podobieństwo lub różnicę między dwoma rzeczami lub osobami.

My daughter is a teacher, like me.
Home, sweet home, there's no place like home.

→ **Like** występuje z takimi czasownikami jak **be, feel, look, smell, sound, taste**.
Po **like** następuje rzeczownik.

It feels like fur. It smells like cheese.

KIEDY UŻYWASZ AS?

1. **As** występuje jako przyimek. Zwróć uwagę na różnicę znaczenia **as** i **like** w poniższych zdaniach.
   Although she is a lawyer, she worked as a history teacher.
   (pracowała jako nauczycielka)
   She taught her children like a real teacher although she didn't have any qualifications.
   (uczyła swoje dzieci jak prawdziwa nauczycielka)
2. **As** występuje także z okolicznikiem czasu.
   As usual, he didn't do his homework.
3. **As** występuje również jako spójnik przed podmiotem i orzeczeniem.
   They did exactly as they promised.

TYPOWE BŁĘDY UWAŻAJ!

Źle: During my summer holidays from school I worked ~~like~~ a waiter in a restaurant.
PODPOWIEDŹ: Nie używaj **like** zamiast **as**. **Jako** i **jak** to nie to samo!
Dobrze: During my summer holidays from school I worked as a waiter in a restaurant.

HOTSPOT!

W mowie potocznej często słyszy się zastępowanie **as** przez **like**, np. **Nobody looks after you like I do** zamiast **Nobody looks after you as I do.** To samo dotyczy **like** używanego w znaczeniu **for example, such as**, np. **I like team sports like football and basketball** zamiast **I like team sports such as football and basketball.** Na egzaminach i w wypowiedziach pisemnych lepiej zastosować tradycyjną wersję tych zdań.

YOUR TURN NOW!

I. Complete the sentences with **like** or **as**.

1. It's raining here every day. I don't like weather _________ this.
2. It can't be lemonade, it tastes _________ water.
3. Kate used to work _________ a taxi driver before she married.
4. Jimmy is very naughty, _________ always.
5. Do it _________ I told you.
6. Mary swims very well, in fact she swims _________ a fish.
7. During Halloween, Ralph dressed up _________ a ghost.
8. I'm so tired, I worked _________ a dog all day.
9. Martin failed his German exam, _________ he expected.

II. Complete the sentences with **like** or **as** and the words in the box.

you   a tour guide   a birthday present   usual   mine
a child   a person   a turkey   a cauliflower

1. My parents gave me this computer __________________.
2. Tom is 30 but sometimes he behaves __________________.
3. Ann has been working __________________ for three years.
4. My mother is cooking something. It smells __________________.
5. My dog snores __________________, just listen to him.
6. Will you phone me at nine, __________________?
7. You speak English very well. I'd like to speak English __________________.
8. Your dress looks exactly __________________.
9. This meat tastes __________________. What is it?

III. Correct these sentences where necessary.

1. Although she is an adult, she sometimes acts as a child.
2. When I was ill, my mother looked after me as a doctor.
3. Susan works like a doctor in a clinic.
4. This woman looks as my English teacher.
5. It's easy, you can do it like this!

Proverb:
Like mother, like daughter.
Like father, like son.

KEY

I. 1. like 2. like 3. as 4. as 5. as 6. like 7. as 8. like 9. as **II.** 1. as a birthday present 2. like a child 3. as a tour guide 4. like a cauliflower 5. like a person 6. as usual 7. like you 8. like mine 10. like turkey **III.** 1. Although she is an adult, she sometimes acts like a child. 2. When I was ill, my mother looked after me like a doctor. 3. Susan works as a doctor in a clinic. 4. This woman looks like my English teacher. 5. OK.

UNIT 49 So/such/so that

Mary is so nice. Mary jest taka miła.
Mary is such a nice girl. Mary jest taką miłą dziewczyną.
Their children are so nice. Ich dzieci są takie miłe.
They have such nice children. Oni mają takie miłe dzieci.
I've never eaten such delicious food before. Nigdy dotąd nie jadłem tak wyśmienitego jedzenia.
It was such a nice day. To był taki ładny dzień.
It was so nice a day! To był taki ładny dzień.
She dances so beautifully! Ona tak pięknie tańczy!
They are such people! To tacy ludzie!
It's such an interesting book. To taka interesująca książka.

KIEDY STOSUJESZ SO/SUCH?

Do podkreślenia cechy osoby lub rzeczy oraz do wzmocnienia przysłówka określającego czynność.

TYPOWE BŁĘDY **UWAŻAJ!**

Źle: He is ~~so~~ nice boy.

PODPOWIEDŹ: **So** występuje tylko przed samym przymiotnikiem. Jeśli po przymiotniku następuje rzeczownik, musisz użyć **such**. Przed rzeczownikiem policzalnym w liczbie pojedynczej musisz użyć **such a/an**.

Dobrze: He is such a nice boy.

Źle: It was such ~~a~~ lovely weather.

PODPOWIEDŹ: Przed rzeczownikiem niepoliczalnym stosuj **such** bez przedimka **a/an**.

Dobrze: It was such lovely weather.

Źle: They are such ~~a~~ nice people.

PODPOWIEDŹ: Przed rzeczownikiem w liczbie mnogiej również stosuj **such** bez przedimka **a/an**.

Dobrze: They are such nice people.

Źle: Pavarotti sings ~~such~~ beautifully.

PODPOWIEDŹ: Przed przysłówkiem a także przed kwantyfikatorami **much/many**, **little/few** stosuj **so**.

Dobrze: Pavarotti sings so beautifully.

HOTSPOT!

Uważaj na konstrukcję typu **so beautiful a view**. Jest ona równoważna z **such a beautiful view**, lecz rzadziej używana w mowie potocznej, częściej spotykana np. w poezji. Jest to typowa pułapka egzaminacyjna!

YOUR TURN NOW!

I. Complete the sentences with **so**, **such** or **such a**.

1. John looks smart. He wears ________ expensive clothes.
2. John's clothes are ________ expensive.
3. I was ________ hungry that I ate all the food from the fridge.
4. I didn't know they live ________ far from London.
5. The food at the school canteen was ______ awful that we felt sick after eating lunch there.
6. Susan is ________ good pupil that she always gets excellent marks at school.
7. Their children are ________ naughty. I can't put up with them.

II. Join the broken sentences.

1. I have so much money
2. My son has so many friends
3. Robert is so silly
4. It was such awful food
5. The weather was so nice
6. It was such a rainy day

A. that nobody wants to play with him.
B. that we couldn't let the dog out.
C. that I don't know what to do with it.
D. that he can't invite them all at one time.
E. that nobody wanted to eat it.
F. that we took the children to the zoo.

III. Choose the correct word.

From: Hania
To: Alice

Hi, Alice,
(1) _So/such_ good to hear from you; thanks for (2) _so/such_ a nice email and (3) _so/such_ fantastic photos. They came when Rick was here, (4) _so/such_ we could both enjoy remembering the good time we had together in Largs. And little Sue is (5) _so/such_ cute! She is sleeping (6) _so/such_ peacefully in your arms. That's my favourite photo. Life here has become as hectic as it always is at the beginning of a new school year – or indeed even more (7) _so/such._ Teaching is (8) _so/such_ hard work! (9) _So/such_, please don't expect long emails from me too often. But it's good to know that you are there at the other end of the email link (10) _so that/such that_, if need be, we can get in touch quickly.
Love,
Hania :)

IV. Correct the mistakes where necessary.

1. Joan is so a beautiful actress.
2. Thomas has so fast car that he always pays fines for overspeeding.
3. We have so little money that we can't go abroad this year.
4. I've met so much people at the party that I can't remember their names.
5. I was such tired yesterday that I didn't do my homework, sorry.

KEY **I.** 1. such 2. so 3. so 4. so 5. so 6. such a 7. so **II.** 1.C 2.D 3.A 4.E 5.F 6.B **III.** 1. so 2. such 3. such 4. so 5. so 6. so 7. so 8. such 9. so 10. so that **IV.** 1. Joan is such a beautiful actress. 2. Thomas has such a fast car... 3. OK 4. I've met so many people at the partty that I can't remember their names. 5. I was so tired yesterday that I didn't do my homework, sorry.

UNIT 50 CONSOLIDATION

I. Fill the gaps with appropriate verbs from the box in the correct tense and form.

share	create	try	walk	contribute	decide	include	put	hope
use	lead	drive	save	cause	replace	take	have	

DO YOUR BIT IN THE GREENHOUSE WAR

Most of us (1)_____________ to the world's environmental problems every day. In Britain, for example, an average adult (2)_____________ 11 tonnes of carbon dioxide per year. Harmful routines (3)_____________, among others, using the car, leaving electronic equipment on standby overnight, printing out numerous copies of a document instead of filing information on the computer, and many others. All this (4)___________ a dramatic rise in global warming, which (5)_________ not only to increased temperatures, but also to abnormal weather conditions such as flooding and drought. So, is there anything we can do to be more eco-friendly? Nicole Wilson, a Birmingham nurse, (6)_____________ some good answers to this question.

She usually (7)____________ to work or (8)____________ public transport; she (9)___________ only when she is on a night shift. She (10) ________________ the car for major shopping, but she does it only once a month, and even then she normally (11)_____________ it with a friend. To cut on domestic waste, she (12)_____________ newspapers, bottles, cans, even old shoes in the recycling bin provided by the city council. She also (13)_____________ to keep domestic rubbish to a minimum. And now, as some of her domestic appliances come to the end of their life, she (14)_____________ to replace them with A-rated, energy-efficient models. Soon she (15)_____________, also, all her lightbulbs with energy-efficient ones. By doing all that she (16)_____________ she (17)_____________ about £ 500 a year, and also cut her household emissions from electricity use by more than 10 per cent.

KEY 1. contribute 2. creates 3. include 4. causes 5. leads 6. has 7. walks 8. takes 9. drives 10. uses 11. shares 12. puts 13. tries 14. has decided 15. is going to replace 16. hopes 17. will save

Interpretacja wyników testu

Jeśli uzyskałeś co najmniej 30 punktów – gratulacje! Możesz przejść do dalszej części książki. Jeśli masz mniej niż 30 punktów, powinieneś przeczytać wybrane partie materiału jeszcze raz. Jeśli nieprawidłowo odpowiedziałeś na któreś z pytań 1-11, przeanalizuj ponownie rozdziały 26-32. Jeśli masz problemy z udzieleniem prawidłowych odpowiedzi do pytań 12-22, wróć do rozdziałów 33-39. Jeśli sprawiły Ci kłopot odpowiedzi na pytania 23-27, wróć do rozdziałów 40-43. Jeśli nie udzieliłeś poprawnej odpowiedzi na pytania 28-31, przeanalizuj ponownie rozdziały 44-46. Jeśli pytania 32-35 sprawiły Ci trudność, wróć do rozdziałów 47-49. Wykonaj ten sam test ponownie po kilku dniach, aby sprawdzić, ile naprawdę pamiętasz. POWODZENIA!

'How to get rid of this broken glass?"
'Throw it out through the hole in your broken kitchen window!'
Are you eco-friendly?

CONSOLIDATION!

Time to check what you have learned from units 26–50. Do these tasks and find out what your results are. Choose the correct form of the words in italics.

1. I need a lot of *paper/papers* to print out my composition.
2. Young people's *life is/lives are* not easy nowadays due to the high level of unemployment in our country.
3. The police *has caught/have caught* a dangerous murderer.
4. Look! There's *a pack of/a swarm of* bees sitting up in the tree.
5. Could you introduce me to your *boy friend/boyfriend*?
6. *The making friends/Making friends* while you are on holiday is interesting.
7. *No getting/Not getting* a present on your birthday is a sad experience.
8. London is the biggest city of *the Great Britain/Great Britain*.
9. Have you ever seen *the Mont Blanc/Mont Blanc*?
10. Adam studies History at *the Warsaw University/Warsaw University*.
11. My mother-in-law is in *the hospital/in hospital*. She is going to have an operation.
12. Mary bought two books and I bought *three/three ones*.
13. Don't worry about your exam. Sit down and *relax/relax yourself*.
14. Children, you are very naughty. Behave *yourself/yourselves*!
15. I don't like these shoes. Could you show me *other/another* pair, please?
16. This student failed the test but the *others/other* students did very well.
17. Jim has eaten *the whole/all* bread. There's nothing left for supper.
18. *Every/All* people must have a rest from time to time.
19. Each of my children *go/goes* to a different school.
20. My neighbours shout *at themselves/each other* every night.
21. Neither of my cousins *like/likes* spinach.
22. Either of these children *speak/speaks* English very well.
23. *There's/It's* too noisy in the classrom, we can't work.
24. *There's/It's* too little coffee, we must buy some.
25. I have *a few/a little* money so I can lend you some, no problem.
26. Mary has *a few/few* friends at school so she feels lonely there.
27. Susan knows *a fewer/fewer* people than Mary.
28. John is e*nough strong/strong enough* to move this wardrobe.
29. He's *too much poor/much too poor* to afford a new Mercedes.
30. Have this *red delicious/delicious red* apple!
31. Anne is a *twelve-years-old /twelve-year-old* girl.
32. Jim is *so/as* tall as his older brother.
33. My friend is a teacher, *as/like* me.
34. Ben is *so/such* good-looking.
35. The Browns are *such nice/such a nice* people.

Proverb:
It is never too late to learn.

KEY

1. paper 2. lives are 3. have caught 4. a swarm 5. boyfriend 6. Making friends 7. Not getting 8. Great Britain 9. Mont Blanc 10. Warsaw University 11. in hospital 12. three 13. relax 14. yourselves 15. another 16. other 17. all 18. All 19. goes 20. each other 21. likes 22. speaks 23. It's 24. There's 25. a little 26. few 27. fewer 28. strong enough 29. much too poor 30. delicious red 31. twelve-year-old 32. as 33. like 34. so 35. such nice

UNIT 51 do/let's do THE IMPERATIVE

Go home! Idź do domu!
Come home, please. Proszę, chodź do domu.
Don't go there! Nie chodź tam!
Let's go home! Chodźmy do domu!
Let's not go there! Nie idźmy tam!
Let him/her do it! Niech on/ona to zrobi!
Be careful! Uważaj!/Bądź ostrożny!

KIEDY UŻYWASZ TRYBU ROZKAZUJĄCEGO?

Do wyrażenia polecenia lub ostrzeżenia, a także sugestii.

Jeśli chcesz wyrazić polecenie z przeczeniem **not**, musisz skorzystać z czasownika pomocniczego (operatora) **do not** (**don't**). Stosujesz tę formę tylko w odniesieniu do drugiej osoby liczby pojedynczej i mnogiej.

Don't buy this sweater, it's awful! Nie kupuj tego swetra, jest okropny!
Don't shout! Nie krzycz!/nie krzyczcie!

Jeśli chcesz wyrazić sugestię wspólnego zrobienia czegoś, stosujesz strukturę **Let's = Let us**.

Let's go to a jazz concert. Chodźmy na koncert jazzowy.
Let's not forget to send Mary a birthday card. Nie zapomnijmy wysłać Marii kartki z życzeniami na urodziny.

Słowo **let** odpowiada polskiemu **niech** w poleceniach skierowanych do trzeciej osoby liczby pojedynczej lub mnogiej i łączy się zwykle z zaimkiem w formie **him/her/them** lub z rzeczownikiem, np.:

Let your brother join our club. Niech twój brat wstąpi do naszego klubu.

→ Pamiętaj o użyciu słowa **please**, które sprawia, że polecenie brzmi uprzejmiej, a nawet jak prośba.

Help me, please. Proszę, pomóż mi.
Shut the door, please. Proszę, zamknij drzwi.

TYPOWE BŁĘDY UWAŻAJ!

Źle: ~~Not~~ drink it!
PODPOWIEDŹ: Przy wyrażaniu polecenia z przeczeniem **not** użyj czasownika pomocniczego **do**
Dobrze: Don't drink it!

Źle: Let ~~he/she/they~~ go to sleep!
PODPOWIEDŹ: Przy tworzeniu polecenia w trzeciej osobie liczby pojedynczej i mnogiej zastosuj zaimek w odpowiedniej formie (tj. w **object case**)
Dobrze: Let him/her/them go to sleep!

YOUR TURN NOW!

I. Rewrite the following questions as commands.

EXAMPLE **Can you open the window? Open the window, please.**

1. Can you fix my computer?
2. Can you take the dog to the vet?
3. Can they go for a walk now?
4. Can we stay here longer?
5. Can he write this report?

II. Complete the sentences with the appropriate verb from the box.

finish go wash invite drink

1. Don't ________ this tea, it's very hot!
2. Let's not ________ the Greens, they are going to ruin our party!
3. Let them ________ the exercise, it's important.
4. ________ your hands, you're going to have a sandwich.
5. Let's ________ to the theatre tonight.

III. Translate into Polish.

4. DO NOT FEED THE MONKEYS

1. Keep off the grass

5. DO NOT LEAVE YOUR LUGGAGE HERE

2. 

3. DO NOT PARK HERE

IV. Correct the mistakes where necessary.

1. Let he not use my computer.
2. Let she come to my party.
3. Let's cook chicken soup.
4. Let they go for a walk.

KEY

I. 1. Fix my computer, please. 2. Take the dog to the vet, please. 3. Let them go for a walk now. 4. Let's stay here longer. 5. Let him write this report. **II.** 1. drink 2. invite 3. finish 4. wash 5. go **III.** 1. Nie deptać trawników. 2. Nie śmiecić. 3. Nie parkować. 4. Nie karmić małp. 5. Nie zostawiać tu bagażu. **IV.** 1. Let him not use my computer. 2. Let her come to my party. 3. OK 4. Let them go for a walk.

UNIT 52 need/don't need/needn't

We need more time for this job. Potrzebujemy (=Potrzeba nam) więcej czasu na tę pracę.
Do you need more money for it? Czy potrzebujecie na to więcej pieniędzy?
We don't need more people. Nie potrzebujemy (= Nie trzeba nam) więcej ludzi.
Susan needs to do it well. (= She must do it well.) Susan musi to zrobić dobrze.
John doesn't need to help us. John nie potrzebuje (=nie musi) nam pomagać.
John needn't come every day. John nie potrzebuje (=nie musi) przychodzić codziennie.

JAK STOSUJESZ CZASOWNIK NEED?

Need wyraża potrzebę dokonania czegoś lub osiągnięcia danego stanu. Zaprzeczone **need** (**needn't, don't need**) oznacza brak takiej potrzeby lub brak przymusu. Formy przeczące czasownika **need** używane są zatem jako przeczenie czasownika **must** lub konstrukcji **have to**.

W czasie teraźniejszym **need** tworzy dwie formy pytań i przeczeń:

1. Jak inne czasowniki, tj. z operatorem **do** w odpowiedniej osobie. W tym wypadku przed czasownikiem głównym trzeba dodać **to** (**He doesn't need to do it**).
2. Jak czasowniki posiłkowe, tj. bez operatora. W tym wypadku stosujesz jedną formę dla wszystkich osób i nie dodajesz **to** przed czasownikiem głównym (**He needn't do it**).

Needn't używane jest rzadziej niż forma z operatorem; gdy nie jesteś pewien, której formy użyć zastosuj **don't/doesn't need**.

→ Gdy chcesz wyrazić brak potrzeby, a nie brak przymusu, używaj wyłącznie przeczenia z operatorem (**He doesn't need more money for his holiday**).

TYPOWE BŁĘDY UWAŻAJ!

Źle: Mary ~~need~~ help.
PODPOWIEDŹ: W trzeciej osobie liczby pojedynczej simple present **need**, jak inne czasowniki, przyjmuje końcówkę **-s**.
Dobrze: Mary needs help.

Źle: Peter ~~needs do~~ it.
PODPOWIEDŹ: W formie twierdzącej **need** wymaga użycia **to** przed czasownikiem głównym.
Dobrze: Peter needs to do it.

Źle: I ~~needn't~~ a new coat this year; the one I bought last year is still quite fashionable.
PODPOWIEDŹ: Wyrażając brak potrzeby, użyj przeczenia z operatorem.
Dobrze: I don't need a new coat this year; the one I bought last year is still quite fashionable.

YOUR TURN NOW!

I. Make the following sentences negative.

1. Kate needs a lot of money for her holiday.
2. Peter needed your help yesterday.
3. They'll need a road map to find their way in France.
4. Jonathan must paint his room this weekend.
5. We need to buy potatoes today.

II. Kasia is going to Scotland for her summer holiday. Read the text and Kasia's notes of what she still needs to do before leaving, and complete the sentences below the text. You may have to use a dictionary!

CLOTHING > The clothes you pack for a holiday in Scotland need to be flexible because of temperature changes. The best way to cope with British weather is to wear layers of clothing – for example, a T-shirt worn under a shirt and a jumper. Sensible walking shoes or trainers are recommended for sightseeing. In winter you will need a warm coat or jacket (preferably water-proof), woolen jumpers and warm footwear. In summer you need to be prepared for rain, so bring an umbrella, light anorak or raincoat and have at least one warm sweater.

1. wyprać koszulki
2. wyczyścić buty
3. naprawić sweter
4. kupić
- parasolkę
- skafander
- ciepły sweter?

EXAMPLE Kasia must wash her T-shirts.

1. She won't n________ a warm coat.
2. She m________ mend her sweater.
3. She'll n________ an anorak.
4. She m________ clean her trainers.
5. She is g________ to b________ an umbrella.

III. Join the broken sentences.

1. Kasia must
2. He needs
3. We don't
4. I needn't

A. have to go there.
B. clean these shoes; they're clean.
C. to have more time for this exercise.
D. phone her parents at once.

IV. Correct the sentences where necessary. Be careful: there may be more than one mistake in each of them – or none at all.

1. During a flight you need drink a lot of water but you musn't eat too much.
2. Look! That man drowning! He need help!
3. What? Peter wanted to borrow some money from you? He certainly doesn't need it; he's a millionaire!
4. She works in very small company; they needn't more staff.

KEY

I. 1. Kate doesn't need a lot of money for her holiday. 2. Peter didn't need your help yesterday. 3. They won't need a road map to find their way in France. 4. Jonathan needn't paint/doesn't need to paint his room this weekend. 5. We needn't buy/don't need to buy potatoes today. **II.** 1. She won't need a warm coat. 2. She must mend her sweater. 3. She'll need an anorak. 5. She must clean her trainers. 6. She is going to buy an umbrella. **III.** 1D 2C 3A 4B **IV.** 1. During a flight you need to drink a lot of water but you mustn't eat too much. 2. Look! That man is drowning! He needs help! 3. OK 4. She works in a very small company; they don't need more staff.

UNIT 53 must/need/have to/have got to NEGATION

You don't have to visit Dr Brown in the clinic. Ask her for a home visit.
Nie musisz iść do dr Brown do przychodni. Poproś ją o wizytę domową.
You don't need to/You needn't visit Mary in the hospital; she's already back home.
Nie musisz odwiedzać Mary w szpitalu; ona jest już w domu.
You mustn't visit Kate in the hospital; she's in intensive care.
Nie wolno ci odwiedzać Kate w szpitalu; ona jest na oddziale intensywnej terapii.

JAK TWORZYSZ PRZECZENIE OD CZASOWNIKA MUST?

Przeczenie **must not** (**mustn't**) wyraża zakaz, a więc **I must not** (**I mustn't**) nie znaczy **nie muszę** lecz **nie wolno mi**. Dla wyrażenia zakazu można również stosować przeczenie **can't** (**You can't do it**), ale **mustn't** (**You mustn't do it**) brzmi bardziej stanowczo.

Gdy chcesz wyrazić brak przymusu, stosujesz przeczenie tworzone od czasownika **need**. W czasie teraźniejszym przeczenie to może być wyrażone albo formą **need not** (**needn't**), taką samą dla wszystkich osób, albo za pomocą **need** + operator **do** w odpowiedniej osobie (np. **I don't need**).

JAK TWORZYSZ PRZECZENIE OD STRUKTURY HAVE TO/HAVE GOT TO?

Przeczenie od struktur **have to** i **have got to** (czyli brak przymusu) tworzysz przy pomocy operatora **do**.

Używasz operatora **do** w odpowiedniej osobie i odpowiednim czasie gramatycznym.

I don't have to go to school today = I needn't/I don't need to go to school today.

Jeśli nie jesteś pewien, czy zastosować przeczenie z **need** czy z **have to**, użyj przeczenia z **have to**.

TYPOWE BŁĘDY **UWAŻAJ!**

Źle: I ~~mustn't~~ do this exercise.
PODPOWIEDŹ: Pamiętaj, że w przeczeniu czasownika **must** występuje zmiana znaczenia.
Dobrze: I don't have to do this exercise./I needn't do this exercise./I don't need to do this exercise.

Źle: I ~~haven't~~ to go there.
PODPOWIEDŹ: Pamiętaj o operatorze, szczególnie gdy tworzysz przeczenie z **have to**!
Dobrze: I don't have to go there.

Źle: Mary ~~musn't~~ come back so late.)
PODPOWIEDŹ: W pisowni **mustn't** (= **must not**) skracasz tylko partykułę **not**.
Pisownia **must** pozostaje bez zmian.

YOUR TURN NOW!

I. Complete the sentences below the road signs. What do they say you must/mustn't do?

EXAMPLE
You mustn't smoke here. 1. You ______ 2. You ______ 3. You ______ 4. You ______

II. Make the following sentences negative.

1. Mary has to practise the piano every day.
2. At the scouts' camp they had to cook their own meals.
3. I must finish this report before I go home.
4. You've got to wait for your exam results.
5. We must send her a Christmas card.

III. Complete the text with the correct forms of **can**, **must**, **need** and **have to**.

In my school lessons begin at 8 a.m. We (1)______ come to school punctually; we (2)______ be late. Our teachers also come on time and the school day begins. We (3)_______ to stand up when the teacher enters the classroom, but we usually do. We (4)_______ be prepared well, or we get bad marks. We often have class tests, and of course we don't like them. Sometimes we (5)_______ ask the teachers to have a class test on another day, but we (6)_______ do that too often. Really, school life (7)_______ be very hard at times!

IV. Join the broken sentences.

1. You mustn't	A. to water the garden today; it's been raining heavily all morning.
2. She doesn't have	B. do any homework because the teachers gave us no homework today!
3. John's got to	C. smoke in here; it's a maternity ward!
4. I needn't	D. spend a lot of time on learning because he has his finals this year.

V. Correct the mistakes where necessary.

1. 'You musn't feed your cats so often', said the vet.
2. Otylia don't have to train every day.
3. He's got to talk to his boss about his new job.
4. She hasn't to do any extra exercises; her English is very good.

KEY

I 1. You must stop here. 2. You mustn't park here. 3. You mustn't overtake here. 4. You must slow down here./You must drive slowly here. **II** 1. Mary doesn't have to practice the piano every day. 2. At the scouts' camp they didn't have to cook their own meals. 3. I don't have to/I needn't/I don't need to finish this report before I go home. 4. You don't have to wait for your exam results. 5. We don't have to/We needn't/We don't need to send her a Christmas card. **III.** 1. must/have to 2. mustn't/can't 3. don't have/don't need 4. 've got/have to 5. can 6. can't/mustn't 7. can **IV.** 1C, 2A, 3D, 4B **V.** 'You mustn't feed your cats so often', said the vet. 2. Otylia doesn't have to train every day. 3. OK 4. She doesn't have to do any extra exercises; her English is very good.

UNIT 54 should/ought to

They should visit their grandparents more often. Oni powinni częściej odwiedzać dziadków.
I ought to learn French more regularly. Powinnam bardziej regularnie uczyć się francuskiego.
Such accidents shouldn't happen; people should be more careful on the road.
Takie wypadki nie powinny się zdarzać; ludzie powinni bardziej uważać na drodze.
This coat is rather expensive. Should I buy it, do you think?
Ten płaszcz jest dość drogi. Jak myślisz, czy powinnam go kupić?
You ought not to smoke here; this is a hospital ward. Nie powinieneś tu palić; to jest oddział szpitalny.

KIEDY UŻYWASZ SHOULD/OUGHT TO?

1. Gdy chcesz powiedzieć, że coś powinno (lub nie powinno) się zdarzyć lub zostać wykonane.
We should finish this exercise now.
Such accidents shouldn't happen.

2. Gdy chcesz wyrazić oczekiwanie graniczące z pewnością, że coś nastapi lub już nastąpiło.
Polański's new film should be good.
She should be home by now.

3. Gdy chcesz udzielić rady lub wyrazić krytykę czyjegoś postępowania
You should hurry up if you want to catch that bus.
You shouldn't miss your English lessons so often.

4. W wypowiedziach oficjalnych (szczególnie w formie pisemnej) gdy chcesz uprzejmie wyrazić nakaz
Guests should deposit the valuables in the hotel safe.

→ We wszystkich tych sytuacjach **should** można zastąpić przez **ought to**, jednakże **should** używane jest znacznie częściej. Po **should** użyj czasownika głównego w formie podstawowej bez **to** (**I should phone my sister**.) **Ought** wymaga użycia **to** przed czasownikiem (**I ought to do it soon.**)

Should, jak **can** i **must**, tworzy pytania przez inwersję. Pytanie z **should** wyraża niepewność (**Should I paint my room red?**). W pytaniach nie zastępuj **should** przez **ought to**; pytanie typu **Ought I to do it?**, choć teoretycznie poprawne, brzmi staroświecko.

W przeczeniach dodajesz **not** bezpośrednio po **should** lub **ought**.
(**You should not smoke here./You ought not to smoke here.**) W obu wypadkach możesz użyć formy skróconej (**shouldn't, oughtn't**).

TYPOWE BŁĘDY UWAŻAJ!

Źle: You should ~~to~~ do it.
PODPOWIEDŹ: Po **should** opuść **to** przed czasownikiem głównym.
Dobrze: You should do it.

Źle: You ought ~~to not~~ smoke here.
PODPOWIEDŹ: W przeczeniach użyj **not** zaraz po **ought**, przed czasownikiem głównym.
Dobrze: You ought not (You oughtn't) to smoke here.

YOUR TURN NOW!

I. Complete the sentences using **can/can't**, **must/mustn't**, **should/shouldn't**.

1. You __________ spend too much time playing computer games. It's bad for your eyes.
2. Cathy's last book was really good, so her new one __________ also be a bestseller.
3. Do you think this dress suits me? __________ I buy it?
4. You __________ take a shower before entering the pool. It's a regulation here.
5. **A written notice** Customers __________ use the parking space provided at the rear.
6. I __________ understand it why nobody is answering the phone. Mary __________ be at home by now.
7. __________ you help me please? This exercise is really hard.
8. You __________ be so angry at Tom. He didn't want to break the vase; it was an accident.
9. Jane __________ use so much make-up. It makes her look much older than she is.

II. Match the problem and the advice.

1. Jean's hands get cold very quickly. She ought to ____
2. Peter isn't very good at maths. Maybe he should ____
3. Eve and Martin want to get a bigger flat. They should ____
4. We are looking for a cheap holiday. We ought to ____

a. investigate some 'last minute' offers.
b. look for a good mortgage.
c. have some extra lessons.
d. buy a pair of woollen gloves.

III. Put the following guidelines for air passengers under the right headings. Write out the guidelines as complete sentences using **should** or **ought to**.

take a gentle stroll, then put your feet up and relax
drink plenty of water
try to adjust gradually to time change
eat a light meal
make your last day at home a relaxed one
stretch your arms and legs at least once an hour
put on loose-fitting, comfortable clothes of natural fibres
avoid alcohol, tea and coffee, and heavy meals
chew gum to ease ear-ache
do breathing exercises

Before the flight	**During the flight**	**After arrival**
You __________	You __________	You __________
You __________	You __________	You __________
You __________	You __________	
	You __________	
	You __________	

KEY **I.** 1. shouldn't/mustn't 2. should 3. Should 4. must 5. should 6. can't, should 7. Can 8. shouldn't 9. shouldn't **II.** 1d 2c 3b 4a **III.** Before the flight you should: make your last day at home a relaxed one; avoid alcohol, tea and coffee, and heavy meals; put on loose-fitting, comfortable clothes of natural fibres. During the flight you should: chew gum to ease ear-ache; drink plenty of water; eat a light meal; do breathing exercises; stretch your arms and legs at least once an hour. After arrival you should: take a gentle stroll, then put your feet up and relax; try to adjust gradually to time change.

UNIT 55 can do/could do/may do/might do

Hilda could read when she was five; now she can read five books a week.
Hilda umiała czytać jak miała pięć lat; teraz może przez tydzień przeczytać pięć książek.
It's a bit stuffy here. Could I open the window? Tu jest trochę duszno. Czy mogłabym otworzyć okno?
May I borrow your book? Czy mogę pożyczyć twoją książkę?
It might be too late to phone Tamara; she usually goes to bed early.
Może być za późno by dzwonić do Tamary; ona zwykle chodzi wcześnie spać.

JAK STOSUJESZ COULD?

1. Jako formę przeszłą od czasownika **can**, wyrażającą przeszłą możliwość lub umiejętność
Ralph could speak Arabic when he was a small boy.

2. Do wyrażenia hipotetycznej umiejętności lub możliwości dokonania czegoś w przyszłości
We could go to Corsica for our next holidays.

3. Do wyrażenia uprzejmie prośby lub pytania o pozwolenie
Could I use your mobile, please?

JAK STOSUJESZ MAY?

1. Jak **can**, do wyrażenia w czasie teraźniejszym możliwości dokonania czegoś; jednak w odróżnieniu od **can**, użycie **may** sugeruje brak pewności, podkreśla hipotetyczność wyrażanej możliwości.

He can do it. On może to zrobić. (100% pewności)
He may do it. On może to zrobić./On to być może zrobi. (30-70% pewności)

2. Jak **can**, do wyrażania pozwolenia i proszenia o nie
You may stay up late tonight. = You can stay up late tonight.

→ **May** jest formą bardziej uprzejmą niż **can**. Stopniem uprzejmości odpowiada formie **could**.
May I open the window? = Could I open the window?

JAK STOSUJESZ MIGHT?

Might jest formą czasu przeszłego czasownika **may**, stosowaną podobnie jak **may**.

→ Formy **may**, **might** i **could** stosowane są w wyrażaniu przypuszczeń dotyczących teraźniejszości i przyszłości (> unit 56) oraz przeszłości (> units 92, 93).

Tak, jak **can**, **could**, **must** oraz **should**, **may/might** również tworzą pytania i przeczenia bez operatora, za pomocą inwersji.

TYPOWE BŁĘDY UWAŻAJ!

Źle: He may ~~to~~ go there.

PODPOWIEDŹ: Jak w przypadku **can/could** i **must**, po **may/might** opuść **to** przed głównym czasownikiem.

Dobrze: He may go there.

YOUR TURN NOW!

I. Complete a well-known anecdote about the difference in the use of **can** and **may**.

A young man was visiting his old aunt. She was very rich, and the nephew had high hopes about the wealth he thought he might inherit. So, he was listening politely to all the boring things his aunt was saying and, without even batting an eyelid, he agreed with all her opinions. The conversation went on for much longer than he wished, and the room was hot and stuffy, so in the end he started feeling sleepy. He hoped that a cigarette might revive him, so he summoned all his courage and asked his aunt: 'Auntie dear, (1) ______ I smoke here?' The aunt looked at him icily and answered: 'Yes, you (2) ______, but you (3) ______ not. And I don't like people who don't speak English properly.' The young man's heart sank.

II. Choose the correct forms of the verbs from the box to fill the blanks. You must use most of the verbs more than once.

can must should may might shouldn't

Dear Ola,

Thanks for your email. You've asked me to give you some advice how best to travel to and in Scotland. I'll tell you only the essentials. You (1) ________ find out more when you come here. First, please remember that London Heathrow is a very large and busy airport with several terminals. So you (2) ________ want to avoid flying there and, instead, fly straight to Edinburgh or Glasgow. Travel agents (3) ________ advise you on good flights to either of these destinations. It (4) ________ cost you much more than flying to London and then taking a train or coach up north, and it (5) ________ save you a lot of hassle. The only problem with changing flights (6) ________ be the transfer of luggage. Luggage does sometimes go missing on such occasions. Please remember that in such a case you (7) ________ report it to the Baggage Control Office of the airline you travelled with. They will ask you to complete a Property Irregularity Form which you (8) ________ do immediately. You (9) ________ keep a copy of this form. This is important because you (10) ________ be entitled to some compensation from the airline.

For cheap travelling within Scotland one of the best ways is to hire a bicycle which (11) ________ appeal to you since you are such a keen cyclist. Bicycles (12) ________ be hired from various places though, so you (13) ________ want to compare the prices before you decide. I (14) ________ send you a list of bicycle hire shops in Edinburgh in my next email if you want. Please remember, though, that nearly all shops require you to put down a deposit which (15) ________ be paid by cheque or with a credit card – no cash, I'm afraid. The deposit will be returned to you when the bicycle is returned in one piece!

I hope this has answered all your questions.

Take care,

Alistair

KEY

I 1. can 2. can 3. may **II** 1. can 2. may/might 3. can 4. shouldn't 5. can/may/might/could 6. might/may/could 7. must 8. should/must 9. must 10. may/could/might 11. should 12. may/can 13. may/might 14. can 15. may/can

UNIT 56 **must be/can't be/could be/may be/might be**

EXPRESSING SUPPOSITIONS: PRESENT AND FUTURE

Please don't wait for me with supper tonight. There's a Christmas party at the office so I may be home late. Nie czekaj na mnie dziś z kolacją, proszę. W biurze jest przyjęcie gwiazdkowe, więc mogę późno wrócić do domu.
He isn't at home. He could/may/might be at the library.
Nie ma go w domu. On może być w bibliotece.
Joanna can't be at home. I saw her going out five minutes ago.
Joanny na pewno nie ma w domu. Pięć minut temu widziałam, jak wychodziła.
Ian's girlfriend broke off with him. I think he must be broken-hearted; he loved her very much.
Dziewczyna Iana zerwała z nim. Myślę, że on musi mieć złamane serce, bo bardzo ją kochał.

JAK WYRAŻASZ PRZYPUSZCZENIA?

Jeśli przypuszczasz, że coś jest lub może być prawdą, ale brak ci całkowitej pewności, użyj odpowiednio **could/may/might**, **can't** lub **must** w połączeniu z **be**.

→ Do wyrażania przypuszczenia można użyć **must** wyłącznie w formie twierdzącej (**He must be well over ninety**), a **can** wyłącznie w formie przeczącej (**He can't be that old!**).

Jeśli użyjesz **could/may/might** (**It could/may/might be true**), wyrażasz niepewność co do swojego sądu. Masz zaledwie 30-70% pewności, że się nie mylisz.

Jeśli użyjesz **can't** (**It can't be true**) lub **must** (**It must be false**), stwierdzasz, że wysnułeś wniosek z zaistniałych faktów i uważasz, że twoja opinia jest prawdziwa lub przynajmniej bardzo prawdopodobna (masz 90-100% pewności).

TYPOWE BŁĘDY **UWAŻAJ!**

Źle: It ~~can~~ be Tom.
PODPOWIEDŹ: Jeśli chcesz wyrazić przypuszczenie oparte na wątłych przesłankach, użyj **could/may/might**. Użycie **can** w formie twierdzącej do wyrażenia przypuszczeń jest nieprawidłowe.
Dobrze: It could/may/might be Tom.

Źle: I'm not expecting Bob to phone tonight. So it can't be ~~he~~.
PODPOWIEDŹ: Choć teoretycznie gramatycznie poprawne, zdanie '**it can't be he**' brzmi bardzo staroświecko. W konstrukcjach z **could/may/might**, **can't** i **must**, wyrażających przupuszczenie zawsze używaj zaimków osobowych w **object case** (np. **him, us, them**).
Dobrze: I'm not expecting Bob to phone tonight. So it can't be him.

YOUR TURN NOW!

I. Fill the gaps in the dialogues with the appropriate forms of **may/might/could**, **can't** or **must**.

1. A Someone's at the door. I hope it's Joe.
   B It _________ be Joe. He's in Paris.
2. A Here's my Gran's old photograph album. Do you want to have a look?
   B Of course. I love old photographs. Look! What a strange hat! Who's that woman, do you know?
   A I'm not sure. It _________ be my aunt Nela. I'll ask Gran if you like.
3. A Are you still here, Carol? It's eight o'clock!
   B It _________ be that late! Oh, Mum, I've missed my school bus again!
4. A Who's on the phone?
   B It's hard to say. The line's weak and I can't recognize the voice. It _________ be your boss, I think.
5. A Do you know that Sue and Mike have split?
   B Oh, dear. That _________ be hard on Sue. She cares for that boy a lot.
6. A Where's the cat? He was sleeping all morning on the sofa here but now he's gone.
   B I think he _________ be in the kitchen, watching Mum cooking dinner, but I'm not sure.
7. A I don't know what's happened. I've been ringing Barry for ages and still there's no answer.
   B Don't worry. He _________ be out. He always goes shopping on Saturday afternoons.
8. A Look! That's Giewont over there.
   B It _________ be Giewont. Giewont has a characteristic shape and a cross on top. Look! There it is.
9. A Are you taking your umbrella?
   B No, what for? It's such a bright day.
   A Yes, but it _________ rain later. At least that's what the weather forecast says.
10. A The telephone's ringing. Shall I get it?
    B No, it's OK. I'll get it. It _________ be Mark. I'm expecting a call from him.
11. A Will Kathryn spend Christmas with us, do you think?
    B She _________ but I think it's most unlikely. I think she'll go to Luxembourg.

II. Correct the mistakes where necessary.

1. What! Tim had an accident? It mustn't be true.
2. Do you mean she didn't lock her car? She can't be that careless!
3. The traffic's so heavy today that Mr Brown must be late for the meeting.
4. I can't believe you've spent all that money on horses! You may be crazy.
5. Are you saying he shouted at his boss? He must be a fool.

KEY

I. 1. can't 2. could/may/might 3. can't 4. could/may/might 5. must 6. could/may/might 7. must 8. can't 9. could/may/might 10. must 11. could/may/ might **II.** 1. What! Tim had an accident? It can't be true. 2. OK 3. The traffic's so heavy today that Mr Brown could/may/might be late for the meeting. 4. I don't believe you've spent all that money on horses! You must be crazy. 5. OK

UNIT 57 I have been doing PRESENT PERFECT CONTINUOUS

We have been flying for three hours now. Lecimy już dwie godziny.
Have you been running? You look tired. Biegłeś? Wyglądasz na zmęczonego.
How long have you been learning English? Jak długo uczysz się angielskiego?
Barbara hasn't been studying much recently. Barbara nie uczyła się dużo ostatnio.

JAK TWORZYSZ CZAS PAST PERFECT CONTINUOUS?

Podmiot + have/has + been + ing (> unit 59)

KIEDY STOSUJESZ CZAS PRESENT PERFECT CONTINUOUS?

1. Do wyrażania czynności, która rozpoczęła się jakiś czas temu i nadal trwa.

I have been doing my homework for four hours.

2. Do wyrażania czynności, która niedawno się zakończyła i jej skutki są oczywiste. W odróżnieniu od czasu **present perfect**, czas **present perfect continuous** kładzie nacisk na samą czynność jako taką i na czas jej trwania, a nie na jej rezultat.

Kate has been crying. Her eyes are red.

→ Czas **present perfect continuous** w zależności od kontekstu wyrażany jest w języku polskim przez czas teraźniejszy lub przeszły.

Ralph has been eating chocolate, that's why his mouth is so brown.
Ralph jadł czekoladę i dlatego ma brązową buzię.
Ralph has been eating chocolate for two hours, he's going to be sick.
Ralph od dwóch godzin zajada się czekoladą, na pewno się rozchoruje.

PORÓWNANIE CZASU PRESENT PERFECT I PRESENT PERFECT CONTINUOUS

Gdy używasz czasu **present perfect continuous**, podkreślasz fakt wykonywania czynności.
Gdy używasz czasu **present perfect**, podkreślasz rezultat tej czynności.

I have been writing letters for two hours. I have written six letters.
I have been repairing my car since the morning. I have repaired it.

TYPOWE BŁĘDY UWAŻAJ!

Źle: I've ~~been reading~~ this book three times.
PODPOWIEDŹ: Jeśli chcesz powiedzieć, ile razy dana czynność wystąpiła, nie możesz użyć **present perfect continuous**. Powinieneś w tym wypadku użyć **present perfect simple**.
Dobrze: I've read this book three times.

Źle: We ~~are playing~~ chess since four o'clock.
PODPOWIEDŹ: Jeśli czynność rozpoczęła się jakiś czas temu i nadal trwa, musisz użyć czasu **present perfect continuous**.
Dobrze: We have been playing chess since four o'clock.

YOUR TURN NOW!

I. Read the sentences and write **T** (True) or **NS** (Not Stated) next to each sentence.

EXAMPLE Jim has been reading the latest issue of Newsweek.
He has read the whole magazine. **NS**

1. Jenny has been typing her letter all morning. The letter is finished. _____
2. Jenny has typed her letter. The letter is finished. _____
3. Tom has been talking on the phone since 10 o'clock. He is still talking. _____
4. Mary has fixed her computer by herself. The computer is working. _____
5. Max has been repairing his bike since last week. He can ride it now. _____
6. Max has been repairing his bike since last week. He still has some work to do. _____
7. Helen has been reading a book all night. She has finished it. _____
8. She has tidied her room. It's clean now. _____

II. Match the broken sentences. Choose the best possible ending for 1-7.

1. Dick has been saving money since October...
2. Martin has been writing his essay for an hour...
3. Jack has been living in Kuwait since 1998...
4. Nick has been painting his room...
5. Bob has been digging his garden...
6. Bill has been jogging for two hours....
7. Mike has been studying hard all night...

A. ...that's why he has a headache now.
B. ... that's why he's wearing a paper hat.
C. ...and so far he has saved $300.
D. ...that's why his shoes are covered with mud.
E. ...but he hasn't finished it yet.
F. ... that's why he's so hot.
G. ...and he still lives there.

III. Choose the correct form.

1. She is crying because she *has cut/has been cutting* onions for the salad.
2. I *have been cleaning/have cleaned* the house for three hours and I need a rest now.
3. Tim *has been smoking/has smoked* the whole packet of cigarettes.
4. Helen *has learnt/has been learning* how to sew. Now she can make pretty clothes for her baby.
5. Sarah *has been looking/has looked* for her mobile all morning and she hasn't found it yet.
6. I *have been using/have used* my car for three years and so far it has never broken down.
7. Mum *has been cooking dinner/has cooked dinner* so we can have it now.
8. Ted *has been cooking/has cooked* dinner for three hours and it isn't ready yet.
9. Elizabeth *has been writing/has written* this article since Monday.

KEY

I. 1NS 2T 3T 4T 5NS 6T 7NS 8T **II.** 1C 2E 3G 4B 5D 6F 7A **III.** 1. has been cutting 2. have been cleaning 3. has smoked 4. has learnt 5. has been looking 6. have been using 7. has cooked 8. has been cooking 9. has been writing

UNIT 58 I had done/I had worked PAST PERFECT

When we opened the door, we realised that someone had broken into our flat.
Kiedy otworzyliśmy drzwi, zdaliśmy sobie sprawę, że ktoś włamał się (wcześniej) do naszego mieszkania.
Had they visited London before they went there last year?
Czy oni odwiedzili (wcześniej) Londyn zanim pojechali tam w zeszłym roku?
Steve hadn't walked his dog before he left for school.
Steve nie wyprowadził psa zanim wyszedł do szkoły.
After I had finished my essay, I played the guitar.
Gdy skończyłem wypracowanie, grałem na gitarze.
After I finished my essay, I went to the cinema.
Gdy skończyłem wypracowanie, poszedłem do kina.

KIEDY UŻYWASZ CZASU PAST PERFECT?

1. Gdy mówisz o czynnościach lub zdarzeniach, które wystąpiły wcześniej niż inna czynność lub zdarzenie w przeszłości. Czynność późniejszą wyrażasz w czasie **past simple**.
   Elizabeth had studied hard before she took her exam in December.
2. Gdy mówisz o czynnościach, zdarzeniach lub stanach, które rozpoczęły się w przeszłości i trwały nadal w momencie wystąpienia innej, późniejszej czynności. Czas **past perfect** jest wówczas odpowiednikiem czasu **present perfect** w odniesieniu do dalszej przeszłości.
   When I met John, he had already lived in Brighton for five years.

→ Czas **past perfect** często występuje z przysłówkami **when, before, after, already, just, for, since, till, until, by, by the time, never**. Z przysłówkami **before** lub **after** możesz użyć czasu **past perfect** lub **past simple** – sens zdania pozostanie niezmieniony.

They went for a walk after it had stopped raining. = They went for a walk after it stopped raining.

→ Jeśli czynności następują bezpośrednio po sobie, używasz **past simple**.

I came home, took off my jacket, washed my hands and turned on the radio.

TYPOWY BŁĄD UWAŻAJ!

Źle: Bob ~~worked~~ in the Institute for five years when I met him.

PODPOWIEDŹ: Jeśli jakaś czynność lub stan wciąż trwały, gdy nastąpiła inna, późniejsza czynność, do wyrażenia wcześniejszej czynności lub stanu musisz użyć czasu **past perfect**.

Dobrze: Bob had worked in the Institute for five years when I met him.

YOUR TURN NOW!

I. Match the halves of these sentences.

1. When we opened the door,
2. We had driven 650 km
3. How long had Jenny been in London
4. By the time Mary arrived at the meeting
5. My wife wanted to know

a) before we finally reached our destination.
b) we had discussed the problem.
c) we realised that someone had broken into our flat.
d) how much money I had spent in the pub.
e) before she met Jim?

II. Complete the text with the verbs. Remember to use the correct tense: **past simple** or **past perfect**.

be make record want go destroy rain look
reach begin shout cannot slip put throw

It was going to be a very important race. The day was sunny but the previous night it (1) _________ heavily, so there (2) _________ puddles on the track. We were standing in line waiting for the start of the race. 'Ready, steady, go!' the man (3) _________. And off we (4) _________. Robby was the fastest and I (5) _________ to be at least the second on the finish. Suddenly I felt I (6) _________ my old trainers on. They were too tight and I (7) _________ run at my top speed. I (8) _________ to march as fast as I could. I didn't notice a banana peel somebody (9) _________ away carelessly on the track. I (10) _________ and fell into the puddle. My shorts and my T-shirt got muddy. When I finally (11) _________ the finish, I was devastated. 'Don't worry!' said Mark. 'I (12) _________ the whole race on my video', he said with a smile. I wanted to kill him. I was furious and started to cry. When I got home, my eyes were red and sore. I (13) _________ at the mirror and regretted I (14) _________ a fool of myself. Then Mark phoned and said he (15) _________ the tape. I was relieved.

III. Correct the mistakes where necessary.

1. When I arrived at school the test already started.
2. Jim was working as a teacher for two years when I first met him.
3. Last year we went to Denmark. We were never there before.
4. Jeff had no idea where his mother put his new CD.
5. I told the policeman I never saw that man before.
6. We knew each other for three years when we got married in 1998.
7. I thanked Jenny for the postcard she sent me from Cyprus the previous year.

KEY

I. 1c 2a 3e 4b 5d **II.** 1. had rained 2. were 3. shouted 4. went 5. wanted 6. had put 7. couldn't 8. began 9. had thrown 10. slipped 11. reached 12. recorded 13. looked 14. had made 15. had destroyed **III.** 1. When I arrived at school the test had already started. 2. Jim had been working /had worked for two years as a teacher when I first met him. 3. We had never been there before. 4. Jeff had no idea where his mother had put his new CD. 5. I told the policeman I had never seen that man before. 6. We had known each other for three years when we got married in 1998. 7. I thanked Jenny for the postcard she had sent me from Cyprus the previous year.

UNIT 59 I had been doing/I had been working
PAST PERFECT CONTINUOUS

Susan had been trying to change the tyre for two hours before Mark helped her.
Susan przez dwie godziny próbowała zmienić oponę zanim Mark jej pomógł.
The police had been looking for my car for two months before they dropped the case.
Policja szukała mojego samochodu przez dwa miesiące zanim umorzyli sprawę.
We hadn't been practising for the exam, that's why we failed it.
Nie ćwiczyliśmy przed egzaminem i dlatego nie zdaliśmy.
Had it still been snowing when you went for a walk that afternoon?
Czy wciąż padał śnieg gdy wyszliście na spacer tego popołudnia?
While we were jogging in the park the paths were slippery, because it had been raining.
Gdy biegaliśmy po parku, ścieżki były śliskie, gdyż wcześniej padało.
While we were jogging in the park the paths were slippery, because it was raining.
Gdy biegaliśmy po parku, ścieżki były śliskie, bo właśnie padał deszcz.

KIEDY STOSUJESZ CZAS PAST PERFECT CONTINUOUS?

1. Gdy chcesz powiedzieć, że jakaś czynność była wykonywana i trwała przez jakiś czas, zanim nastąpiła inna czynność w przeszłości. Czas **past perfect continuous** zawsze występuje w relacji z innym wydarzeniem w przeszłości.
He had been working in the coal mine for ten years when the accident happened.

2. Do wyciągnięcia wniosków w stosunku do wydarzeń z przeszłości.
Her eyes were red and swollen. It was obvious that she had been crying.

→ Czas **past perfect continuous** jest odpowiednikiem czasu **present perfect continuous** w odniesieniu do przeszłości. Bardzo często występuje w mowie zależnej (> unit 69).

TYPOWY BŁĄD **UWAŻAJ!**

Źle: ~~I had been talking~~ on the phone at 10 o'clock yesterday.
PODPOWIEDŹ: Jeśli chcesz powiedzieć, że jakaś czynność miała miejsce w danym momencie w przeszłości, nie używaj **past perfect continuous**. Wystarczy **past continuous**.
Dobrze: I was talking on the phone at 10 o'clock yesterday.

YOUR TURN NOW!

I. Match the result with its cause.

1. He was out of breath...
2. His hands were dirty...
3. He was wet all over...
4. He was sad ...
5. He had a hoarse voice...
6. His mouth was brown...

A. ...because he was planting strawberries in the garden.
B. ...because he had been quarreling with his girlfriend.
C. ... because he had been screaming at his children.
D. ...because he had been eating chocolate.
E. ...because he had been walking in the rain.
F. ... because he had been running all the way.

II. Complete the text with the correct verb from the box. Use **past perfect** or **past perfect continuous** forms.

drive pour leave try spend shake turn go change take

It happened exactly three months ago. I remember it very well. I (1)________ the previous day at the club playing cards till morning, so when I came home I was dying for a good sleep. When I made myself comfortable in bed, the telephone rang. It was my sister. She was in trouble. She had to be in Brighton before 11 because she had an important lecture there. She (2)_______ for an hour and was about a hundred kilometres before Brighton when her car stopped and she couldn't start it again. She (3)________ different tricks but nothing worked. She asked me to for help. At first I wasn't very eager to get dressed again and drive in that cold rainy weather. Yet Sarah sounded so miserable that I felt I had to go. I put on a pair of jeans and a jacket, keeping my pyjamas top on. I didn't want to waste time looking for some clean shirt.

I (4)_______ as fast as possible for an hour when I saw my poor sister standing next to her old car. After I (5)______ the key, I realised something was wrong with the ignition. I decided to buy a set of new spark plugs. There was a big shopping centre nearby so I went there. After I (6)_____ my car in the car park, I waved to my sister and headed for the entrance. I was surprised to see a group of smartly dressed people at the gate. There were flowers, the logo of the shop was proudly displayed, but I didn't think much about it. I wanted to buy the plugs and help my sister.

'996, 997, 998.... ' the people at the gate were counting loudly. '...999, a thousand!' they yelled and stopped me. They (7)_______ my hand and patting me on my back for a long while before I understood what was going on. 'You are our thousandth customer! Congratulations!" the manager explained. 'Yeah? ' I asked impatiently. 'As our dear customer you are receiving this brand new Opel Corsa. Happy driving, sir.' I couldn't believe it. The rain (8)_______ since the morning and there I was, my jacket unbuttoned and my old pyjamas top popping from under it. They (9)________ pictures and the following day I saw my picture in the local paper. How I regretted that I (10)__________ to a shirt that morning.

KEY

I. 1F 2A 3E 4B 5C 6D II.1. had spent 2. had been driving 3. had tried/had been trying 4. had been driving 5. had turned 6. had left 7. had been shaking 8. had been pouring 9. had been taking 10. hadn't changed

UNIT 60 He does/He will do PRESENT HABITS

On Sundays Mark usually gets up late. W niedziele Marek zwykle wstaje późno.
On Sundays Mark will usually get up late. W niedziele Marek zwykle wstaje późno.
When Betty has a problem to solve, she will work at it until she finds a solution.
Kiedy Betty ma problem do rozwiazania, pracuje nad nim aż znajdzie sposób.
When Tom has a problem to solve, he will ask his girlfriend for advice.
Kiedy Tom ma problem do rozwiązania, prosi swoją dziewczynę o radę.
Ben is strange – he'll sit for hours staring at the window and saying nothing to anybody.
Ben jest dziwny – przesiaduje godzinami gapiąc się w okno i nie odzywając się do nikogo.

KIEDY STOSUJESZ PRESENT SIMPLE, A KIEDY WILL?

Czynności powtarzające się, zwyczajowe, możesz wyrazić w czasie teraźniejszym przy pomocy czasu **present simple** lub przy pomocy operatora **will**. Form czasu **present simple** używa się częściej, natomiast **will** – szczególnie w opowiadaniach. Operator **will** kładzie nacisk na oczywistość czyjegoś postępowania, a więc podkreśla przewidywalność danej czynności. Może być skrócony do formy **'ll**.

W przykładowych zdaniach podanych w ramce można zamiennie stosować **present simple** lub **will** bez zmiany znaczenia.

→ Jeśli chcesz podkreślić, że czyjś powtarzający się sposób postępowania drażni cię, użyj **present continuous** (> unit 14) lub operatora **will**. Operator **will** wyrażający czyjś denerwujący zwyczaj nigdy nie ulega skróceniu do **'ll**, przeciwnie – jest akcentowany.

What I dislike about my sister is that she will always borrow my best clothes without asking.

Sens wypowiedzi pozostanie niezmieniony, jeśli użyjesz **present simple**:

What I dislike about my sister is that she always borrows my best clothes without asking.

Użycie operatora **will** podkreśla jednak fakt twojego niezadowolenia.

→ Podobnie użycie operatora **won't (will not)** w odniesieniu do rzeczy (nie osób) wyraża naszą krytykę. Wówczas najczęściej stosowana jest forma skrócona **won't**.

My car won't start on a frosty morning.

To samo zdanie wyrażone w formie **present simple** stwierdza fakt, nie wyraża niezadowolenia:

My car doesn't start on a frosty morning.

TYPOWY BŁĄD UWAŻAJ!

Źle: Greg is quite cheeky. ~~He often will argue with his parents.~~

PODPOWIEDŹ: Jeśli używasz operatora, np. **will**, przysłówki typu **always, often, never** umieszczasz między operatorem a czasownikiem głównym.

Dobrze: Greg is quite cheeky. He will often argue with his parents.

YOUR TURN NOW!

I. Replace the underlined verb by **will+infinitive**.

EXAMPLE: He never says 'hello' to his neighbours.
He won't say 'hello' to his neighbours.

1. My children love computer games. They spend all days at the computer.
2. George is absent-minded. He often forgets about his appointments.
3. My English teacher is very strict. She gives us tests every week.
4. Helen always leaves the light on in the bathroom, which annoys me.
5. Every day is the same: Steve gets up, makes himself a cup of coffee and takes a shower.
6. This new secretary always argues whenever you ask her to stay in the office after five.

II. Complete the dialogues with **will** or **won't**. Choose a suitable verb from the box. There are two extra verbs which you will not need.

enter buy turn come reply go interrupt start finish

1. A: Why are you and Jeff arguing so much?
   B: He never listens to me. He ______________ the TV on and watch football matches.
2. A: Are you having problems with your new computer?
   B: Yes. Sometimes it jams and ________ start again.
3. A: Why are you angry with Maggie, your flat-mate?
   B: You know, when nobody is looking she ________ to the kitchen and steal my yoghurts.
4. A: Do you enjoy your English classes?
   B: Not at all. All lessons are the same. Our teacher ________ the classroom, open her book and dictate us grammatical rules. It's so boring!
5. A: Steve is impossible!
   B: Why do you think so?
   A: He __________ me whenever I try to tell a joke.
6. A: I'm bored with Lucas.
   B: Why is that?
   A: He is so predictable. Everyday he ________ from work, kick his shoes off and watch TV.
7. A: Our new neighbour is so strange. I can't stand him!
   B: What's the problem?
   A: He pretends he doesn't recognize me and __________ to my greeting.

KEY

I. 1. They will spend all days at the computer. 2. He will often forget about his appointments. 3. She will give us tests every week. 4. Helen will always leave the light on in the bathroom. 5. Steve will get up, make himself a cup of coffee and take a shower. 6. This new secretary will always argue whenever you ask her to stay in the office after five. **II.** 1. He will turn the TV on and watch football matches. 2. Sometimes it jams and won't start again. 3. You know, when nobody is looking she will go to the kitchen and steal my yoghurts. 4. Our teacher will enter the classroom, open her book and dictate us grammatical rules. 5. He will interrupt me whenever I try to tell a joke. 6. Every day he will come from work, kick his shoes off and watch TV. 7. He pretends he doesn't recognize me and won't reply to my greeting.

UNIT 61 used to do/would do PAST HABITS AND STATES

When I was a teenager I used to wear mini-skirts. Kiedy byłam nastolatką, nosiłam spódniczki mini.
There used to be a small shop in my street, and now they are building a huge supermarket here. Na mojej ulicy był kiedyś mały sklepik, a teraz budują tu ogromny supermarket.
He never used to leave the garage door open. On nigdy nie zostawiał otwartych drzwi do garażu.
Fifty years ago the British didn't use to go abroad for holidays as often as they do now. Pięćdziesiąt lat temu Brytyjczycy nie mieli w zwyczaju tak często jak teraz spędzać wakacji za granicą.
John would often hum while he was working. John zwykł był często nucić podczas pracy.

KIEDY UŻYWASZ FORM USED TO (DO) I WOULD (DO)?

Used to używasz, gdy chcesz powiedzieć, że w przeszłości jakaś czynność lub stan powtarzały się regularnie, były czymś zwyczajem. Powtarzalność danej czynności w przeszłości można także wyrazić w **past simple**. W odróżnieniu od **simple past**, konstrukcja **used to** podkreśla fakt, że dana czynność lub stan już nie mają miejsca i należą do przeszłości.

Before he retired, for forty years he used to catch the same bus to get to work.

Would (do) używa się podobnie jak **used to (do)** do podkreślenia powtarzalności jakiejś czynności w przeszłości.

Before he retired, for forty years he would catch the same bus to get to work.

→ **Would (do)** w tym znaczeniu używa się tylko do wyrażania przeszłych czynności, nie stanów, a więc wyłącznie z **action verbs**, nigdy ze **state verbs**. (> Unit 95)
Would (do) używa się przede wszystkim w wypowiedziach pisemnych, np. w opowiadaniach, szczególnie gdy podkreślone są okoliczności, w których dana czynność występowała.

→ Do tworzenia pytań i przeczeń **used to** używa dla wszystkich osób operatora **did** (**Did you use to smoke when you were a schoolboy? In the past he didn't use to work as much as he does now**). Często przeczenia tworzy się przy pomocy **never** (**In the past he never used to work as much as he does now**).
Konstrukcja **would to** wyrażająca zwyczajową czynność w przeszłości używana jest tylko w formie twierdzącej.

TYPOWY BŁĄD UWAŻAJ!

Źle: Before she lost her mother Mary ~~would~~ be a very happy child.

PODPOWIEDŹ: Do wyrażania przeszłych stanów, nie czynności, można użyć **used to do** lub **past simple**, nigdy **would**.

Dobrze: Before she lost her mother, Mary used to be a very happy child./Mary was a very happy child.

HOTSPOT!

W zeszłym roku odwiedziliśmy Londyn. (czynność jednorazowa) = **Last year we visited London.**
Gdy podajesz termin jakiegoś zdarzenia z przeszłości, musisz użyć **past simple**. Jeśli jednak chcesz podkreślić powtarzalność danego stanu lub czynności, użyj formy **used to** i dla wyjaśnienia dodaj odpowiedni przysłówek. **W zeszłym roku odwiedzaliśmy Londyn.** (czynność powtarzana) = **Last year we used to visit London regularly.**

YOUR TURN NOW!

I. Rewrite the sentences to make it clear that some of the actions or states were repeated in the past. Remember to change the verb forms where necessary.

1. Before they got married Ed bought Sylvia flowers every day, but he doesn't do it any longer.
2. When I was at school I regularly wrote letters to my friends, but now I am too busy to do that.
3. Betty read lots of books when she was younger, but now she only reads fashion magazines.
4. Not long ago Alex helped Jean in household chores, but now he watches television all evening.
5. My cat was lovely when she was a kitten but now she is a bit too fat.

II. Complete the text with the phrases from the box.

would take time off work would start used to sell would sing used to hurry would lose would do used to store would peel would tiptoe used to have would spend would take out would climb used to add

When we were children, our family celebrated Christmas in a very traditional way. About a week before Christmas Eve our Mother (1) ________________ all kinds of preparations. First, she (2) ________________ the shopping in small local shops which (3) ________________ about everything. When all the necessary ingredients were in the larder, she (4) ________________ all days cooking and baking in our big kitchen. My sisters and I (5) ________________ back home after school to be the first to scrape the bowl. And we helped Mother, too. We (6) ____________, cut and slice, sieve, whip and stir, but it was always Mother who (7) ________________ the final, masterly touches to every dish and cake. It was hard work, and she was a demanding boss, but it was also fun to work together.

Yet, for me, real fun began only on Christmas Eve. On that day Father, usually too busy to spend much time with the children, (8) ________________ and join us in the preparations. His job was to decorate the Christmas tree. We (9) ________________ huge Christmas trees, reaching up to the ceiling in our spacious sitting-room. Father (10) ________________ big boxes of Christmas decorations, which we (11) ________________ from year to year – each year adding a few new items – and, to begin, he (12) ________________ a ladder to put a silvery tinsel star on top of the tree. From that moment, the kitchen and all the goodies there (13) ________________ all their appeal for me. I (14) ________________ to the dining room and ask Father to let me help him. The main attraction was that while working on the tree he (15) ________________ Christmas carols. He had a wonderful singing voice and I loved singing the carols with him.

When I now think back of those times, what stands out in my mind is our working together and singing together. This feeling of togetherness and sharing is what Christmas joy means for me.

KEY

I. 1 Before they got married Ed would/used to buy Sylvia flowers every day, but he doesn't do it any longer. 2. When I was at school I would/used to write letters to my friends, but now I am too busy to do that. 3. Betty would/used to read lots of books when she was younger, but now she only reads fashion magazines. 4. Not long ago Alex would/used to help Jean in household chores, but now he watches television all evening. 5. My cat used to be lovely when she was a kitten but now she is a bit too fat. **II.** 1. would start 2. would do 3. used to sell 4. would spend 5. used to hurry 6. would peel 7. used to add 8. would take time off work 9. used to have 10. would take out 11. used to store 12. would climb 13. would lose 14. would tiptoe 15. would sing

UNIT 62 used to do/be used to do/get used to do

In the past, my Grannie didn't have a washing machine. W przeszłości moja babcia nie miała pralki.
She used to do her washing by hand. Robiła swoje pranie ręcznie.
She wasn't used to using a washing machine. Nie była przyzwyczajona do używania pralki.
Recently I've bought her a washing machine and now Grannie is getting used to washing her things in it.
Ostatnio kupiłam jej pralkę i teraz babcia przyzwyczaja się do prania w niej swoich rzeczy.

KIEDY UŻYWASZ USED TO DO/BE USED TO DO/GET USED TO DO?

1. Gdy chcesz wyrazić stan lub czynność, które powtarzały się regularnie w przeszłości, były czyimś zwyczajem, lecz obecnie nie mają miejsca, użyj **used to** (> unit 61).

2. Gdy chcesz podkreślić czyjeś przyzwyczajenie do jakiejś osoby, rzeczy lub czynności, użyj **be used to (something/doing something)** w odpowiedniej formie osobowej i we właściwym czasie. Czynność będącą przyzwyczajeniem wyrażasz rzeczownikiem odsłownym z końcówką **–ing** (> patrz **gerund**, unit 30).

The British are used to bad weather.
When he was a boy, Philip was used to getting up early.

→ Konstrukcja **be used to** wyraża stan przyzwyczajenia do czegoś.

3. Gdy chcesz podkreślić proces przyzwyczajania się do czegoś/kogoś, użyj konstrukcji **get used to (something/doing something)**.

At first, Mark was afraid to bathe the baby, but gradually he got used to it.
I hope Francesca will soon get used to living in Scotland.

4. Przyzwyczajenie można także wyrazić używając konstrukcji **be accustomed to (something/doing something)**.

Ever since he was a boy Richard has been accustomed to taking his medicine against asthma.

TYPOWE BŁĘDY UWAŻAJ!

Źle: When I was in London, ~~I'm used~~ to drive on the left.
PODPOWIEDŹ: Jeśli chcesz powiedzieć, że w przeszłości zwykłeś regularnie wykonywać jakąś czynność, ale obecnie już tego nie robisz, użyj **used to**.
Dobrze: When I was in London, I used to drive on the left.

Źle: I'm used to ~~drive~~ on the left.
PODPOWIEDŹ: Jeśli chcesz powiedzieć, że jesteś przyzwyczajony do wykonywania jakiejś czynności, użyj formy **-ing**.
Dobrze: I'm used to driving on the left.

HOTSPOT!

Wymowa **used** [ju: st] w formie **used to** różni się od wymowy form czasownika **use** [ju: z].
Tak więc **I used** [ju: st] **to do it** oraz **I was used/got used** [ju: zd] **to it** wymawiamy inaczej!

YOUR TURN NOW!

I. Choose the correct answer to complete the mini-dialogues.

1. A: Has Bob always lived in Edinburgh?
   B: No, when he was a boy he ________________ to live in Ayrshire.
   a) got used b) used c) was used
2. A: Did you find learning to drive difficult?
   B: Yes, I did at first. But I soon ________________ to it.
   a) used b) was used c) got used
3. A: You are looking tired.
   B: I ________________ to getting up so early.
   a) 'm not used b) didn't use c) don't get used
4. A: Helen isn't happy in her new school.
   B: I think she ________________ to such strict discipline before.
   a) didn't use b) didn't get used c) wasn't used
5. A: Peter and Jean have moved to Crete.
   B: Oh, really? They ________________ to live in the Netherlands, didn't they?
   a) used b) got used c) were used
6. A: Have you ever lived in the country?
   B: No, but I hope we will soon ________________ to it.
   a) used b) get used c) be used

II. Join the broken sentences.

1. Maggie is used to eating lots of strawberries
2. Marissa has been used to going to church every Sunday
3. Elizabeth used to spend her holidays in the West of Ireland
4. Mary has got used to getting up early
5. Lucy was used to looking after her baby sister
6. Helen will soon get used to her new school

A. although she didn't like it at first.
B. while her parents were at work.
C. but now she prefers going to Spain.
D. because her mother is very religious.
E. although she doesn't like it now.
F. because they grow them on their farm.

III. Match each sentence with its correct meaning.

When I was a teenager

1. I got used to doing my own cooking.
2. I was used to doing my own cooking.
3. I used to do my own cooking.

A. I treated doing it as something normal.
B. I did it regularly then, but I don't do it now.
C. I gradually became accustomed to doing it.

KEY

I. 1b 2c 3a 4c 5a 6b **II.** 1F 2D 3C 4A 5B 6E **III.** 1C 2A 3B

UNIT 63 to do/to be doing/to have done/to be done/to have been done
THE INFINITIVE

To be or not to be; that is the question. Być albo nie być – oto jest pytanie.
Chris is happy to be getting married to Joan. Chris jest szczęśliwy, że żeni się z Joanną.
It is better to have loved and lost than never to have loved at all.
Lepiej jest kochać i stracić niż nigdy nie kochać.
Ann is lucky to have been working for such a good firm.
Anna ma szczęście, że pracuje dla tak dobrej firmy.

Forma bezokolicznika jest identyczna z formą podstawową czasownika, zwykle poprzedzoną partykułą **to**. Forma ta ulega jednak pewnym modyfikacjom:

present infinitive	**to do**
present continuous infinitive	**to be doing**
perfect infinitive	**to have done**
perfect continuous infinitive	**to have been doing**
present infinitive passive	**to be done**
perfect infinitive passive	**to have been done**

Present infinitive (w formie czynnej i biernej) oraz **present continuous** infinitive oznaczają czynność odbywającą się w tym samym czasie, co czynność wyrażona czasownikiem w formie osobowej.

I am sorry to be keeping you after hours but we have a very urgent contract to write.

Perfect infinitive (w obu stronach) oraz **perfect continuous infinitive** oznaczają czynność, która poprzedzała czynność wyrażoną czasownikiem w formie osobowej.

I am sorry to have kept you after hours but now that we've finished we can go home.

TYPOWY BŁĄD UWAŻAJ!

Źle: We meant ~~to stay~~ there for a week but the weather was so bad that we left after two days.

PODPOWIEDŹ: Jeśli chcesz wyrazić, że coś w przeszłości zawiodło twoje nadzieje lub oczekiwania, użyj **perfect infinitive**.

Dobrze: We meant to have stayed there for a week but the weather was so bad that we left after two days.

HOTSPOT!

W języku polskim nie istnieją odpowiedniki wszystkich angielskich form bezokolicznika. W tłumaczeniu z języka polskiego na angielski, lub przy pisaniu własnych tekstów po angielsku staraj się uwzględnić relacje czasowe wyrażone w tych formach.

DID YOU KNOW?

According to the British Medical Journal, twins are less likely to commit suicide than others, but more susceptible to become mentally ill. This news comes from Denmark, where scientists are reported to have studied 21,653 pairs of twins. These findings back the widely-accepted view that strong family ties and commitments cut the risk of suicidal behaviour.

YOUR TURN NOW!

I. With or without **to**? Add **to** where necessary.

1. Peter wants _______ speak to you about his project.
2. She ought _______ tell you all about her problems.
3. Mark is a champion. He can _______ swim a mile in no time.
4. You should learn how _______ compromise.
5. We mustn't _______ take photographs in the museum.
6. He believes _______ have been framed by the police.
7. She liked _______ be praised.
8. They couldn't _______ believe the horrible news.
9. He pretended not _______ have been listening.
10. We might just as well _______ stay at home tonight.
11. I am sorry _______ have broken my promise.
12. No matter how careful we are, accidents will _______ happen.
13. Bob thinks it is very difficult _______ save money nowadays.
14. It may _______ be best _______ look this word up in a dictionary.

II. Use the verbs from the box to complete the sentences with the correct infinitive. In one sentence more than one answer is possible.

offer earn re-elect go poach escape work make

1. Sheila was lucky to _______________ serious injury in that car accident.
2. George was happy to _______________ a rise.
3. The President of Farlandia will be glad to _______________.
4. Old Macpherson is known to _______________ salmon for years.
5. Peter likes to _______________ loads of money by doing as little work as possible.
6. 'To _______________ the same mistake twice was unforgivable,' my boss said before he fired me.
7. Bessie is a workaholic. She is likely to _______________ even at New Year.
8. In all euro-zone countries prices tended to _______________ up last year.

KEY

I. Peter wants to speak to you about his project. 2. She ought to tell you all about her problems. 3. Mark is a champion. He can swim a mile in no time. 4. You should learn how to compromise. 5. We mustn't take photographs in the museum. 6. He believes to have been framed by the police. 7. She liked to be praised. 8. They couldn't believe the horrible news. 9. He pretended not to have been listening. 10. We might just as well stay at home tonight. 11. I am sorry to have broken my promise. 12. No matter how careful we are, accidents will happen. 13. Bob thinks it is very difficult to save money nowadays. 14. It may be best to look this word up in a dictionary. **II.** 1. Sheila was lucky to have escaped serious injury in that car accident. 2. George was happy to have been offered a rise. 3. The President of Farlandia will be glad to be re-elected. 4. Old Macpherson is known to have poached/have been poaching salmon for years. 5. Peter likes to earn loads of money by doing as little work as possible. 6. 'To have made the same mistake twice was unforgivable', my boss said before he fired me. 7. Bessie is a workaholic. She is likely to be working even at New Year. 8. In all euro-zone countries prices tended to have gone up last year.

The telephone was invented in 1876. Telefon został wynaleziony w 1876 r.
The bank has been robbed. Obrabowano bank.
The programme is being recorded at the moment. Program jest nagrywany w tym momencie.

KIEDY STOSUJESZ STRONĘ BIERNĄ (THE PASSIVE)?

Strona bierna w języku angielskim jest stosowana znacznie częściej niż w języku polskim. Odpowiednikiem angielskich zdań w stronie biernej jest często konstrukcja bezosobowa w języku polskim. Często nie jest istotne, kto jest wykonawcą czynności.

A new supermarket has been opened here.

Jeśli chcesz położyć nacisk na wykonawcę czynności, użyj przyimka **by**.

This photo was taken by my father.

JAK TWORZYSZ STRONĘ BIERNĄ?

ACTIVE	PASSIVE
We bake bread every day.	Bread is baked every day.
We are baking bread at the moment.	Bread is being baked at the moment.
We have baked bread.	Bread has been baked.
We baked bread.	Bread was baked.
We were baking bread.	Bread was being baked.
We are going to bake bread.	Bread is going to be baked.
We will bake bread.	Bread will be baked.
We can bake bread.	Bread can be baked.

Strona bierna od czasów **present perfect continuous** i **past perfect continuous** nie jest używana. Wszystkie czasowniki modalne tworzą stronę bierną tak jak **can** w powyższym przykładzie.

TYPOWE BŁĘDY UWAŻAJ!

Źle: The window is ~~been~~ cleaned once a month.
PODPOWIEDŹ: Strona bierna składa się z czasownika **be** i tzw. trzeciej formy czasownika, czyli **past participle**.
Dobrze: The window is cleaned once a month.

Źle: Your room ~~is cleaned~~ at the moment.
PODPOWIEDŹ: W czasach typu **continuous** strona bierna zawiera formę **being**.
Dobrze: Your room is being cleaned at the moment.

HOTSPOT!

Jeśli wykonawca czynności jest oczywisty, nie wymieniaj go niepotrzebnie.
The magazine is published twice a month ~~by the publisher~~.

YOUR TURN NOW!

I. Change these sentences into **passive**.

1. Someone will iron your shirts. Your shirts ______________.
2. They are discussing the problem of unemployment. The problem ______________.
3. Someone has stolen my car. My car ______________.
4. Someone is going to meet you at the airport. You ______________.
5. The police have arrested the thief. The thief ______________.
6. Mary is repairing her bike. Mary's bike ______________.
7. Ralph walks the dog three times a day. The dog ______________.
8. They mended our washing machine yesterday. Our washing machine ______________.
9. They were discussing the topic before the lunch break. The topic ______________.
10. They have printed all the documents. All the documents ______________.
11. Nobody has seen Jeff since Monday. Jeff ______________.
12. They won't issue the next bulletin until May. The next bulletin ______________.
13. They may commit a crime. The crime ______________.
14. Somebody can steal the money. The money ______________.

II. Read the article on crimefighters at Sunshine Secondary School and put the verbs in the correct **passive** form.

Crimefighters is a programme that helps prevent crime and vandalism at Sunshine Secondary School in Bishopton. Students (1) _________ *(allow)* to report crime and remain anonymous, and make some cash. **Crimefighters** (2) _________ *(establish)* in 2002 by Jim Thompson, the headmaster. During the first year the programme has helped the administration in solving 12 cases of vandalism and theft. Special forms (3) _______ *(issue)* and if students have information on a crime that has, or may (4) _______ *(commit)*, they can fill the form and put it in a special box next to the reception desk. When the crime (5) _________ *(solve)*, students can get their cash reward from the bookkeeper's office. Rewards are from £5 to 30, depending on the situation. The money for cash rewards (6) _______ *(donate)* by the Bishopton Police Department. Since the programme started, more than £300 (7) ______ *(give)* in rewards for the students who have informed the school authorities about drug dealing, theft, acts of vandalism and similar cases.

KEY

I. 1. Your shirts will be ironed. 2. The problem of unemployment is being discussed. 3. My car has been stolen. 4. You are going to be met at the airport. 5. The thief has been arrested (by the police). 6. Mary's bike is being repaired. 7. The dog is walked three times a day. 8. Our washing machine was mended yesterday. 9. The topic was being discussed before the lunch break. 10. All the documents have been printed. 11. Jeff hasn't been seen (by anybody) since Monday. 12. The next bulletin won't be issued until May. 13. The crime may be comitted. 14. The money can be stolen. **II.** 1. are allowed, 2. was established, 3. have been issued, 4. be committed, 5. has been solved, 6. has been donated, 7. has been given

UNIT 65 I was told/We were given THE PASSIVE (2)

Every year the lucky winner is given a prize. Co roku szczęśliwemu zwycięzcy wręcza się nagrodę.
I have been shown his latest painting. Pokazano mi jego najnowszy obraz.
A well-qualified applicant will be offered a high salary.
Wysoka pensja zostanie zaoferowana odpowiednio wykwalifikowanemu kandydatowi.
I was told about their wedding. Powiedziano mi o ich weselu.
Mary was given flowers at the end of her lecture. Na zakończenie wykładu wręczono Marii kwiaty.
How much were you paid for doing this job? Ile ci zapłacono za wykonanie tej pracy?
I wasn't promised any pay-rise. Nie obiecano mi podwyżki.

KIEDY STOSUJESZ KONSTRUKCJĘ TYPU I WAS TOLD?

Jest to specyficzna konstrukcja w stronie biernej, która nie ma odpowiednika w języku polskim, a zatem jest trudna do przetłumaczenia.

W języku angielskim formę bezosobową można wyrazić na dwa sposoby:

Flowers were given to Mary. = Mary was given flowers.

Wybór formy zależy od tego, na co chcemy położyć nacisk: na czynność (co zostało zrobione) czy na adresata czynności (kto był przedmiotem czynności). W pierwszym zdaniu ważniejszy jest fakt dania kwiatów, w drugim natomiast obdarowana nimi osoba.

JAKIE CZASOWNIKI MOŻNA STOSOWAĆ W KONSTRUKCJI TYPU I WAS TOLD?

Czasowniki, które mają dwa dopełnienia (bliższe i dalsze) mogą występować w zdaniach z konstrukcją typu **I was told**. Są to np. **advise, allow, bring, declare, expect, hand, give, lend, pay, promise, recommend, sell, send, show, speak, suppose, teach, tell**.

They handed Mary a letter. = A letter was handed to Mary. = Mary was handed a letter.

Obydwa dopełnienia: **a letter** (dopełnienie bliższe) oraz **Mary** (dopełnienie dalsze) mogą być podmiotami zdania w stronie biernej.

TYPOWY BŁĄD UWAŻAJ!

Źle: ~~We supposed~~ to complete the exam paper before 12 o'clock.

PODPOWIEDŹ: Strona bierna wymaga użycia czasownika **be** w odpowiedniej formie.

Dobrze: We are supposed to complete the exam paper before 12 o'clock.

HOTSPOT!

COMPARE: I was shown the room. = Pokazano mi pokój.
I was shown to the room. = Zaprowadzono mnie do pokoju.

YOUR TURN NOW!

I. Change the emphasis of the sentences.

EXAMPLE: The key was given to the cleaning lady. The cleaning lady was given the key.

1. A reward will be given to the best student. The best student ____________.
2. Will the details be sent to me? Will I ____________?
3. A surprise present was handed to me. I ____________.
4. A new car was lent to me. I ____________.
5. A promotion was promised to Ann. Ann ____________.
6. A legacy of 1000,000 euros was left to Jim. Jim ____________.
7. A fake piece of jewellery was sold to her. She ____________.
8. A long holiday was recommended to Steve. Steve ____________.

II. Rewrite the sentences in the **passive**.

1. They asked you to call the manager. You ____________.
2. Everybody speaks English here. English ____________
3. They paid me 100 euros for the article. I ____________.
4. They allow patients one visit a day. Patients ____________.
5. They advised Susan to apply for the job. Susan____________.
6. My boss told me the news. I ____________.
7. They expect us to leave soon. We ____________.
8. They taught him how to use e-mail. He ____________.
9. The librarian brought me the book. I ____________.
10. Someone should show him our new office. He ____________

III. Answer the questions using the **passive**.

1. What should be recommended to a student who is overworked?
   The student ____________.
2. If you write a letter of application, what might you be sent?
   You ____________.
3. What job would you like to be offered?
   I ____________.
4. How much is the Member of the European Parliament paid?
   A Member____________.

KEY

I. 1. The best student will be given a reward. 2. Will I be sent the details? 3. I was handed a surprise present. 4. I was lent a new car. 5. Ann was promised a promotion. 6. Jim was left a legacy of 1000,000 euros. 7. She was sold a fake piece of jewellery. 8. Steve was recommended a long holiday. **II.** 1. You were asked to call the manager. 2. English is spoken here. 3. I was paid 100 euros for the article. 4. Patients are allowed one visit a day. 5. Susan was advised to apply for the job. 6. I was told the news. 7. We are expected to leave soon. 8. He was taught how to use e-mail. 9. I was brougt the book by the librarian. 10. He should be shown our new office. **III. Possible answers:** 1. The student should be recommended to get some rest. 2. You might be sent an invitation to an interview. 3. I would like to be offered a job of a dustman. 4. A Member of the European Parliament is paid 8,000 euros a month.

UNIT 66 He is said to be bossy/It is said that THE PASSIVE (3)

He is said to be the best footballer. Mówi się o nim, że jest najlepszym piłkarzem.
He is believed to have organised the strike. Uważa się, że on zorganizował strajk.
It was reported that four people had been wounded.
Zakomunikowano, że cztery osoby odniosły rany.

KIEDY STOSUJESZ KONSTRUKCJĘ HE IS SAID TO + VERB / IT IS SAID THAT...?

Gdy chcesz wyrazić powszechną opinię na jakiś temat, możesz posłużyć się stroną bierną takich czasowników jak **believe, consider, hope, know, report, say, think + bezokolicznik**. Forma bezokolicznika zależy od tego, czy wyrażana opinia dotyczy sytuacji współczesnej, czy przeszłej (różne formy bezokoliczników > unit 63)

He is said to live in this house. Mówi się, że on mieszka w tym domu.
He is said to have lived in this house. Mówi się, że on mieszkał tym domu.

Zdania te możesz także wyrazić przy pomocy konstrukcji **It is said**.

It is said that he lives in this house. Mówi się, że on mieszka w tym domu.
It is said that he lived in this house. Mówi się, że on mieszkał w tym domu.

Odpowiednikiem tych zdań w stronie czynnej są następujące wypowiedzi:
People say he lives in this house. People say he lived in this house.

TYPOWE BŁĘDY UWAŻAJ!

People say he is working as a reporter.
Źle: He is said ~~to work~~ as a reporter.
PODPOWIEDŹ: Jeśli chcesz zachować **present continuous** w stronie biernej, użyj bezokolicznika w formie ciągłej.
Dobrze: He is said to be working as a reporter.

People say he was teaching maths.
Źle: He is said ~~to be teaching~~ maths.
PODPOWIEDŹ: Jeśli czynność, o której mówisz, miała miejsce w przeszłości i jest wyrażona w formie **past continuous** lub **present perfect continuous**, użyj bezokolicznika **to have been + ing**.
Dobrze: He is said to have been teaching maths.

People say he was involved in drug trafficking
Źle: He is said ~~to be involved~~ in drug trafficking.
PODPOWIEDŹ: Jeśli czynność, o której mówisz, jest wyrażona w stronie biernej w czasie **present perfect**, **past simple** lub **past perfect**, użyj bezokolicznika w formie **to have been + past participle**.
Dobrze: He is said to have been involved in drug trafficking.

I. Choose the correct form in these sentence transformations.

1. People say Jim has been ill recently.
   Jim is said *(to be ill/to have been ill)* recently.
2. People say Julie works for the gang.
   Julie is said *(to work/to be working)* for a gang.
3. Everyone expects that the President will attend the meeting.
   The President is said *(to attend/to be attending)* the meeting.
4. Journalists suppose that Nick was a spy during the war.
   Nick is said *(to be/to have been)* a spy during the war.
5. People say that Robert was murdered.
   Robert is said *(to be/to have been)* murdered.
6. People say the Smiths have bought a house.
   The Smiths are said *(to buy/to have bought)* a house.
7. They say John is in prison.
   John is said *(to be/to have been)* in prison.
8. They say that Susan spent two years in the USA.
   Susan is said *(to spend/to have spent)* two years in the USA.

II. Transform these sentences so that their meanings remain the same.

1. Journalists report (that) the Minister has had a heart attack.
   a) It is reported ______________________________.
   b) The Minister is reported ______________________________.
2. Lots of people believe (that) Steve is travelling in the Middle East.
   a) It is believed ______________________________.
   b) Steve is believed ______________________________.
3. People say (that) Napoleon was sleeping in this room.
   a) It is said ______________________________.
   b) Napoleon is said ______________________________.
4. People say (that) Mr Brown has arrived in Australia.
   a) It is said ______________________________.
   b) Mr Brown is said ______________________________.
5. Everyone says (that) he was a good leader.
   a) It is said ______________________________.
   b) He is said ______________________________.

KEY

I. 1. to have been ill 2. to work 3. to attend 4. to have been 5. to have been 6. to have bought 7. to be 8. to have spent **II.** 1a) It is reported (that) the Minister has had a heart attack. b) The Minister is reported to have had a heart attack. 2a) It is believed (that) Steve is travelling in the Middle East. b) Steve is believed to be travelling in the Middle East. 3a) It is said (that) Napoleon was sleeping in this room. b) Napoleon is said to have been sleeping in this room. 4a) It is said (that) Mr Brown has arrived in Australia. b) Mr Brown is said to have arrived in Australia. 5a) It is said (that) he was a good leader. b) He is said to have been a good leader.

I have my windows cleaned every month. Co miesiąc ktoś myje mi okna.
Last month I had new tiles put in my bathroom.
W zeszłym miesiącu położono mi nowe kafelki w łazience.
Jim is having his car repaired. Właśnie naprawiają Jimowi samochód.
I'm going to have my flat painted. Mam zamiar zlecić komuś pomalowanie mieszkania.
We didn't have a new roof put because it was too expensive.
Nie położyliśmy nowego dachu (nie zleciliśmy położenia nowego dachu), gdyż było to za drogie.
Did you have your hair cut or did you cut it yourself?
Byłaś u fryzjera czy sama obcięłaś włosy (obcięto ci włosy czy sama je obcięłaś)?

KIEDY STOSUJESZ KONSTRUKCJĘ TO HAVE SOMETHING DONE?

W języku polskim gdy zlecasz komuś do wykonania jakąś pracę, zwykle posługujesz się stroną czynną, np.: **Położyłam nowe kafelki w łazience**.
W języku angielskim posługujesz się wówczas konstrukcją **to have something done**.

→ W mowie potocznej często zamiast **have something done** stosuje się **get something done**, np. **We must have our car checked = We must get our car checked.**

JAK TWORZYSZ KONSTRUKCJĘ TO HAVE SOMETHING DONE?

	HAVE	SOMETHING	DONE	
Jane	has	her hair	cut	every month.
You should	have	your eyes	tested.	
I must	have	my washing machine	fixed.	
Mary	is having	her computer	serviced	at the moment.
The Browns	are having	new windows	put	now.
My mother	had	her jacket	cleaned	last week.

TYPOWE BŁĘDY UWAŻAJ!

Someone has installed a dishwasher for me.
Źle: ~~I have installed a dishwasher.~~
PODPOWIEDŹ: Jeśli zlecasz komuś jakąś pracę, użyj konstrukcji **to have something done**.
Dobrze: I have had a dishwasher installed.

Someone is cooking lunch for Bob.
Źle: Bob ~~has~~ his lunch cooked.
PODPOWIEDŹ: Jeśli czynność odbywa się w momencie mówienia o niej, użyj formy ciągłej **to be having something done**.
Dobrze: Bob is having his lunch cooked.

YOUR TURN NOW!

I. Look at the pictures and write a suitable sentence describing what is going on. Use the verbs in the box.

fix fill test

1. The dentist is __________ her tooth. She is ____________________.
2. The optician is __________ her eyes. She is ____________________.
3. Father is __________ Mark's bike. Mark is ____________________.

II. Read about each situation and write suitable sentences. Use **have something done** in the correct form.

1. Lynne is walking her dog while someone is cleaning her coat.
   Lynne ______________________________ cleaned.
2. My mother hired somebody to clean her windows.
   My mother______________________________ cleaned.
3. Luke asked someone to do his homework.
   Luke ______________________________ done.
4. The lock of our front door is broken. We are going to hire someone to repair the lock of our front door. We ______________________________ repaired.
5. My car is dirty and I have no time to wash it. I must ask someone to wash my car.
   I ______________________________ washed.

III. Correct the sentences in column B according to the situations described in column A.

A	B
1. Someone has posted Mary's letters.	Mary has her letters posted.
2. Someone will tidy Jenny's room.	Jenny will be having her room tidied.
3. The haidresses is dyeing Claudia's hair.	Claudia is dyeing her hair.
4. Someone irons Tom's shirts.	Tom irons his shirts.
5. The tailor has made this suit for Michael.	Michael has this suit made.

KEY

I. 1. The dentist is filling her tooth. She is having her tooth filled. 2. The optician is testing her eyes. She is having her eyes tested. 3. Father is fixing Mark's bike. Mark is having his bike fixed. **II.** 1. Lynne is having her coat cleaned. 2. My mother had her windows cleaned. 3. Luke had his homework done. 4. We are going to have the lock of our front door repaired. 5. I must have my car washed. **III.** 1. Mary has had her letters posted. 2. Jenny will have her room tidied. 3. Claudia is having her hair dyed. 4. Tom has his shirts ironed. 5. Michael has had this suit made.

One should do something about it. Trzeba coś z tym zrobić./Powinno się coś z tym zrobić.
You should do something about it. Trzeba coś z tym zrobić./Powinno się coś z tym zrobić.
One can learn how to drive in two weeks' time.
Można nauczyć się prowadzić samochód w ciągu dwóch tygodni.
You can learn how to drive in two weeks' time.
Można nauczyć się prowadzić samochód w ciągu dwóch tygodni.
One mustn't park here. Nie wolno tu parkować.
You mustn't park here. Nie wolno tu parkować.
One shouldn't drop litter on the pavement. Nie należy rzucać odpadków na chodnik.
You shouldn't drop litter on the pavement. Nie należy rzucać odpadków na chodnik.
How does one make an omelette? Jak się robi omlet?
How do you make an omelette? Jak się robi omlet?

KIEDY STOSUJESZ ZDANIA Z PODMIOTEM ONE/YOU?

Zdania z podmiotem **one/you** są odpowiednikiem zdań z podmiotem bezosobowym w języku polskim, zaczynających się od słów **Powinno się, Trzeba, Nie wolno, Nie należy**.
W tym kontekście **one** i **you** odnosi się do ogółu ludzi, a nie do konkretnej osoby.

Zaimek **one** używany jest jako podmiot bezosobowy w wypowiedziach oficjalnych a w języku mówionym zazwyczaj przez osoby starsze, z wyższych sfer, np. **One just doesn't eat fish with a knife.**

→ Często zaimek **you** w wypowiedziach typu **How do you get from Edinburgh to Glasgow?** jest mylnie interpretowany przez Polaków jako zapytanie danej osoby o to, jak ona jeździ z Edynburga do Glasgow. Tymczasem pytanie to ma charakter ogólny i należy je tłumaczyć **Jak dojechać z Edynburga do Glasgow?** Jeśli zaakcentujesz **you**, pytanie będzie miało na celu uzyskanie informacji, jak twój rozmówca zwykle dojeżdża do Glasgow.

TYPOWY BŁĄD UWAŻAJ!

Poszedłby na imprezę, ale jest zbyt zmęczony.
Źle: ~~One would like to go to the party but one is too tired.~~

PODPOWIEDŹ: Użycie zaimka **one**, gdy masz na myśli konkretna osobę, brzmi niezręcznie i pretensjonalnie.

Dobrze: He'd like to go to the party but he's too tired.

HOTSPOT!

One w znaczeniu podmiotu bezosobowego występuje tylko w brytyjskiej odmianie języka angielskiego i w zasadzie tylko w wypowiedziach oficjalnych. W amerykańskiej angielszczyźnie takiego użycia **one** nie spotyka się. Amerykanie preferują użycie **you**.

I. Match these English sayings with their Polish equivalents.

1. One cannot live on love. **B. Natury nie zmienisz.**

2. One cannot make an omelette without breaking eggs. **F. Raz się jest młodym.**

3. One cannot put back the clock. **E. Nie da się cofnąć czasu.**

4. One cannot be at two places at once. **K. Jak się nie ma, co się lubi, to się lubi, co się ma.**

5. One cannot change human nature. **C. Gdzie drwa rąbią, tam wióry lecą.**

6. One is never too old to learn. **G. Nie da się być w dwóch miejscach naraz.**

7. One is only young once. **J. Człowiek cale życie się uczy.**

8. One should try everything once. **A. Na naukę nigdy nie jest za późno.**

9. One only lives once. **D. Nie samą miłością się żyje.**

10. One is always learning. **I. Wszystkiego trzeba spróbować.**

11. When one doesn't have what one likes, one likes what one has. **H. Żyje się raz.**

II. Jim used to live with his parents where he had everything done for him. Now he has moved to his new flat. He is not used to living on his own and has a lot of problems. He's going to phone his parents and his friends and ask for advice. Write his questions next to each problem.

EXAMPLE: 'I'm hungry and I have some eggs but I don't know how to cook eggs. How do you cook eggs?'

1. My shirts are dirty but I don't know how to wash shirts.
How ______________________________?
2. My plants are dying but I don't know how often to water them.
How ______________________________?
3. I was sent an electricity bill but I don't know how to pay it.
How ______________________________?
4. I need a bank account but I don't know how to open a bank account.
How ______________________________?
5. My cups and plates are dirty but I don't know how to use a dishwasher.
How ______________________________?
6. I have a computer but I don't know how to get the Internet installed.
How ______________________________?
7. The tap in my bathroom is leaking but I don't know how to fix it.
How ______________________________?
8. I love pancakes but I don't know how to make them.
How ______________________________?

KEY

I. 1D 2C 3E 4G 5B 6A 7F 8I 9H 10J 11K **II.** 1. How do you wash shirts? 2. How often should you water plants? 3. How do you pay electricity bills? 4. How do you open a bank account? 5. How do you use a dishwasher? 6. How do you get the Internet installed? 7. How do you fix the tap in the bathroom? 8. How do you make pancakes?

UNIT 69 He said he was at home. REPORTED SPEECH (1) REPORTING STATEMENTS

Our teacher says (that) we must study harder. Nasz nauczyciel mówi, że musimy więcej się uczyć.
Betty said (that) she was tired. Betty powiedziała, że jest zmęczona.
Tom told her (that) he would cook lunch. Tom powiedział jej, że ugotuje lunch.
I said (that) I didn't have time to buy bread. Powiedziałam, że nie mam czasu kupić chleba.

JAK TWORZYSZ REPORTED SPEECH?

Jeśli chcesz zrelacjonować czyjąś wypowiedź podaną w formie zdania twierdzącego lub przeczącego, najczęściej używasz czasowników **say** i **tell**. Przytoczone zdanie zostaje nieco zmienione.

DIRECT SPEECH	REPORTED (INDIRECT) SPEECH
'I am from Manchester,' said Jack.	Jack said (that) he was from Manchester.
'I haven't read this book,' said Jack.	Jack said (that) he hadn't read that book.
'You will win the lottery,' the fortune-teller said.	The fortune-teller told me I would win the lottery.

→ Jeśli czasownik wprowadzający zdanie w mowie zależnej jest w czasie teraźniejszym (**says, tells me**), to czas w zdaniu przytoczonym pozostaje niezmieniony,

'I can swim', says Ben. = Ben says (that) he can swim.

→ Jeśli czasownik wprowadzający mowę zależną jest w czasie przeszłym (**said, told me**), to w przytaczanym zdaniu w większości wypadków stosuje się zasadę tzw. **backshift** („cofnięcia" czasów gramatycznych)
np. **present simple** → **past simple**, **present continuous** → **past continuous**, **present perfect** → **past perfect**, **will** → **would**, **can** → **could** itd.
Zmiany obejmują również następujące wyrażenia: **this** → **that**, **these** → **those**, **here** → **there**, **now** → **then**, **today** → **that day**, **tomorrow** → **the following day**, **yesterday** → **the day before**, **next week** → **the following week**.

→ Gdy używasz **tell**, musisz dodać, komu coś zostało powiedziane, np. **Mary told me (her, him, us, them) that she was leaving on Monday.** Gdy używasz **say**, masz dwie możliwości: **Mary said that she was leaving on Monday** lub **Mary said to me that she was leaving on Monday.**

TYPOWY BŁĄD UWAŻAJ!

Źle: ~~Mark told that he can't drive this old car.~~

PODPOWIEDŹ: Czasownika **told** wymaga podkreślenia, komu coś zostało powiedziane. Konieczne jest też „cofnięcie" czasu w relacjonowanym zdaniu oraz zamiana **this** na **that**.

Dobrze: Mark told us (that) he couldn't drive that old car.

HOTSPOT!

Past simple może pozostać niezmieniony w **reported speech** lub możesz użyć **past perfect**.

DIRECT SPEECH **Tom said: 'I had a headache so I didn't go to school.'**

REPORTED SPEECH **Tom said he had/had had a headache so he didn't go/hadn't gone to school.**

YOUR TURN NOW!

I. Report these sentences changing **direct speech** to **reported (indirect) speech**.

EXAMPLE: 'I can't find my keys,' said Anne.
Anna said she couldn't find her keys.

1. 'I must leave now,' said Jeff. ____________
2. 'We have seen this film,' Tom and Jerry said. ____________
3. 'Susan can't swim,' said her mother. ____________
4. 'I'm going to visit Edinburgh next month,' said Mary. ____________
5. 'They will help us,' said Ralph. ____________
6. 'I have lived here for ten years,' said Ben. ____________
7. 'I work in a bank' said Jim. ____________

II. Write the original sentences (change **reported speech** to **direct speech**).

EXAMPLE: Martin said he was going out.
'I'm going out,' said Martin.

1. Martin said (that) he had a lot of homework to do. ____________
2. Martin said (that) he had been sick for a few days. ____________
3. Martin said (that) he would finish this job soon. ____________
4. Martin said (that) he had had a good time at the party the previous day.
____
5. Martin said (that) he was writing his essay. ____________
6. Martin said (that) he wanted to go to Wales the following week.
____
7. Martin said (that) he was going to take a driving test. ____________

III. Correct the mistakes.

1. Mary told she would buy a printer this week.
2. Brian said me that he wanted to go to Spain next month.
3. I told to him that I had to go to work now.
4. Dave said that there was no time left and we must hurry.
5. Jim told to me that they have been waiting for me for two hours.

KEY

I. 1. Jeff said (that) he had to leave then. 2. Tom and Jerry said (that) they had seen that film. 3. Susan's mother said (that) Susan couldn't swim. 4. Mary said (that) she was going to visit Edinburgh the following month. 5. Ralph said (that) they would help us. 6. Ben said (that) he had lived there for ten years. 7. Jim said he worked in a bank. **II.** 1. I have a lot of homework to do. 2.I have been sick for a few days. 3. I will finish this job soon. 4. I had a good time at the party yesterday. 5. I am writing my essay. 6. I want to go to Wales next week. 7. I am going to take a driving test. **III.** 1. Mary said (that) she would buy a printer./Mary told me (that) she would buy a printer that week. 2. Brian said (that) he wanted to go to Spain the following month./Brian told me (that) he wanted to go to Spain the folloing month. 3. I told him that I had to go to work then. 4. Dave said that there was no time left and we had to hurry. 5. Jim told me that they had been waiting for me for two hours./Jim said to me (that) they had been waiting for me for two hours.

UNIT 70 She asked if he loved her REPORTED SPEECH (2) REPORTING QUESTIONS

Tom wants to know who has written to me. Tom chce wiedzieć, kto do mnie napisał.
Mary asks if we can meet on Saturday. Maria pyta, czy możemy się spotkać w sobotę.
Ben asked if I wanted to go for a walk. Ben zapytał, czy chcę iść na spacer.
Susan asked how much the apples were. Susan zapytała, ile kosztują jabłka.
The police officer asked what my name was. Policjant zapytał, jak się nazywam.
Sam asked me where I lived. Sam zapytał, gdzie mieszkam.

Relacjonowanie pytań w języku angielskim następuje wg odmiennych zasad niż w języku polskim.

→ Szyk zdania pytającego w mowie zależnej zawsze ulega zmianie i przyjmuje formę zdania oznajmującego: najpierw podmiot, potem orzeczenie. Nie ma znaku zapytania na końcu.

→ Jeśli czasownik wprowadzający mowę zależną jest w czasie teraźniejszym (**asks, wants to know**), to czas w zdaniu przytoczonym pozostaje niezmieniony. Jeśli jednak czasownik ten jest w czasie przeszłym, co zdarza się znacznie częściej (**asked, wanted to know**), relacjonowane pytanie ulega dalszej modyfikacji, tak jak zdania oznajmujące. (> unit 69)

Yes/No questions, czyli pytania zaczynające się od czasownika pomocniczego **Do/Did/Are/Is/Has** itp. w mowie zależnej wymagają użycia **if** lub **whether**.
Whether brzmi bardziej oficjalnie niż **if.**

'Do you like winter sports?' 'Yes, I do.'
Mary asked if I liked winter sports. = She wanted to know whether I liked winter sports.

Wh-questions, czyli pytania zaczynające się od **Where/Why/When/Who/What/How**, w mowie zależnej zachowują słowo pytające **Wh-.**

Where were you yesterday? She wanted to know where I had been/was yesterday.

TYPOWE BŁĘDY **UWAŻAJ!**

Źle: Tom asked ~~what was the time?~~
PODPOWIEDŹ: Relacjonowane pytanie ma szyk zdania oznajmującego i nie kończy się znakiem zapytania.
Dobrze: Tom asked what the time was.

Źle: Mary wanted to know ~~did I enjoy the party?~~
PODPOWIEDŹ: Pytanie typu **Yes/No** wymaga użycia w mowie zależnej słowa **if** lub **whether**.
Dobrze: Mary wanted to know if I enjoyed/had enjoyed the party.

YOUR TURN NOW!

I. Look at the picture and write the questions in reported speech.

EXAMPLE: 'Are you tired?' asked Elizabeth.
Elizabeth asked if Mary was tired.

1. Elizabeth wanted to know ______________________________.
2. Elizabeth asked ______________________________.
3. Elizabeth asked ______________________________.
4. Elizabeth asked ______________________________.
5. Elizabeth asked ______________________________.
6. Elizabeth asked ______________________________.
7. Elizabeth wanted to know ______________________________.
8. Elizabeth asked ______________________________.
9. Elizabeth wanted to know ______________________________.

1. Where have you been?
9. Are you happy you are back home?
2. How long were you in Edinburgh?
6. Did you see Bob?
3. Where did you stay?
5. What did you buy?
8. Who brought you to the airport?
7. When did you see him?
0. Are you tired?
4. Was it raining?

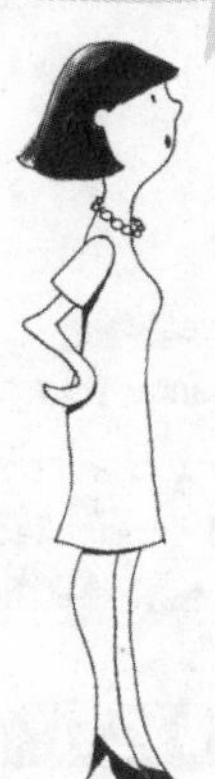

II. Read the text and find five **reported questions**. Then write down the original questions.

Yesterday I was stopped by a police officer for speeding. He asked me a few questions. First, he wanted to know how long I had had my driving licence.
Then he asked why I had been driving so fast. He also wanted to know if the speedometre in my car was working properly. He also asked if I had been using a radar detector.
He asked me if I was ready to pay the fine immediately.

1. How long ______________________________?
2. Why ______________________________?
3. Is ______________________________?
4. Have ______________________________?
5. Are ______________________________?

KEY

I. 1. Elizabeth wanted to know where Mary had been. 2. Elizabeth asked how long Mary was/had been in Edinburgh. 3. Elizabeth asked where Mary stayed/had stayed. 4. Elizabeth asked if it was/had been raining. 5. Elizabeth asked what Mary bought/had bought. 6. Elizabeth asked if Mary saw/had seen Bob. 7. Elizabeth wanted to know when Mary saw/had seen Bob. 8. Elizabeth asked who brought/ had brought Mary to the airport. 9. Elizabeth wanted to know if Mary was happy she was back home. **II.** 1. How long have you had your driving licence? 2. Why were you driving so fast?/Why have you been driving so fast? 3. Is the speedometre in your car working properly? 4. Have you been using a radar detector? 5. Are you ready to pay the fine immediately?

UNIT 71 He told me to listen REPORTED SPEECH (3)
REPORTING REQUESTS/COMMANDS

The teacher told me to write the essay.
Nauczyciel kazał mi napisać wypracowanie/Nauczyciel powiedział, abym napisał wypracowanie.
Tom asked me to help him. Tom poprosił, abym mu pomogła.
Jeff told me not to open the door. Jeff powiedział mi, abym nie otwierała drzwi.
The guide told us not to feed the monkeys. Przewodnik powiedział nam, abyśmy nie karmili małp.

JAK WYRAŻASZ PROŚBY I POLECENIA W REPORTED SPEECH (W MOWIE ZALEŻNEJ)?

Do bezpośredniego wyrażania próśb i poleceń używasz czasownika w podstawowej formie, czyli bezokolicznika bez **to** (> patrz unit 51). Do wyrażania próśb i poleceń w mowie zależnej używasz najczęściej czasownika **tell** lub **ask** (przeważnie w **simple past**) oraz bezokolicznika z **to**.

→ Jeśli polecenie lub prośba zawierają przeczenie, w mowie zależnej musisz zastosować **not to + verb**.

DIRECT SPEECH	REPORTED (INDIRECT) SPEECH
Sit down!	He told me to sit down.
Don't waste your time!	He told me not to waste my time.
Please, don't leave yet.	He asked me not to leave yet.
Could you please change your shoes?	She asked me to change my shoes.

W mowie zależnej, przy relacjonowaniu próśb i poleceń, obowiazują podobne zasady co w przypadku relacjonowaniu zdań oznajmujących i pytań: **this → that, today → that day, tomorrow → the following day, here → there** (> unit 69).

TYPOWE BŁĘDY UWAŻAJ!

Don't leave the door unlocked, please.
Źle: She asked me ~~don't leave the door unlocked.~~
PODPOWIEDŹ: Użycie **don't** w mowie zależnej jest niewłaściwe. Musisz posłużyć się bezokolicznikiem poprzedzonym słowem **not**.
Dobrze: She asked me not to leave the door unlocked.

Come home before lunch!
Źle: She ~~said~~ me to come home before lunch.
PODPOWIEDŹ: Bezpośrednio po czasowniku **said** nie można stosować zaimka osobowego. Chociaż forma **She said to me** jest możliwa, znacznie częściej używana jest forma **She told me.**
Dobrze: She told me to come home before lunch.

YOUR TURN NOW!

I. Helen is very unhappy. Everybody is telling her what to do. Report these commands and requests.

EXAMPLE: **The teacher told her: 'You mustn't come late to school again!'**
The teacher told her not to come late to school again.

1. Her mother said: 'Tidy up your room now!'
   Her mother told her ______________________________________.
2. Her sister said: 'Don't leave your shoes in the bathroom!'
   Her sister told her ______________________________________.
3. The doctor said: 'Take up more exercise and go on a diet.'
   The doctor told her ______________________________________.
4. Her boyfriend said: 'Don't phone me tonight!'
   Her boyfriend told her ____________________________________.
5. Her neighbour said: 'Never smoke in the lift!'
   Her neighbour told her ____________________________________.
6. Her friend said: 'Don't wear this ugly sweater to school!'
   Her friend told her ______________________________________.

II. Now write these commands and requests in **direct speech**.

EXAMPLE: **Mary told me not to change anything in that composition.**
Mary said: 'Don't change anything in this composition!'

1. Alex told me to stay where I was.
   Alex said: '______________________________!'
2. Julie told me not to give out her secret.
   Julie said: '______________________________!'
3. Ben asked me to help him with his old car.
   Ben said: '______________________________.'
4. The receptionist asked us not to allow our children to play with the lift.
   The receptionist said: '__________________________________.'
5. The host told me not to bring my dog into the dining room.
   The host said: '______________________________________.'
6. The doctor told me to take those pills twice a day and stay in bed for a week.
   The doctor said: '______________________________________.'

KEY

I. 1. Her mother told her to tidy up her room then. 2. Her sister told her not to leave her shoes in the bathroom. 3. The doctor told her to take up more exercise and go on a diet. 4. Her boyfriend told her not to phone him that night. 5. Her neighbour told her never to smoke in the lift. 6. Her friend told her not to wear that ugly sweater to school. **II.** 1. Stay where you are! 2. Don't give out my secret! 3. Help me with my old car, please. 4. Please don't allow your children to play with the lift. 5. Don't bring your dog into the dining room. 6. Take these pills twice a day and stay in bed for a week.

UNIT 72 Could you tell me EMBEDDED QUESTIONS

Can you tell me what time the bus leaves? Czy możesz mi powiedzieć, o której odjeżdża autobus?
Could you tell me how much this watch is? Czy mógłby mi pan powiedzieć ile kosztuje ten zegarek?
Do you know if the shops are open on Sunday? Czy wiesz, czy sklepy są otwarte w niedzielę?
I'd like to know where Tom lives. Chciałabym wiedzieć, gdzie mieszka Tom.
I wonder why they decided to sell their house. Zastanawiam się, dlaczego postanowili sprzedać dom.

KIEDY STOSUJESZ EMBEDDED QUESTIONS?

Jeśli chcesz, aby twoje pytanie zabrzmiało bardziej uprzejmie, powinieneś zastosować konstrukcję **embedded questions**, czyli poprzedzić swoje pytanie zwrotem typu **Can you tell me** itp.

→ **Embedded questions** mają zawsze szyk wyrazów jak w zdaniu oznajmującym, a więc najpierw podmiot, potem orzeczenie. Nie stosuje się operatorów **do/did**.

Embedded questions rozpoczynające się od zwrotów **Can you tell me/Could you tell me** kończą się znakiem zapytania, natomiast poprzedzone zwrotami typu **I wonder/I'd like to know** mają na końcu kropkę, jak wszystkie zdania oznajmujące.

JAK TWORZYSZ EMBEDDED QUESTIONS?

Pytania typu **Wh-** zachowują słowo pytające **what/where/when** itp., zmieniając jednak szyk wyrazów.

When is your birthday?
Can you tell me when your birthday is?/I wonder when your birthday is.

Pytania typu **Yes/No** wymagaja użycia **if** lub **whether**.

Did you enjoy the party?
Could you tell me if (whether) you enjoyed the party?/I wonder if (whether) you enjoyed the party.

Whether brzmi bardziej oficjalnie niż **if** i dlatego w mowie potocznej jest używane rzadziej.

TYPOWE BŁĘDY UWAŻAJ!

Źle: Could you tell me what time ~~is it~~?

PODPOWIEDŹ: Pytanie poprzedzone wprowadzeniem **Could you tell me** ma szyk wyrazów jak w zdaniu oznajmującym, a więc inwersja **is it** jest błędem.

Dobrze: Could you tell me what time it is?

Źle: I wonder how ~~did they~~ make so much money~~?~~

PODPOWIEDŹ: Pytania zaczynające się od **I wonder** kończą się kropką i mają strukturę zdania oznajmującego, a więc użycie operatora **did** jest niepotrzebne.

Dobrze: I wonder how they made so much money.

YOUR TURN NOW!

I. Kate is very straightforward. Make her questions sound more polite.

EXAMPLE: **What time is the meeting?**
Could you tell me what time the meeting is?

1. What's Mark's telephone number? I wonder ______________________.
2. Did you have an English test yesterday? Could you ______________________?
3. Why are you so hot? I wonder ______________________.
4. Have you had lunch yet? Can you tell me ______________________.
5. Is this your umbrella? I wonder ______________________.
6. Where is the bus stop? Do you know ______________________.
7. When is Mary's birthday? I'd like to know ______________________.
8. How to use this scanner? Could you show me ______________________?
9. Are you coming to Jeff's party tomorrow? I wonder ______________________.
10. What present are you going to bring him? Can you tell me ______________________.

II. Mike has written a letter to a travel agency. Read the extract from his letter. Find six mistakes and correct them.

I have a few questions concerning the trip to Brighton on Wednesday 17 September. I would like to know what time does the coach leave? Could you possibly tell me is there a TV on the coach? Do you know if there is a break for lunch during the trip? Could you also inform me will we have an opportunity to stop in Canterbury?
I have been told that I need to take a sleeping bag. Could you tell me do I really need to take one? And one more question. I have a pet dog. I wonder can I take her with me? Could you inform me if pets are allowed on the coach?
My last question concerns the possibility of getting a refund. Can you inform me is it possible to get my money back if I am dissatisfied with your service?

Yours sincerely,
Mike Smith

KEY

I. I wonder what Mark's telephone number is. 2. Could you tell me if you had an English test yesterday? 3. I wonder why you are so hot. 4. Can you tell me if you have had lunch yet? 5. I wonder if this is your umbrella. 6. Do you know where the bus stop is? 7. I'd like to know when Mary's birthday is. 8. Could you show me how to use this scanner? 9. I wonder if you are coming to Jeff's party tomorrow. 10. Can you tell me what present you are going to bring him? **II.** I have a few questions concerning the trip to Brighton on Wednesday 17 September. I would like to know what time the coach leaves. Could you possibly tell me if there is a TV on the coach? Do you know if there is a break for lunch during the trip? Could you also inform me if we will have an opportunity to stop in Canterbury? I have been told that I need to take a sleeping bag. Could you tell me if I really need to take one? And one more question. I have a pet dog. I wonder if I can take her with me. Could you inform me if pets are allowed on the coach? My last question concerns the possibility of getting a refund. Can you inform me if it is possible to get my money back if I am dissatisfied with your service? Yours sincerely, Mike Smith.

UNIT 73 You're free, aren't you? QUESTION TAGS

Mark doesn't work in a bank, does he? Marek nie pracuje w banku, prawda?
Your children can speak English, can't they? Twoje dzieci potrafią mówić po angielsku, prawda?
Dave hardly works, does he? Dave prawie nie pracuje, prawda?
She is a nice girl, isn't she? To miła dziewczyna, prawda?

Question tags są to krótkie pytania dodane na końcu zdania, odpowiadające polskiemu **prawda/nieprawdaż? Question tags** używasz, gdy chcesz, aby twój rozmówca potwierdził lub zaprzeczył temu co, mówisz, a także gdy chcesz, by twoja wypowiedź brzmiała bardziej uprzejmie. **Question tags** są rzadko używane w oficjalnym, pisanym języku.

→ **Intonacja wznosząca** ↗ oznacza, że oczekujesz rzeczywistej odpowiedzi na swoje pytanie.
Intonacja opadająca ↘ oznacza, że oczekujesz potwierdzenia swojej wypowiedzi.

Question tags tworzysz poprzez inwersję **be, can, must** lub przy pomocy operatora **do/does/did** lub **have/has/had** zgodnego z orzeczeniem w zdaniu głównym. Jeśli zdanie jest twierdzące, **question tag** jest przeczący, i odwrotnie – do zdania przeczącego dodajesz twierdzący **question tag**. Jeśli zdanie zawiera przysłówek typu **hardly, scarcely** – **question tag** jest twierdzący.

SZCZEGÓLNE PRZYPADKI TWORZENIA QUESTION TAGS

I am	I am clever, **aren't I?**
need (negative)	He doesn't need to come tomorrow, **does he?** He needn't come tomorrow, **need he?**
must/may/might	We must pay duty on our cigarettes, **mustn't we?**
ought to	We really ought to phone them, **oughtn't we/shouldn't we?**
Let's	Let's go to the pub, **shall we?**
Request	Bring me some water, **will you?**
Nobody	Nobody was there, **were they?**

Czasami stosuje się twierdzący **question tag** po zdaniu oznajmującym. Służy to wyrażeniu sympatii lub współczucia rozmówcy. **Oh, things are really difficult, are they?** (intonacja rosnąca). Jeśli zastosujesz intonację opadającą, zdanie zabrzmi sarkastycznie.

TYPOWY BŁĄD UWAŻAJ!

Źle: The shops close at seven, ~~isn't it~~?
PODPOWIEDŹ: Forma czasownika w **question tag** musi być zgodna z orzeczeniem zdania głównego.
Dobrze: The shops close at seven, don't they?

HOTSPOT!

Czasem słyszy się **question tag** w postaci **innit?** Nie jest to uznawane za poprawne gramatycznie.

YOUR TURN NOW!

I. Here are some sentences that people said at the party. Match each sentences with an appropriate **question tag**.

1. Lovely party,
2. These cookies are delicious,
3. Jim and Jenny have been invited,
4. Susan hasn't made this salad,
5. You are Steve Brown
6. You know Jack,
7. Let's have a dance,
8. You weren't in Paris last week,
9. Jeff is very friendly,
10. We must leave now,
11. Nobody has phoned,

A. have they?
B. aren't you?
C. isn't it?
D. were you?
E. has she?
F. aren't they?
G. isn't he?
H. mustn't we?
I. shall we?
J. don't you?
K. haven't they?

II. Choose the correct option.

1. These are the flowers for Susan, ____________?
   a) aren't they? b) aren't those? c) are these d) aren't these
2. We've never done anything like that before, ___________?
   a) haven't we? b) didn't we? c) have we? d) did we?
3. Pass me the sugar,
   a) do you? b) can you? c) will you? d) yes?
4. Someone has been drinking from my glass, ___________?
   a) has he? b) hasn't he? c) have they? d) haven't they?
5. I am cute, ___________?
   a) am I? b) aren't I? c) do I? d) don't I?
6. Something should be done about this, _____________?
   a) should it? b) shouldn't it? c) should they? d) shouldn't they?
7. Don't annoy Martin, ______________?
   a) do you? b) won't you? c) don't you? d) will you?

III. Write **T** (True) or **F** (False) next to these sentences.

1. With a rising intonation of a question tag you express a genuine request for information. **T/F**
2. With a falling intonation of a question tag you ask for conformation. **T/F**
3. With negative adverbials such as *hardly, never, scarcely* question tags are negative. **T/F**

KEY

I. 1C 2F 3K 4E 5B 6J 7I 8D 9G 10H 11A **II.** 1a 2c 3c 4d 5b 6b 7d **III.** 1T 2T 3F

UNIT 74 I'm hungry. Are you? ECHO QUESTIONS

A: We can take the number 195 bus. A: Możemy pojechać autobusem 195.
B: Can we? B: Tak? 195?

A: I'm going to London. A: Wyjeżdżam do Londynu.
B: Are you? B: Wyjeżdżasz?

A: We mustn't miss the train. A: Nie możemy spóźnić się na pociąg.
B: Mustn't we? B: Nie możemy?

Echo questions są to pytania stanowiące echo czyjejś wypowiedzi. Służą do wyrażania zdziwienia lub zainteresowania wypowiedzią naszego rozmówcy, a więc przede wszystkim podtrzymaniu rozmowy. Zdaniu twierdzącemu towarzyszy echo wypowiedzi w formie twierdzącej, natomiast zdaniu przeczącemu – echo w formie przeczącej.

W odróżnieniu od **question tags** (> unit 73), **echo question** jest wypowiadane przez drugą osobę (rozmówcę). **Echo question** jest to więc osobne zdanie pytające, reakcja na czyjąś wypowiedź.

JAK TWORZYSZ ECHO QUESTIONS?

Echo questions tworzy się przy pomocy odpowiedniej formy czasownika **be**, czasowników pomocniczych (operatorów) **do, does, did, have, has, had**.

Możliwe jest również tworzenie **Echo question** poprzez powtórzenie całego pytania twojego rozmówcy, z tym że zastępujesz część zdania słowem pytającym typu **Wh-** i akcentujesz je.

A: Have you been to the National Museum?
B: Have I been to what? Have I been where?

INTONACJA

Jeśli używasz wznoszącej się intonacji, okazujesz swojemu rozmówcy uprzejme zainteresowanie.

A: I met a very interesting man yesterday.
B: Did you? ↗

Opadająca intonacja towarzyszy często przeczącym **echo questions** i wyraża poparcie dla rozmówcy.

A: That was the best film we've ever seen!
B: Yes, wasn't it? ↘

TYPOWY BŁĄD UWAŻAJ!

Źle: A: I really like swimming.
B: Oh, ~~don't~~ you?

PODPOWIEDŹ: Nie myl **echo questions** z **question tags**. Twierdzenie lub przeczenie zdania pierwotnego przenosi się na **echo question** jeśli chcesz wyrazić swoje zdziwienie lub zainteresowanie.

Dobrze: B: Oh, do you?

YOUR TURN NOW!

I. Choose the correct **echo question**.

1. We haven't seen Anne for ages.	A. Is she?
2. You won't need an umbrella.	B. Aren't you?
3. Margaret is always tired.	C. Should they?
4. We won!	D. Have you?
5. You could borrow my camera, no problem.	E. Haven't you?
6. They should be here by now.	F. Doesn't he?
7. We must hurry.	G. Must we?
8. Mark doesn't smoke cigarettes.	H. Did you?
9. I've got to go.	I. Won't I?
10. I'm not going to phone Mark.	J. Could I?

II. Write the correct **echo question** next to each sentence.

1. Susan wants to be a doctor.	A. _______________? How nice.
2. You look beautiful in this dress.	B. _______________? Thank you.
3. The party at Ken's was great.	C. Yes, _______________? He's a good host.
4. Mike has just left.	D. Oh, _______________? What a pity!
5. You know, Dave sold his old car yesterday.	E. Oh, _______________? I wonder why.
6. Have you heard, Kathy's going to have a baby!	F. _______________? Are you kidding?
7. Guess what, Tom proposed to Jenny!	G. _______________? Wow, that's great!
8. We must wear school uniforms.	H. _______________? I didn't know that.
9. You should take up more exercise, I'm afraid.	I. Oh, _______________? I'll try.
10. I've passed the exam!	J. _______________? Congratulations!

III. Write **T** (True) or **F** (False) next to each sentence.

1. Echo question with a rising intonation shows a polite interest and surprise at what the other speaker has said. **T/F**
2. Echo question with a falling intonation expresses confirmation of what the other speaker has said. **T/F**
3. An echo question isn't used in response to a statement. **T/F**
4. In response to a negative statement, an echo question isn't always negative. **T/F**

KEY

I. 1E 2I 3A 4H 5J 6C 7G 8F 9D 10B **II.** A. Does she? B. Do I? C. Yes, wasn't it? D. Oh, has he? E. Oh, did he? F. Is she? G. Did he? H. Must you? I. Oh, should I? J. Have you? **III.** 1T 2T 3F 4F

UNIT 75 CONSOLIDATION

I. Read the text written by a 6th Form student, Rebecca, do the crossword and find the clue.

At the beginning of my high school education, I used to be a very shy girl. Once, I remember it clearly, I made a complete fool of myself. I was walking down the steep hill that used to be in our school grounds (now there's a football pitch in this place) and I slid all the way down on my bottom. Everybody was watching me and some people laughed. I felt so stupid and so embarrased. I wasn't used to being the centre of attention. All I could think about was how dumb I was. My trousers were torn here and there and covered in mud. My ankle hurt. When I was walking into the school hall I tried to become invisible. I had been crying for a while in the bathroom when my classmate arrived. She asked me to turn round and so I did. She told me not to worry and promised to help me clean my trousers. When my trousers didn't look like a disaster anymore, I was so grateful to her and forced myself to smile. Since then she has been my best friend. A friend in need is a friend indeed. That's right, isn't it?

CROSSWORD

1. Something unpleasant happened to Rebecca at the beginning of her high school _________.
2. She didn't use to be an outgoing person, just the oppposite, she was _______.
3. The hill was _______.
4. Rebecca wasn't used to being the _______ of attention.
5. What got torn and muddy?
6. Her classmate helped her _______ the mud off.
7. Her new friend asked her to turn _______.
8. Rebecca thought that she made a _______ fool of herself.

CROSSWORD KEY 1. education, 2. shy, 3. steep, 4. centre, 5. trousers, 6. clean, 7. round, 8. complete **clue:** CHEER UP

Interpretacja wyników testu

Jeśli uzyskałeś co najmniej 30 punktów – gratulacje! Możesz przejść do dalszej części książki. Jeśli masz mniej niż 30 punktów, powinieneś przeczytać wybrane partie materiału jeszcze raz. Jeśli nieprawidłowo odpowiedziałeś na któreś z pytań 1-7, przeanalizuj ponownie rozdziały 51-56. Jeśli masz problemy z udzieleniem prawidłowych odpowiedzi do pytań 8-12, wróć do rozdziałów 57-59. Jeśli sprawiły Ci kłopot odpowiedzi na pytania 13-17, wróć do rozdziałów 60-62. Jeśli nie udzieliłeś poprawnej odpowiedzi na pytania 18-26, przeanalizuj ponownie rozdziały 63-68. Jeśli pytania 27-35 sprawiły Ci trudność, wróć do rozdziałów 69-74. Wykonaj ten sam test ponownie po kilku dniach, aby sprawdzić, ile naprawdę pamiętasz. POWODZENIA!

CONSOLIDATION!

Time to check what you have learned in units 51 – 74. Do these tasks and find out what your results are. Choose the correct form from the words in italics.

1. Let's *don't go/not* go to the forest today!
2. Let *she/her* come with us for a walk!
3. We don't need *to buy/buy* any food today.
4. We *mustn't/needn't* go to school tomorrow; it's Sunday.
5. You *don't have to/mustn't* do this exercise now. You can do it later.
6. We *should/ought to* leave earlier than yesterday.
7. It *mustn't/can't* be true. Are you joking?
8. Why are you so hot? Have you *run/been running*?
9. Mark has *eaten/been eating* biscuits since morning. He's going to have a stomach ache.
10. When I met Jack in 2002, he *lived/had lived* in Bishopton for 10 years.
11. When Jenny arrived home, Jim *had already cooked/already cooked* the dinner.
12. Tom *had tried/had been trying* to solve that problem for two days before he found a solution.
13. *She'll/will* sit all day and stare at people. That's typical for her.
14. We *would/used to* live in the city but two years ago we moved to the village.
15. There *used to/would* be a small cinema in this street. Now they're building a car park here.
16. When I lived in the country I *used to/was used to* farm animals.
17. I was used to *have/having* a tiny kitchen when I lived in a flat.
18. Their bid was the first *to discuss/to be discussed.*
19. I promise, I will get used to *drink/drinking* tea with milk, if you insist.
20. 'Look, they are painting the gate.' 'Yes, the gate is *painted/being painted*.'
21. 'They say that Anne works as a paramedic.' 'Yes, she is said to *work/have worked* as a paramedic.'
22. 'They say Zenon worked as a postman.' 'Yes, he is said to *work/have worked* as a postman.'
23. Mary went to the dentist and *filled her toot in/had her tooth filled.*
24. Susan asked somebody to paint the walls in her flat. She *painted the walls/had the walls painted.*
25. A letter was handed to the Prime Minister. Yes, the Prime Minister *was handed/handed* a letter.
26. How do *one/you* roast turkey?
27. Mark said he *would finish/will finish* the book the following day.
28. Sally asked *if did I meet/if I met* her son at school.
29. Mary asked why *were I/I were* so happy.
30. Ben told me *not to use/to don't use* his computer.
31. Could you tell me where *is the cash dispenser/the cash dispenser is*?
32. I wonder why *is he so suntanned/why he is so suntanned.*
33. I don't know what time *is it/ it is.*
34. Bob is listening to music, *is he/isn't he*?
35. 'Mary went skiing.' 'Oh, *did she/didn't she*?'

KEY

1. not go 2. her 3. to buy 4. needn't 5. don't have to 6. should 7. can't 8. been running 9. been eating 10. had lived 11. had already cooked 12. had been trying 13. will 14. used to 15. used to 16. was used 17. having 18. to be discussed 19. drinking 20. being painted 21. to work 22. have worked 23. had her tooth filled 24. had the walls painted 25. was handed 26. you 27. would finish 28. if I met 29. I were 30. not to use 31. the cash dispenser is 32. why he is so suntanned 33. it is 34. isn't he? 35. did she?

1. Czasy teraźniejsze: *Present Simple* i *Present Continuous (Present Progressive)*

1. W 3. osobie liczby pojedynczej w czasie *Present Simple* czasowniki mogą mieć różne końcówki. Wpisz podane czasowniki w odpowiednie kolumny.

rely ✔ carry rush fetch mix show buy lie relax marry
say copy grow

Końcówka	-es	-ies	-s
	....	*relies,*	....
	....	....	....
	....	....	....

2. Oto pięć możliwości stosowania czasu teraźniejszego prostego *Present Simple* – zaznacz w okienku, zgodnie z którą regułą zostało utworzone każde zdanie.

a. stwierdzenia ogólne
b. stwierdzenia dotyczące życia poszczególnych osób
c. stwierdzenia dotyczące przyrody
d. przysłowia
e. regularnie powtarzające się czynności

1 My lunch break is at twelve thirty. ☐
2 The restaurant opens at 9 am and closes at midnight. ☐
3 In the United States shops tend to be open 24 hours a day. ☐
4 Too many cooks spoil the broth. ☐
5 I grow flowers on my balcony. ☐
6 As a professional football player you earn a lot of money. ☐
7 My girlfriend buys expensive clothes. She thinks they last longer. ☐
8 When in Rome, do as the Romans do. ☐
9 In summer, days are longer than in winter. ☐

3. A teraz to samo z czasem teraźniejszym ciągłym – *Present Continuous (Progressive)*. Zaznacz w okienku, która reguła dotyczy danego zdania.

a. jeszcze nie zakończone czynności, mające określony czas trwania
b. właśnie trwające czynności
c. trwające, zachodzące zmiany
d. zaplanowane wydarzenia, mające nastąpić w przyszłości
e. prognozy dotyczące przyszłości lub nadawanie pytaniom bardziej uprzejmej formy

1 Your pancakes are getting better and better. ☐
2 I'm drinking a glass of water. ☐
3 We're leaving for France tomorrow. ☐
4 I'm usually preparing lunch when the kids come home from school. ☐
5 For the time being I am sharing a flat with my brother. ☐
6 His health is gradually deteriorating. ☐
7 ● What are you doing? ▲ I am cleaning the kitchen. ☐
8 I am sorry, but I can't answer the phone right now. I'm taking a shower. ☐
9 I'm afraid I am not supporting you in this matter. ☐

4. Wpisz czasownik w odpowiedniej formie: w czasie *Present Simple* lub *Continuous.*

to play As a professional tennis player, my brother ...*plays*... tennis regularly. I'm afraid you can't talk to him right now, because he .... ① a match right now. I'm sure it'll be over in an hour or so. He .... ② against our grandfather, you see. In summer they .... ③ twice a week.

to rain Look, it .... ④. What a shame! We can't go for a walk now. You don't mind the weather, do you? You're used to it. In Scotland, where you come from, it always .... ⑤ at this time of the year.

to stay My husband is in London at the moment. He .... ⑥ at the Savoy Hotel. He normally .... ⑦ there when he's in London.

work/not ● My computer .... ⑧. I've had it for five years now. Never a problem. But yesterday it broke down. May I use your computer?

▲ I'm afraid my computer .... ⑨ In fact, it hasn't worked for years.

to write I .... ⑩ a new novel. I never .... ⑪ short stories. I'm not good at expressing myself in so few pages.

to bake Whenever I visit her, grandmother .... ⑫ a cake. I never .... ⑬ cakes. My neighbour .... ⑭ biscuits every Saturday. She always .... ⑮ some for me.

5. ***Present Simple czy Continuous*? Zwróć uwagę, na użycie jakiego czasu wskazują słowa takie jak *always*, *usually*, *regularly*. Pamiętaj o umieszczeniu przymiotnika we właściwym miejscu!**

1 You are such a messy person. You .... (to leave / always) your things around.

2 Our neighbour downstairs .... (to complain / always) about us. He doesn't like the music we're playing. And it's too loud, he says. Listen, he .... (to play / now) the saxophone. He .... (to play / usually) the sax at about 5 o'clock. That man has such a nerve!

3 He .... (to go away / always) for weekends leaving his wife and kids alone. The poor woman. Well, my husband .... (to go away / regularly) for weekends, too. But I don't mind. I enjoy having the weekends for myself.

4 We .... (to have / always) roast beef on Sundays. Why can't we have pork for a change. I am sick and tired of beef. My mother .... (to serve / always) chicken on Sundays. I think Sunday is a good day for chicken.

6. ***„Z wizytą u ekscentrycznej rodziny – rozmowa o północy". Present Simple czy Continuous?***

● *the guest* ▲ *the host*

● Who *is making* (to make) that terrible noise?

▲ It .... (to be) ① our grandfather. He sometimes .... (to practise) ② the violin at night. He .... (to play/not) ③ well, does he?

● But it .... (to be) ④ after midnight. Surely, he .... (to make) ⑤ too much noise?

● Oh, that noise .... (to matter / not) ⑥. We .... (to be) ⑦ all used to it. Look, the moon .... (to shine) ⑧ brightly. Grandad .... (to be) ⑨ moonstruck, you see. Sometimes he .... (to go) ⑩ swimming in the moonlight, or he .... (to dig) ⑪ holes in the garden.

● Listen, it .... (to get) ⑫ noisier and noisier.

▲ That is just my father. He .... (to snore) ⑬. Dad always .... (to snore) ⑭. But I .... (to warn) ⑮ you. There .... (to be) ⑯ more to come. My brother .... (to talk) ⑰ in his sleep and my little sister .... (to be) ⑱ a real sleep-walker.

● I think your sister .... (to walk) ⑲ around now. I can hear her steps.

▲ No, no, these .... (to be) ⑳ our family ghosts. I haven't told you about them yet. They .... (to dance) ㉑ upstairs in the attic. We .... (to call) ㉒ them Fred and Ginger because they .... (to love) ㉓ dancing. They .... (to be) ㉔ extremely polite. Sometimes they even come down and talk to us.

● You .... (to joke) ㉕, aren't you? You .... (to tell / not) ㉖ the truth.

▲ I always .... (to tell) ㉗ the truth. Listen, someone .... (to knock) ㉘ at the door. I .... (to wonder) ㉙ who that can be.

2. Czasy przeszłe: prosty *(Past Simple)* i ciągły *(Past Continuous)*

1. Wpisz czasowniki w odpowiednie kolumny.

walk ✔ play reply travel suffer plug ✔ pull prefer listen marry watch try label hurry benefit

Końcówka -ed	(podwojona spółgłoska) -ed	-y > -ied
walked, ...	............plugged, ...	....
....	....	....
....	....	....
....	....	....

2. Savoir vivre! – Uzupełnij zdania odpowiednimi czasownikami w czasie *Past Simple*.

disappear encounter live marry ✔ move pour prefer scrub suffer unplug use

1 I married........ my wife in 1955. She .... in France when she was a teenager. That's where she .... the French style of savoir vivre.

2 At the beginning of our marriage I always .... dusting the furniture to doing the washing up.

3 I .... from a dreadful backache. But when we .... into our new house and bought a new hoover the pain ....

4 Yesterday I .... the floor for hours, and it still looks filthy.

5 By mistake I .... a bucket of water over the TV set. But I .... the TV immediately.

6 I .... to lead a boring life before I met her.

3. Od podanych rzeczowników utwórz czasowniki, nadaj im formę czasu *Past Simple* i uzupełnij nimi zdania.

collection loss meeting miss panic tip try walk wedding ✔

1 My father always .... to work.

2 I .... my wife at a party. We *married* one year later.

3 My boss is a very quiet person, but yesterday he .... his patience.

4 My grandpa .... stamps. Now they are worth a fortune.

5 When the fire broke out, people ....

6 Yesterday evening everyone .... the waiter generously. He was very nice and deserved a good tip.

7 Normally, my brother always scores during a basketball game. But in the decisive match he .... too hard. He .... five times.

4. *Twój Yellow Langenscheidt-Cocktail* odniósł ogromny sukces na wczorajszym przyjęciu. Opowiedz, jak go przyrządziłeś!

You need:	Halve a melon and remove the seeds. Make melon balls with a scoop and chill them.
1 melon 1 grapefruit 2 lemons water sugar mint leaves lemon twists	Peel a grapefruit with a sharp knife. Cut the fruit into segments. Sprinkle the grapefruit segments with sugar. Allow them to stand at room temperature for 30 minutes. Grate enough rind from two lemons to give 2 tablespoons. Squeeze the juice of 2 lemons. Add the grapefruit and melon balls, then purée everything in a blender. Add enough water to give half a litre of liquid. Stir well. Taste and add sugar if desired. Serve the cocktail in frosted glasses. Sprinkle the glasses with lemon grind. Garnish the cocktail with green mint leaves and a slice of lemon.

How I made that gorgeous cocktail? Well, I halved a melon and removed the seeds. Then ...

5. ***„Dzień z życia gospodyni domowej"*. Połącz zdania, stosując czas *Past Simple* lub *Continuous*.**

1	I cleared the breakfast table.	My husband left for work.
2	I did the ironing.	I watched TV.
3	I took the dog out for a walk.	I thought about a nice birthday present for my mother-in-law.
4	I remembered that I had to pick up clothes at the dry-cleaner's.	I put the dirty clothes into the washing machine.
5	I made the beds.	I listened to the radio.
6	I worked in the garden.	The postman rang the doorbell.
7	I cleaned the windows.	It started raining.
8	I hoovered the flat.	I realized it was time to think about dinner.
9	I looked through my cookery book.	I discovered a nice recipe for fish and chips.
10	I peeled the potatoes and cut them into sections.	My mother dropped in for a cup of tea.
11	I laid the table.	My husband came home from work.
12	I opened a bottle of wine.	He sat at the table and looked forward to his dinner.

1 *While I was clearing the breakfast table my husband left for work.*
2 ....
3 ....
4 ....
5 ....
6 ....
7 ....
8 ....
9 ....
10 ....
11 ....
12 ....

6. **„*Wieczór z lordem Sinclairem*". Przeczytaj, co Lord Sinclair zazwyczaj robi, kiedy spędza wieczór w teatrze.**

Once a week Lord Sinclair goes to the theatre. On these occasions he always wears his morning suit. It consists of a long black coat, striped trousers and a waistcoat. He loves wearing a white shirt and a grey tie with his morning suit. Two hours before the start of the play he gets dressed. His butler prepares his top hat and cleans his shoes. Lord Sinclair has a glass of port in the library, and then his chauffeur drives him to the theatre. He takes his seat in the family box and follows the first act. During the break between the first and second act he has a glass of champagne. After the second act he always calls his mother to tell her about the play. When the curtain falls he usually feels hungry. After the performance he has supper at his club. Afterwards he and his friend play a game of bridge. Then he returns to his flat and goes to bed.

7. **Uzupełnij rozmowę telefoniczną, którą lord prowadzi ze swoją matką następnego dnia, po wizycie w teatrze.**

● *Lord Sinclair's mother* ▲ *Lord Sinclair*

● Did you go to the theatre last night?

▲ Yes, of course I *went*....... to the theatre.

● Why didn't you call me?

▲ I .... ① you because I .... (to fall asleep) ② during act two. The play .... (to be) ③ very boring.

● Did you wear your morning suit?

▲ Yes, I .... ④ my morning suit with the long black coat, the striped trousers and my waistcoat.

● Did you wear a white shirt and a grey tie?

▲ Yes, I .... ⑤ a white shirt and a grey tie.

● Did James prepare your top hat?

▲ Yes, he .... ⑥ my top hat, and as always he also .... ⑦ my shoes.

● Did you have a glass of port in the library before you .... (to leave) ⑧?

▲ Yes, I .... ⑨ my usual glass of port. Benton .... ⑩ me to the theatre.

● Did you take a seat in the family box?

▲ Yes, of course I .... ⑪ a seat in the family box.

● Did you have a glass of champagne after the first act?

▲ I'm afraid I can't remember how many glasses of champagne I .... ⑫. All I remember is that I suddenly .... (to feel) ⑬ very tired. After the second act, Humbert .... (to wake up / me) ⑭ up. I immediately .... ⑮ to the flat and .... ⑯ to bed.

● You must have a double then. I just .... (to talk) ⑰ to Lucinda, and she told me that her niece, whom I dislike very much, as you know, ... (to spend) ⑱ a wonderful evening at the Ritz yesterday with someone who .... (to look) ⑲ exactly like you.

8. Uzupełnij tabelkę.

bezokolicznik	3. os., czas teraźniejszy Present Simple	Past Continuous	Past Simple
....	....	....	*said*
to choose	....	....	....
....	*tries*	....	....
....	....	....	*did*
....	....	*having*	....
....	....	*eating*	....
to hope	....	....	....
....	....	....	*supplied*
to begin	....	....	....
....	*develops*	....	....
....	....	....	*agreed*
to argue	....	....	....

3. Czasy *Past Simple* i *Present Perfect*

1. *Past Participle*, czyli tzw. trzecia forma czasownika, której musimy tu użyć, we wszystkich niżej podanych wyrazach jest identyczna z formą czasu *Past Simple*.

buy ✔ feed have hear make pay read spend travel

Money, money, money

1 What type of car have you ..*bought*..... ?

2 How much money have you .... for the car?

3 Have you .... all your money on a new limousine?

Leisure time and food

4 How many Italian operas have you .... recently?

5 What American short stories have you ....?

6 When have you .... lunch today?

7 Have you .... coffee yet?

8 Has he .... the cats?

9 Have you often .... by boat?

2. W tym ćwiczeniu będzie nieco trudniej, ponieważ formy, które należy wstawić, nie pokrywają się z formami czasu *Past Simple*.

1 How many times have you .... (to be) to the theatre this month?

2 What colour have you .... (to choose) for your new car?

3 How many banks have you .... (to rob)?

4 Where have you .... (to hide) the money?

5 Have you ever .... (to eat) snails?

6 How many bottles of champagne have you .... (to drink) this week?

7 Have you .... (to see) the latest Steven Spielberg movie?

3. „*Dziennik hipochondryka*". Przyporządkuj objawy chorób do ich przyczyn.

1 My eyes are sore.
2 I've got a stiff neck.
3 My breath smells.
4 I'm feeling tired.
5 My back aches.
6 I've got indigestion.
7 I'm coughing.
8 I'm suffering from a hangover.
9 My feet hurt and I have several blisters.
10 I've got sunburn.
11 I've caught a cold.
12 I'm sweating.

do too many stretching exercises
smoke too many cigarettes
sunbathe all day
eat too many garlic and onion canapés
walk in the rain
watch television all night ✔
not get enough sleep
carry heavy shopping bags
spend too much time sitting at the computer
eat too many chocolates
walk around in high heels all day
drink too much

I am so miserable!

1 My eyes are sore *because I have been watching television all night.*
2 I've got a stiff neck ....
3 My breath smells ....
4 I'm feeling tired ....
5 My back aches ....
6 I've got indigestion ....
7 I'm coughing ....
8 I'm suffering from a hangover ....
9 My feet hurt and I have several blisters ....
10 I've got sunburn ....
11 I've caught a cold ....
12 I'm sweating ....

4. ***For* i *since* – wstaw czasowniki w odpowiedniej formie – *Past Simple* lub *Present Perfect*.**

to live	I .... ① here for the past 15 years. I love this part of town and I enjoy living here. Hemingway also .... ② here for two years – from 1944 to 1946.
to move, to be able to	Since we .... ③ to London in 1960, I .... ④ to improve my English.
to attend	I .... ⑤ evening classes for 2 or 3 months now.
to smoke/not	My mother .... ⑥ for several days.
to see	We .... ⑦ him a fortnight ago, but nobody .... ⑧ him since.
to go, to be	It is a long time since we .... ⑨ dancing together, isn't it? In fact, I don't think we .... ⑩ to a disco for more than ten years.
to be, to turn up/not	I .... ⑪ waiting here for more than an hour. But my mother .... ⑫ yet, so I'm still sitting here.

5. ***Past Simple* czy *Present Perfect*? Zwróć uwagę na podkreślone wyrażenia, charakterystyczne dla każdego z tych czasów.**

1 <u>Some time ago</u> my father ...*had*..... (to have) a stroke. He ....*has recovered*.... (to recover) <u>now</u>.

2 <u>Last year</u> my parents .... (to stay) at home during their holidays. But <u>this year</u> they .... (to make) a trip around the world.

3 I .... (to lose) his address and .... (to find/not) it <u>yet</u>.

4 I .... (to see/not) my brother <u>since last Christmas</u>.

5 David, why .... (to come/not) for breakfast <u>this morning</u>?

6 I .... (to finish) <u>just</u> .... my translation.

7 .... (to be) you <u>ever</u> .... to the USA? Yes, <u>last week</u> I .... (to visit) New York.

6. „*Szukamy pracy*". Uzupełnij poniższą rozmowę kwalifikacyjną, stosując czas teraźniejszy, *Present Perfect* lub *Past Simple*.

● *Ms Callman, Head of the Personnel Department* ▲ *Maria*

● Tell me something about your work experience.

▲ I *worked*........ (to work) for John Baxter Ltd. for about 10 years.

● Your English is good. You .... (to live) ① here for a long time, haven't you?

▲ Yes, I .... (to live) ② here for the past 16 years.

● Your surname is Sanchez. That sounds Spanish.

▲ Yes. My family .... (to be) ③ Spanish. I .... (to be) ④ born in Madrid.

● What does your father do?

▲ He .... (to be) ⑤ a teacher, but he .... (to work/not) ⑥ at the moment.

● How long .... (to be) ⑦ learning French?

▲ I .... (to be) ⑧ taking French lessons for 2 years now.

● What about German?

▲ I .... (to begin) ⑨ learning German 6 months ago.

● How many times .... (to change) ⑩ your job?

▲ I .... (to have) ⑪ three jobs since I .... (to leave) ⑫ school.

● Well, thank you very much. I'll call you tomorrow.

7. „*Kłótnia*". Zastosuj *Present Perfect Continuous*.

● *the husband* ▲ *the wife*

▲ Do you realize that we *have been quarrelling*..... (to quarrel) ever since we got married?

● Well, I .... (to ask) ① you to mend the roof for at least 5 years.

▲ Which means that we .... (to argue) ② about this roof for more than 5 years.

● That's because you .... (to listen/not) ③ to anything I said during our marriage.

▲ Ever since we met you .... (to try) ④ to boss me around.

● And you .... (to neglect) ⑤ me ever since you started your job.

4. Czas *Past Perfect*

1. Uzupełnij zdania czasownikami w czasie *Past Simple* lub *Past Perfect*.

All the things that can go wrong if you are a scatterbrained person!

1 I .... (try) to open the door to the flat for half an hour when I suddenly noticed that it was my neighbour's door, not mine. No wonder the key didn't fit.

2 I .... (search) for my glasses all morning when I realized that I had them on. I .... (wear) them all the time without noticing.

3 It .... (rain) all day long when I remembered that I .... (forget) to take the washing inside. So I couldn't wear my pink dress for the party that evening because it was still soaking wet. It served me right.

4 I had a date with my new boyfriend. We .... (arrange) to meet in a pub. I .... (wait) there for half an hour wondering why he .... (not turn up) when it occurred to me that we wanted to meet at a pub called The Wellington and not at The Nelson.

5 I .... (shop) around for quite some time when it suddenly dawned on me that I .... (forget) to turn off the lights of the car. I went back to the car. The car battery was too weak. I couldn't get the car started. My brother had to pick me up.

6 I .... (enjoy) the first half hour of a beautiful film at the cinema with popcorn and Coke when I remembered that I might .... (forget) to turn off the cooker in the kitchen. I left the cinema in a hurry and raced home, straight into the kitchen. Everything was o.k. I .... (forget) to turn off the cooker after all. How stupid of me!

7 I .... (walk) up and down the road for quarter of an hour wondering where on earth I .... (park) the car when I remembered my husband telling me that he needed it that day. What a waste of time!

2. *„Straszne przyjęcie"*. **Kronika katastrofalnych wypadków pewnego wieczora... Opowiedz przebieg zdarzeń!**

1	He ate most of the party sandwiches.	All the other guests arrived.	BY THE TIME
2	He ate too much.	He was sick.	BECAUSE
3	He forgot to dance with his girlfriend.	She was very angry and decided to ignore him all evening.	BECAUSE
4	He spilt some red wine.	A horrible stain appeared on the white table cloth.	WHEN
5	He drank too much at the party.	He couldn't go home by car and had to walk home.	BECAUSE
6	He annoyed so many people at the party.	Nobody wanted to drive him home.	BECAUSE
7	He forgot to put on his coat and it was raining.	He got soaking wet.	BECAUSE
8	He remembered that he carried a raincoat in his rucksack.	He caught a cold.	BY THE TIME
9	He walked ten miles in the pouring rain.	A car stopped and offered him a ride.	BEFORE
10	The rain stopped.	He arrived home.	BY THE TIME
11	He lost his keys.	He couldn't open the door to his flat.	BECAUSE
12	He rang his neighbour's door bell.	All of a sudden he remembered the spare key under the doormat.	WHEN
13	His friendly neighbour made him a pot of coffee.	He only suffered from a slight hangover the next morning.	BECAUSE

1 *By the time the other guests arrived he had eaten most of the party sandwiches.*

5. Formy czasu przyszłego

1. Uzupełnij zdania za pomocą to be *going* to lub *will*. W rozmowie chodzi o sprawy rodzinne i ogólne prognozy na przyszłość.

1 Last year my aunt bought a farm in Canada. She and her husband *are going to* leave Europe for good. Perhaps my cousin *will* join them. But he hasn't made up his mind yet.

2 My parents .... lend us some money. I've asked them and they have agreed to do so. I'm sure my grandparents .... lend us the rest when we ask them and tell them that we need the money to buy a house.

3 My brother .... help me to clear the attic. He's big and strong and I'm sure he won't mind. The only problem is that he is always so busy.

4 My sister and her family .... stay with us over the Christmas holidays. They've done so for the past few years.

5 My mother-in-law has decided to have a big birthday party. She .... invite all her children and grandchildren.

6 If you ask him, my nephew .... surely give you a lift in his car.

7 I reckon my uncle .... be mayor of our little town one day.

8 My daughter has just enrolled at university. She .... study maths and physics. I think she .... be a famous scientist one day.

9 Her in-laws .... probably look after the baby if she asks them. They live just round the corner. If they say no, she .... have to get a baby-sitter.

10 My niece is an emancipated young woman. She and her boyfriend have agreed to share the household chores. He .... do the cooking and she .... be in charge of the shopping. But they haven't decided who .... do the cleaning in their flat. I suppose they .... get someone to do it for them.

2. *„Tydzień z życia szefa"*. **Oto kalendarz Twojego szefa z planami na przyszły tydzień. Powiedz mu, co ma zaplanowane, używając niżej podanych czasowników.**

to have ✔ to have to give to meet to appear to play to give to arrive to leave to attend

Monday	*12.30 am: lunch with the Prime Minister*
Tuesday	*10 am: psychiatrist*
	9 pm: squash with Joe
Wednesday	*10-12 am: business meeting*
	3-5 pm: university lecture: "Efficient Time Management"
	8 pm: Julia for dinner at Bellini's
Thursday	*2 pm: Live Talk Show / BBC*
Friday	*10 am: train departure to Edinburgh / 1 pm: arrival*
	3 pm: talk at the Scottish Whisky Convention
	8.30 pm: train departure / 11.30 pm: arrival London

1 On Monday at 12.30 am you *are having* lunch with the Prime Minister.

2 On Tuesday at 10 am you .... an appointment with your psychiatrist.

3 And at 9 pm you .... squash with Joe.

4 On Wednesday you .... a business meeting from 10 to 12 am.

5 From 3 to 5 pm you .... a university lecture on "Efficient Time Management".

6 At 8 pm you .... Julia for dinner at Bellini's.

7 On Thursday you .... at a live Talk Show at the BBC at 2 pm.

8 On Friday at 10 am you .... for a business trip to Edinburgh.

9 At 3 pm you .... a talk at the Scottish Whisky Convention.

10 At 11.30 pm you .... in London.

ĆWICZENIA Formy czasu przyszłego

3. Plany, plany, plany! – Czas teraźniejszy *Present Simple* czy *Continuous*? Chodzi tu o plany i dokonane ustalenia. Uwaga: czasowniki, które musisz wstawić, są w każdym zdaniu podane w porządku alfabetycznym!

	You need:
1 We are taking the children to the zoo this afternoon. We'll be back at 7 o'clock. The zoo closes at 6 pm, and the bus .... an hour from the zoo to our part of town.	to close ✔ to take ✔ to take
2 We .... to the cinema tonight. The late night performance .... at 10 o'clock.	to go to start
3 Our friends .... us tomorrow. Their train .... at 5 o'clock in the afternoon.	to arrive to visit
4 My daughter .... university this year. The summer term .... in March and .... in July.	to end to start to start
5 I .... not .... till the end of the play. My last train .... at midnight and I mustn't miss it.	to leave to stay
6 We .... a big party next week. It .... father's birthday.	to be to have
7 I .... to the dentist's next week. I .... an appointment on Friday at 10 o'clock.	to go to have
8 We .... tickets for the football match next week. The tickets .... ,25. They .... very expensive.	to be to buy to cost

4. **„*Randka w ciemno*". Czas przyszły *Future Simple* czy *Continuous*?**

● *Linda*

▲ *Patricia*

● .... ① with us on Saturday night?
to go out / you

▲ No, I won't. I .... ② on a blind date with a guy named John. My
to go
brother arranged it. He reckons John is just my type. He thinks we .... ③ like a house on fire.
to get on

● How .... ④ him?
to recognise / you

▲ He .... ⑤ a copy of the Financial Times in his pocket and a red
to have
rose in his hand.

● How .... ⑥ it's you?
to know / he

▲ He'll recognise me when he sees me. I .... ⑦ a bright red dress
to wear
and a big red hat.

● .... ⑧ you up at home?
to pick (up) / he

▲ No, he won't. I .... ⑨ him at the Lonely Hearts Cafe at 8 pm.
to meet

● What .... ⑩ all night?
to do / you

▲ We probably .... ⑪ dinner first. And later we .... ⑫
to have / to go
dancing.

● Do you think you .... ⑬ spending time with a man you've never
to enjoy
met before?

▲ Well, John .... ⑭ my tenth blind date and I'm sure I .... ⑮
to be / to have
a wonderful time on Saturday.

5. Uprzejme pytania tworzymy za pomocą formy *will*. Utwórz pytania i przyporządkuj je do podanych wypowiedzi.

open the window ✔ speak up ring for a taxi close the window sign the letter get us some tea or coffee remind me to phone the baker's excuse me send off the invitations pass on a message

1 It's absolutely stifling in this room.
Will you open the window, please?

2 It's freezing in here.
....

3 I think it's time for a drink now. We could all do with a break.
....

4 I'm afraid I couldn't hear what you just said.
....

5 It's much too late now. I've just missed the last underground.
....

6 I'm afraid I have to make a quick phone-call. I'll be back in a minute.
....

7 I urgently need to talk to the manager. It's a shame he's not in his office.
....

8 I mustn't forget to order the chocolate cake for my son's birthday party.
....

9 The secretary is going to the post-office.
....

10 The company's celebrating its 50th anniversary in June.
....

6. „*Pesymistyczne i optymistyczne spojrzenie w przyszłość*". Uzupełnij rozmowę przyjaciółek, odbywającą się na krótko przed końcem roku, stosując formy Future Perfect.

☺ *Sandra, the optimist* ☹ *Patti, the pessimist*

☹ Next year, my husband and I will have been married for ten long and endless years. (to be)

☺ Next year, my husband and I .... ① ten years of joy and happiness together. (to have)

☹ Next summer, I .... ② in the same job with the same company for over seven years. (to work)

☺ Next summer, I .... ③ the pinnacle* of my career. (to reach)

☹ Statistically speaking, five years from now, the first half of my life .... ④ over. (to be)

☺ Statistically speaking, five years from now, I .... ⑤ going through my second adolescence. (to start)

☹ I'll be 35 in February. The enthusiasm of youth .... ⑥ by then. (to fade away)

☹ By the end of next year, I .... ⑦ completely grey. (to go)

☺ By the end of next year, I .... ⑧ all the colours of the rainbow. (to try)

☹ By then my husband .... ⑨ bald. (to go)

☺ By then my husband and I .... ⑩ that he looks just as sexy as Kojak. (to decide)

☹ Next year at New Year's Eve I .... ⑪ a bitter and depressed woman. (to become)

☺ No, you won't. Next year at New Year's Eve we'll be sitting here again – same time, same place.
Cheers and a Happy New Year!

* **pinnacle** the highest level of fame or success

ĆWICZENIA

6. Strona bierna

1. Sformułuj zasady obowiązujące w kuchni, używając strony biernej.

1 We serve tea in a tea pot.
Tea *is served* in a tea pot.

2 We boil potatoes in a pot.
Potatoes .... in a pot.

3 We prepare salads in bowls.
Salads .... in bowls.

4 We fry eggs in a pan.
Eggs .... in a pan.

5 We serve coffee in cups or mugs.
Coffee .... in cups or mugs.

6 We serve wine in glasses.
Wine .... in glasses.

2. Produkty i typowe dla nich opakowania. Najpierw przyporządkuj opakowania do produktów, a później ułóż zdania w stronie biernej.

flasks ✔ jars barrels bags tubs tub tins cartons or bottles bottles crates packets

1 We sell our perfume in *flasks.* *Our perfume is sold in flasks.*
2 The distillery stores whisky in ....
3 But our customers buy whisky in ....
4 You fill milk in ....
5 One can buy marmalade in ....
6 We pack crisps in ....
7 We deliver bottled beer in ....
8 We distribute our catfood in ....
9 We sell chewing-gum in ....
10 We offer ice cream in ....
11 I buy margarine in a ....

3. *„Jak zostać bogatym i sławnym pisarzem"* – Część 1. Zastąp podkreślone rzeczowniki i wyrażenia odpowiednimi zaimkami osobowymi.

1 The writer jots down the main ideas of the story.

2 He writes an outline of the story.

3 He fleshes out the characters and the plot.

4 He finishes the novel.

5 He sends the manuscript to the editor of his local newspaper.

6 The editor prints excerpts in the weekend edition.

7 The author offers the novel to a publisher.

8 If he likes it, he will publish the novel as a hardcover book.

9 Later, the bookshops offer the paperback edition.

10 The shops sell 50 million copies in the first year.

11 Leading literary translators translate the novel into many languages.

4. Teraz napisz powyższe zdania w stronie biernej. Użyj zaimków jako podmiotów.

1 *They are jotted down by the writer.* ....

2 ....

3 ....

4 ....

5 ....

6 ....

7 ....

8 ....

9 ....

10 ....

11 ....

5. „*Jak zostać bogatym i sławnym pisarzem*" – część 2. To tytuł artykułu o Tobie, ponieważ prasa śledzi przebieg Twojej kariery. Stosując podane konstrukcje, utwórz zdania w stronie biernej w czasie przyszłym.

It is believed	.... 1	Critics review the novel.
It is known	.... 2	A Hollywood film producer buys the property.
It is reported	.... 3	The producer asks the author to turn the novel into a film script.
It is understood	.... 4	A distributor releases the film based on the novel.
It is alleged	.... 5	Cinemagoers all over the world love the film.
It is said	.... 6	The jury awards the Nobel prize for literature to the author.
It is understood	.... 7	The Hollywood film producer wins the Oscar in the category Best Film Production of the Year.

1 *It is believed that the novel will be reviewed by critics.* ....

....

2 ....

....

3 ....

....

4 ....

....

5 ....

....

6 ....

....

7 ....

....

6. Które wydarzenie lub dzieło związane jest z którym nazwiskiem? Używając podanych czasowników zbuduj zdania w stronie biernej: dopasuj „Kamienie milowe historii ludzkości" do ich „twórców".

Shakespeare Mary Quant James Watt James Cook
Sir Christopher Wren George Gershwin ✔ Vivien Leigh
John F. Kennedy William the Conqueror David Lean

1 The opera "Porgy and Bess" .... *to compose*

2 Many famous churches and other buildings in London .... *to design*

3 In 1066 England .... *to conquer*

4 The miniskirt .... *to create*

5 The part of Scarlett O'Hara in "Gone with the Wind" .... *to play*

6 The films "Lawrence of Arabia" and "Doctor Zhivago" .... *to direct*

7 The play "King Lear" .... *to write*

8 Australia and New Zealand .... *to discover*

9 The steam engine .... *to invent*

10 The phrase "Ich bin ein Berliner" .... *to coin*

1 *The opera "Porgy and Bess" was composed by George Gershwin.*

2 ....

3 ....

4 ....

5 ....

6 ....

7 ....

8 ....

9 ....

10 ....

7. *„Czy słyszałaś ostatnią nowinę?"* Oto najnowsze plotki. Przekształć podane zdania, stosując stronę bierną.

1 People say that Lord Sinclair was a spy for the KGB.
He is said to have been a spy for the KGB.

2 The newspapers report that his wife had a nervous breakdown when she heard about her husband's secret service activity.
She is reported ....

3 Friends of ours believe that their son regularly uses the personal services of Madame Fifi.
He is believed ....

4 I hate to be bitchy*, but have you heard about my boss? At the office it is said that his wife has left him.
She is said ....

5 They also think that she now lives with a male model twenty years younger than herself.
She is thought ....

6 My sister Dorothy knows her cosmetic surgeon. According to Dorothy, he facelifted her ten times over the past two years.
She is said ....

7 Rumour has it that she spends a fortune on clothes.
She is said ....

8 Reliable sources think that her handsome young lover will allow her to marry him because she is rolling in money.
He ....

9 Well, we all know that he had an affair with Lord Sinclair's younger daughter and that he dropped her when the other woman came along.
He ....

10 The papers report that she gave a live interview on television talking about all the details of their love life.
She ....

11 People say that she is not capable of keeping anything to herself.
She ....

I really loathe people who bitch about others, don't you?

* **bitchy** in a malicious manner

7. *Gerund* a bezokolicznik

1. **„*Nasz kinoman obejrzał ostatnio dużo filmów*". Znajdź w diagramie odpowiednie czasowniki, dodaj końcówkę -ing i uzupełnij tytuły filmów. Pomogą Ci w tym podane nazwiska aktorów.**

		Starring
1	*Missing*............	Jack Lemmon
2	.... John Malkovich	John Malkovich
3	.... Down	Michael Douglas
4	Stop .... Sense	David Byrne
5	.... the Faith	Ben Stiller
6	She's .... a Baby	Kevin Bacon
7	.... Rita	Michael Caine
8	Dirty	Patrick Swayze
9	.... by Numbers	Joan Plowright
10	.... for Richard	Al Pacino
11	The .... Fields	Sam Waterston
12	.... on Heaven's Door	Til Schweiger

```
A R T H O S M H G V E I J X W M S K
E S E U(M I S S)F N S E N V E R F G
E S D S E N A U A S A H B R P B E N
G L U A U B B U L S T E I G E N R E
N T C R O K I L L N U M F N R A K B
S C A H R N I T B M A K E H A V E I
V O T L E O E N B E N D R O W N E G
E N E O S C G D A N C E N A C H P I
N A N O U K E N E I N V I E L E E G
R U S K E A N P L S B I T R E N N X
Y A O S T L N K L S B X R N X T J U
S T A X J M U R S A K C R Q F S T A
```

2. „*To, co lubimy robić*!" Połącz części zdań, tworząc formę *Gerund* (*-ing*). Uwaga: czasami trzeba dodać przyimek (*in*, *of*, *on* lub *to*)!

1 I'm a real movie buff. That's why I love
2 I study economics. Therefore I think it is worthwhile
3 I like animals. Therefore I am very keen
4 I'm a keen supporter of Manchester United. That's why I enjoy
5 I love New York City. Therefore I dream
6 I've always been a great fan of Gene Kelly and Fred Astaire. In fact, I wouldn't mind
7 I'm a real bookworm. I like all kinds of literature but I'm particularly fond
8 One of my hobbies is water colour painting, but I'd be interested
9 Many people say I'm something of polyglot because I'm keen
10 They also call me a real cosmopolitan because I always look forward
11 I'm afraid I'm not a very active person. I really love
12 I'm a sociable person. I think it's great fun

a to move to the United States.
b to read novels and short stories.
c to go to the cinema regularly. ✔
d to know more about other painting techniques.
e to hang around in cafés and meet friends.
f to go to Old Trafford to see my favourite team playing.
g to try tap dancing myself.
h to support the World Wildlife Fund and similar organisations.
i to read the Financial Times every day.
j to do nothing or to lie in bed and watch an old Hollywood movie on television.
k to learn languages.
l to organise my next trip around the world.

1 I'm a real movie buff. That's why I love *going to the cinema regularly.*

2 I study economics. Therefore I think it is worthwhile ....

3 I like animals. Therefore I am very keen ....

4 I'm a keen supporter of Manchester United. That's why I enjoy ....

....

5 I love New York City. Therefore I dream ....

6 I've always been a great fan of Gene Kelly and Fred Astaire. In fact, I wouldn't mind ....

7 I'm a real bookworm. I like all kinds of literature but I'm particularly fond

....

8 One of my hobbies is water colour painting, but I'd be interested ....

....

9 Many people say I'm something of a polyglot because I'm keen ....

....

10 They also call me a real cosmopolitan because I always look forward ......

....

11 I'm afraid I'm not a very active person. I like ....

12 I'm a sociable person. I think it's great fun ....

3. ***Nowy dyrektor otrzymał zadanie wyciągnięcia firmy z kryzysu. Oto jego pierwsze przemówienie do pracowników.***
Wpisz czasownik + formę *-ing* lub czasownik + *to*.

Ladies and Gentlemen,

1 We can't afford .... (to spend) too much money on restructuring our company.

2 We managed .... (to improve) our corporate image. We mustn't forget .... (to improve) the quality of our products, too.

3 I'm worried because competition seems .... (to get) tougher.

4 We failed .... (to develop) a new product line.

5 Our management tends .... (to be) too optimistic.

6 We decided .... (to adopt) new marketing strategies.

7 We promised our shareholders .... (to come up) with better sales figures.

8 I suggest .... (to get) in touch with a consulting firm.

9 We even considered .... (to reduce) our workforce.

10 But we better postpone .... (to dismiss) workers. Otherwise the trade unions might threaten .... (to go) on strike. I hope .... (to be able) to solve our problems.

4. „*Jak ludzie się zmieniają*!" Opisz, jaka kiedyś była Twoja przyjaciółka (używając konstrukcji *used to* + bezokolicznik) i przedstaw zmiany, jakie ostatnio u niej nastąpiły.

1 Veronica ***used to believe*** (to believe) in marriage and having many children. Now she ***thinks*** (to think) it's much better staying single and .... (to have) a new boyfriend every month.

2 Everybody said she .... (to be) a bit of a loner because she always liked to do things on her own. But now she .... (to be) a rather sociable person.

3 She .... (to live) in the country. Now she .... (to be) a city-dweller.

4 She .... (to eat) healthy wholefood. But now she .... (to be) into fast food.

5 She .... (to love) the beautiful, unspoilt countryside. But now city life really .... (to suit) her.

6 She .... (to hate) cars. But now she .... (to drive) a fast sports car.

7 She .... (to prefer) quiet and peaceful evenings at home. But she has become a real party animal. She .... (to enjoy) parties and likes to dance all night.

8 People .... (to call) her a country bumpkin. But now she .... (to be) considered a city-slicker because she .... (to think) she knows more about fashion and culture than country bumpkins.

8. Imiesłów

1. ***Jeszcze jeden zwykły dzień*! Opisz przebieg dnia. Zwróć uwagę na to, że niektóre wydarzenia odbywają się równocześnie (są napisane obok siebie), a inne następują jedno po drugim (i napisane są jedno pod drugim).**

1 be woken up by the sound of the alarm clock
get up

2 take a shower
get dressed

3 have breakfast — watch breakfast TV

4 drive to work — listen to the news on the radio

5 work from 9 to 5
go home

6 eat something
go to the local pub

7 drink 2 pints of beer — talk to colleagues and friends

8 come home
set the alarm clock

9 think about what happened during the day — fall asleep

1 ***Having been woken up by the sound of the alarm clock, I get up.***

2 ....

3 ....

4 ....

5 ....

6 ....

7 ....

8 ....

9 ....

2. Tu znajdziesz osoby o niezbyt przyjemnych charakterach. Utwórz zdania, przyporządkowując im typowe dla nich zachowania.

bore coward fusspot gossip narcissist ✔ pessimist scaremonger yes-man

1 He can't pass a mirror without looking into it and admiring himself, because he is such a vain person.

Being such a narcissist, he can't pass a mirror without looking into it and admiring himself.

2 Our neighbour spreads stories about burglars in our area which make us feel frightened. She likes to cause public fear.

...., our neighbour spreads stories about burglars in our area which make us feel frightened.

3 The man ran away instead of helping the poor woman who was attacked by two criminals. He showed no courage whatsoever.

...., the man ran away instead of helping the poor woman who was attacked by two criminals.

4 All she's interested in is buying clothes and reading fashion magazines. She doesn't seem to take an interest in anything else.

...., all she's interested in is buying clothes and reading fashion magazines.

5 Grandma tends to think that horrible things are more likely to happen than good things. Sometimes she's a real prophet of doom.

...., Grandma tends to think that horrible things are more likely to happen than good things.

6 My aunt loves talking about other people's private lives although it's none of her business whatsoever.

...., my aunt loves talking about other people's private lives although it's none of her business whatsoever.

7 Your mother is always complaining about everything and never satisfied with anything.

...., your mother is always complaining about everything and never satisfied with anything.

8 He agrees with everything other people say because he wants to please them.

...., he agrees with everything other people say.

3. **Podkreślone wyrazy to czasowniki oznaczające postrzeganie za pomocą zmysłów. Jaką formę należy nadać czasownikom po nich występującym: formę *-ing* (*Present Participle*) czy bezokolicznik?**

A night of horrors!

1 I was sitting in the library with my sister. First, my sister startled me. I didn't hear her ***come***..... (to come) in. In fact, I hadn't noticed her .... (to leave) the room in the first place.

2 Then I could feel something .... (to crawl) up my leg. It was a black spider.

3 I suddenly felt someone .... (to touch) me on the shoulder. I turned round. There was nobody there. It must have been my imagination.

4 We listened to our neighbour's dog .... (to howl) .

5 My sister asked me whether I had locked the door. I answered: "No, but I heard Richard .... (to lock) the door."

6 Then all of a sudden we heard a noise. Checking the living room, we watched someone .... (to climb) through the window.

7 We heard this person .... (to whisper) something.

8 Then I could smell something .... (to burn) .

9 Then there was an abrupt noise and we heard someone .... (to swear) loudly. It was then that we recognized our grandad's voice. He had just lit his pipe. He was a bit drunk and had forgotten his keys. He had been trying to get into the house without waking us up.

9. Zdania z *if*

1. *If* czy *when*? – Oto jest pytanie!

1 I'm off to the party. I hope to be back by midnight. Don't worry ..*if*... I'm late.

2 I'm afraid you can't talk to my husband right now. He's on a business trip in London. I'm sure he'll get in touch with you .... he gets back. .... there is an urgent problem, however, I can give you his mobile number.

3 I'm going shopping soon. .... you want anything, let me know. .... I'm back, we'll have a cup of coffee. But .... I'm not in by 5 o'clock I suggest you have coffee without me.

4 My brother might phone this evening. .... he does, please tell him to pick me up at the airport tomorrow.

5 .... you can spare the time, please come and see me in my office. I'd be interested in your advice on some of our new projects.

6 I'm going to London next week. .... I'm there I'll contact our British representative immediately. Mind you, ... it's not raining I might go for a long walk around Hyde Park first.

7 I suggest we leave at one o'clock. But .... you can't make it, please leave a message on my answering machine. I'll call you .... I get back.

8 I've arranged to have the company car repaired on Wednesday. I'd be very surprised .... it gets fixed* by Friday. But I'm not sure. .... you need the car, however, I'll call the garage* . ... I speak to the mechanic in charge, I'll ask .... the car will be ready for collection.

* **to fix something** to repair or mend something

* **garage** motor vehicles are repaired and serviced in a garage

2. Dziesięć sposobów na to, by powiedzieć „nie".

1 I really can't come to your party tomorrow evening because I have to work.

If I didn't have to work, I would come to your party.

2 Oh dear, we can't go for a walk because it looks like it's going to rain any minute.

....

3 I'm sorry, but I can't go out with you because I have this terrible headache.

....

4 I'm always so busy. That's the reason why I don't visit you very often.

....

5 No, I can't have lunch with you today because I've arranged to meet my parents.

....

6 I can't have dinner with you. You're always talking with your mouth full.

....

7 What a shame. I can't babysit for you this Saturday. I have visitors this weekend.

....

8 I'm not asking you to come upstairs for a drink because my place is in a complete mess.

....

9 I promised my girlfriend to go shopping with her. So I can't help you with your packing.

....

10 I'm not going to marry you because we're not a bit alike and have absolutely nothing in common.

....

3. *„Jaki rodzaj sportu chcesz uprawiać?"* Nie jesteś w dobrej formie i szukasz odpowiedniego dla siebie sportu. Odpowiedz na pytania. Przyporządkuj każdemu rodzajowi sportu właściwe mu cechy i do pytania dopasuj radę, której udziela Ci trener. Kieruj się odpowiedziami, które zakreśliłeś.

Motor racing is your cup of tea.
Ice-hockey is the type of sport that I would recommend. ✔
You should join a rugby club or play American football.
I recommend cricket.
Tennis seems to be your kind of sport.
You should go in for horse racing or other equestrian sports.
Playing basketball or doing the highjump would be a good idea.
I recommend marathon running.
You should try paragliding or parachuting, or even hang-gliding maybe.

1 Do you like the combination of teamsports, bodychecks and ice-skating?

☒ Yes, I do. ☐ No, I don't.

***If you like** the combination of teamsports, bodychecks and ice-skating, ice-hockey **is** the type of sport that I would recommend.*

☐ Yes, I do. ☒ No, I don't.

***If you like** the combination of teamsports, bodychecks and ice-skating, ice-hockey **is not** the type of sport that I would recommend.*

2 Do you admire people like Boris Becker or Andre Agassi?

☐ Yes, I do. ☐ No, I don't.

....

....

3 Is altitude sickness a problem for you?

☐ Yes, it is. ☐ No, it isn't.

4 Are you very tall?

☐ Yes, I am. ☐ No, I'm not.

....

....

5 Do you like horses?

☐ Yes, I do. ☐ No, I don't.

....

....

6 Do you have good stamina and do you like long-distance running?

☐ Yes, I do. ☐ No, I don't.

....

....

7 Do you like fast cars and are you obsessed with speed?

☐ Yes, I do. ☐ No, I don't.

....

....

8 Do you prefer team sports and games that go on for hours, if not for days on end?

☐ Yes, I do. ☐ No, I don't.

....

....

9 Do you like rough sports?

☐ Yes, I do. ☐ No, I don't.

....

....

4. „*Nicka Hornby'ego sposób na życie*". Nick Hornby jest zagorzałym kibicem piłki nożnej. Co by było, gdyby...?

1 I had absolutely no time at all. I watched television all day.

If I hadn't watched so much television, I *would have had* more time.

2 In fact, I spent the whole day in front of the television. They showed live football matches all day long.

.... so many live football matches, I .... so much time in front of the TV.

3 I didn't study for my final exams – I didn't have enough time.

.... more time, I .... harder for my final exams.

4 I didn't cover all the material that we were supposed to learn. I just didn't work hard enough.

.... harder, I .... all the material.

5 I didn't learn all the topics. As a consequence, I was nervous and panicky.

.... all the topics, I .... more confident and less nervous and panicky.

6 I didn't sleep well the night before the exam because I had terrible nightmares about failing.

.... such nightmares, I .... better.

7 During the exam, I wasn't able to concentrate. That's why I made so many mistakes.

.... to concentrate better, I .... so many mistakes.

8 In the end, I failed the exam. But I followed all the reports on the football matches.

.... all the reports, I .... the exam.

9 But I'm proud to say that I wrote a good essay on the commercial side of sports! That was only possible because I watched the entire soccer World Cup on TV.

.... the entire soccer World Cup on TV, I .... such a good essay.

10. Czasowniki pomocnicze

1. **Oto cztery możliwości powiedzenia, że coś „ma” lub „miało” być lub stać się. Podkreślone fragmenty zdań zastąp wyrażeniami podanymi poniżej (1–4). Zwróć uwagę, że w niektórych zdaniach trzeba wprowadzić zmiany, tak żeby były one gramatycznie poprawne!**

1	2	3	4
said to (do) supposed to (do)	supposed to (do)	meant to (be) intended to (be)	was to be
rumour	arrangement	purpose	destiny

1 People say that Joe drinks three bottles of whisky every day.

Joe is said to drink three bottles of whisky every day.

2 Rumour has it that he eats ten hard-boiled eggs for breakfast.

....

3 His manager claims that he sleeps on a bed of nails.

....

4 The purpose of such torture is to gradually kill off all feelings of pain.

....

5 Some people reckon that he had robbed fifty banks when he was younger.

....

6 The reason for the bank robberies was to show the whole world that rules and regulations were not for him and that he is in a class of his own.

....

7 It is alleged that he has 30 children.

....

8 He wanted to prove that he is a real womanizer.

....

9 It is believed that he killed a lion with his bare hands.

....

10 Well, it runs in the family. People say that Joe's father Jim was a hunter in Africa and a famous bullfighter in Spain.

....

11 Jim <u>was bound to</u> become an ardent admirer of Ernest Hemingway.

....

12 And later, Jim, too, <u>became</u> the hero of many little boys – including his own son.

....

13 A film producer <u>plans</u> to do a documentary about Joe's many adventures.

....

14 <u>Rumour has it that</u> Joe will publish some of his poems next year. <u>The idea</u> is to show that he's got brains, not just brawn.

....

15 After that Joe <u>will</u> write his memoirs in order to increase his popularity.

....

16 He <u>will</u> do a promotional tour to sell the book.

....

17 <u>It was arranged that</u> this would be the start of his second career as a writer.

....

2. Zdecyduj, czy czasownik can w podanych zdaniach wyraża umiejętność (U) zrobienia czegoś, czy pozwolenie (P) na coś.

	U	P	
1	☐	☐	Can you lend me some money?
2	☐	☐	Would you ask your mother whether you can lend me some money or not?
3	☐	☐	Can my brother borrow your car?
4	☐	☐	I can use your pocket calculator, can't I?
5	☐	☐	I can play the piano quite well.
6	☐	☐	I can play the piano between 3 and 6 o'clock in the afternoon.
7	☐	☐	My sister can't play tennis, but my brother is very good at it.

3. Z poprzedniego ćwiczenia wybierz cztery zdania, w których *can* można zastąpić przez *may*.

1 ....

2 ....

3 ....

4 ....

4. *Must, mustn't, can, to be (not) allowed*. Uzupełnij zdania wyjaśniające tablice z zakazami.

1 | NO SMOKING |

You might see this in the non-smoking area of a restaurant. You ***mustn't*** smoke there. You .... accept the fact that smoking cigarettes or cigars .... You .... to smoke there.

2 | PLEASE DO NOT TOUCH |

You might find this sign in a museum. Visitors to the museum .... look at the exhibits, but they .... to touch them.

3 | NO LITTER |

You might come across this sign in a picnic area. It means that you .... take all your rubbish with you. You .... leave any rubbish behind.

4 | NO THOROUGHFARE. PRIVATE ROAD |

This is a road sign. Vehicles .... to continue beyond this sign. They .... turn round and try a different road. Driving on ....

5 EMERGENCY EXIT ONLY

Customers might read this in a department store for example. They .... to use this exit in case of an emergency. But otherwise they .... use it. If there is no emergency, they .... try and find another exit.

6 NO CHILDREN UNDER 12

You might come across this notice at the entrance to a pub. It means that children under the age of 12 years .... enter the pub.

7 ENTER WHEN YOUR NUMBER COMES UP

That means that you .... proceed to the counter when your number appears on the screen.

8 NO DOGS

You .... bring dogs here. You might see this sign in a public garden or in a building. Exercising your dogs ....

5. Nie posłuchałeś dobrych rad – teraz tego żałujesz!

What my teacher, my parents, my friends, simply everyone always told me:

1 Work harder.

I should have worked harder.

2 Attend classes more regularly.

....

3 Don't miss so many lessons.

....

4 Do your homework every day.

....

5 Go out less.

....

6 Listen to your professor's lectures more carefully.

....

7 Don't oversleep so often.

....

8 Don't always be late for classes.

....

9 Spend the weekends studying rather than partying.

....

10 Try to avoid last year's mistakes.

....

11 Convince yourself that school isn't so bad after all.

....

If I had remembered all those things I wouldn't have failed my exam.

6. Wybierasz się w podróż. Tam, gdzie jedziesz, trzeba przestrzegać pewnych zasad. Wstaw *mustn't*, *must/have to* lub *needn't*.

1 While in the jungle, never leave your group. You ***mustn't*** walk around alone. You .... stay with your group.

2 The number-one rule is you .... drink the water. That includes tap water, ice and water from the lakes and rivers. Only drink purified boiled water. Of course you .... buy the expensive brands of bottled water, the cheaper ones will also do.

3 Only eat what our cook prepares for you. Tour members .... eat fruit or vegetables from the plants that grow in the forest.

4 Do not touch the plants. They might be poisonous. You .... pick flowers or tear off branches.

5 In order to be fit for our long walks, try going to bed early. You .... stay awake all night. But you .... go to bed at sunset.

11. Mowa zależna

1. **Jaka miła niespodzianka! Patricia, przyjaciółka Jill, mówi jej, że spodziewa się dziecka. Oczywiście, Jill musi tę wiadomość przekazać dalej! Zwróć uwagę na zmiany, które trzeba wprowadzić w zdaniach, oprócz zmian czasów.**

1 I have wonderful news.

Patricia told me that she had wonderful news.

2 Yesterday I had a pregnancy test done.

....

3 I am three months pregnant.

....

4 The baby is due in March next year.

....

5 I should have known myself because every morning I woke up feeling ill.

....

6 I felt sick in the mornings during the first couple of days of my pregnancy.

....

7 I gave up smoking when I found out.

....

8 I've been reading many books about how to be a good mother.

....

9 We're going away for a few days because I need a rest.

....

10 Eventually, I'm going to give up work.

....

11 You can come and babysit for me if you like.

....

2. **Przy tej okazji Jill musi również opowiedzieć, co nowego u niej słychać. Te wiadomości Patricia oczywiście przekazuje dalej.**

1 Two months ago John asked me to marry him.

Jill said that John had asked her to marry him two months before.

2 I've been in love with him for many years now.

She said that ....

3 So I said yes.

....

4 We're getting married on 5th June.

....

5 This will be the happiest day of my life.

....

6 Will you be able to come to our wedding?

....

7 We'll spend our honeymoon on the Bahamas.

....

3. **Znajdź w diagramie 10 czasowników, które mogą znajdować się na początku zdania w mowie zależnej.**

```
O Z G S F M K H J T Q X S C L
H S C P K A E N Z S T A T E Q
K A D M I T X Z E A L D M A S
G Y A S R E P L Y K R I E N T
S V B N R L L K H G E W E R T
U S E X P L A I N T M S A T R
D R A S A M I W E R A D D W E
E Z U M S A N S W E R F T U P
P H L T E L B M A N K Z U I O
X W M N K X Y O A D M S T V G
Q S I M J Y E Z U C A B S R N
```

4. Roberta spotyka w stołówce swoją koleżankę Fionę. Dla Fiony jest to pierwszy dzień po urlopie. Przeczytaj ich rozmowę.

● *Roberta*
▲ *Fiona*

● What was your holiday like?
▲ It was marvellous. We had a great time.
● Where did you go?
▲ We went to the Greek island of Rhodes.
● Who did you go with?
▲ I went with my husband.
● Where exactly did you stay?
▲ We stayed at a small hotel.
● What was the weather like?
▲ The weather was great. We had sunshine every day.
● How did you spend your time?
▲ We went for walks in the evening and did a lot of sunbathing.

5. Wieczorem Roberta opowiada rozmowę z Fioną swojemu mężowi. Uzupełnij jej opowiadanie.

1 I asked her *what her holiday had been like.*
She answered that *it had been marvellous and that they had had a great time.*

2 I wanted to know ....
She answered that ....

3 I asked her ....
She replied that ....

4 I asked ....
She answered that ....

5 I wanted to know ....
She answered that ....

6 I asked her ....
She replied that ....

6. **Ponieważ urlop był bardzo udany, Roberta i John chcą obejrzeć zdjęcia i umawiają się z Fioną przez telefon na spotkanie. Roberta uzgadnia z mężem odpowiedzi na pytania, które zadaje Fiona.**

Fiona's questions:

- Are you free next Saturday?
- Is 7 pm too early?
- Would you like to have dinner at our place?
- Are you interested in last year's photographs, too?
- Will you come by car or will you take the underground?
- Do you want me to draw a map to show you how to get to our house?
- Will you bring your kids?

"John, Fiona asks ...

1 *whether we are free next Saturday."*

2 ....

3 ....

4 ....

5 ....

6 ....

7 ....

7. **„*Przyjęcie*". Jackie i Joanne przychodzą na przyjęcie. Okazuje się, że Joanne miała o nim zupełnie inne wyobrażenie. Robi wymówki Jackie. Uzupełnij rozmowę.**

● *Jackie* ▲ *Joanne*

● Did you hear that? Our boss and his wife are coming to the party. How awful!

▲ But you told me *they weren't coming to the party.* .... You know I don't like them.

● Look, they're only serving drinks, and no food.

▲ Didn't you say .... ①. I'm starving!

- ● It is a fancy dress party! Everyone is wearing fancy clothes!
- ▲ I thought you said that .... ②. We're the only ones wearing normal clothes!
- ● There won't be any live music.
- ▲ But you said .... ③. What a shame!
- ● Everybody's giving presents to the hosts.
- ▲ I thought you said that .... ④. How embarrassing!

8. Zakazy i nakazy. W British Museum otrzymałeś informację o zasadach tam obowiązujących. Opowiadasz o nich w domu.

General Information

1. You may have to wait five or ten minutes at the entrance.
2. Queue at the end of the line.
3. Don't jump the queue.
4. Don't take bags or umbrellas into the museum rooms.
5. You needn't worry about your belongings – our cloakroom is never unattended.
6. You mustn't leave the marked path.
7. You can take photographs provided you don't use a flash.
8. You must follow the directions of our personnel.

"They gave us a leaflet which told us ...

1 ....

2 ....

3 ....

4 *not to take bags and umbrellas into the museum.* ....

5 ....

6 ....

7 ....

8 ....

Klucz do ćwiczeń

1. Czasy teraźniejsze: *Present Simple* i *Present Continuous* (*Present Progressive*)

1

Końcówka -es: rushes, fetches, mixes, relaxes
Końcówka -ies: relies, carries, marries, copies
Końcówka -s: shows, buys, lies, says, grows

2

1 – b; 2 – a; 3 – a; 4 – d; 5 – b; 6 – a; 7 – b; 8 – d; 9 – c

3

1 – c; 2 –b; 3 – d; 4 – b; 5 – a; 6 – e; 7 – b; 8 – b; 9 – e

4

1 is playing; 2 is playing; 3 play; 4 is raining; 5 rains; 6 is staying; 7 stays; 8 isn't working; 9 doesn't work; 10 am writing; 11 write; 12 is baking (*lub:* bakes); 13 bake; 14 bakes; 15 bakes

5

1 are always leaving (*lub:* always leave); 2 is always complaining (*lub:* always complains), is now playing, usually plays; 3 is always going away (*lub:* always goes away), regularly goes away; 4 are always having, always serves

6

1 is; 2 practises; 3 doesn't (*lub:* does not) play. 4 is; 5 is making; 6 doesn't (*lub:* does not) matter; 7 are; 8 is shining; 9 is; 10 goes; 11 digs; 12 is getting; 13 is snoring; 14 snores; 15 am warning (*lub:* warn); 16 is; 17 talks; 18 is; 19 is walking; 20 are; 21 are dancing; 22 call; 23 love; 24 are; 25 are joking; 26 are not telling; 27 tell; 28 is knocking; 29 wonder

2. Czasy przeszłe: prosty (*Past Simple*) i ciągły (*Past Continuous*)

1

Końcówka -ed: walked, played, suffered, pulled, listened, watched,
Podwojenie ostatniej spółgłoski i końcówka -ed: travelled, plugged, labelled, preferred, benefitted

-y > -ied: married, tried, hurried, replied

2

1 married, lived, encountered; 2 preferred; 3 suffered, moved, disappeared; 4 scrubbed; 5 poured, unplugged; 6 used

3

1 walked; 2 met, married; 3 lost; 4 collected; 5 panicked; 6 tipped; 7 tried, missed

4

I <u>halved</u> a melon and removed the seeds. Then I <u>made</u> melon balls with a scoop and <u>chilled</u> them. I <u>peeled</u> a grapefruit with a sharp knife. I cut the fruit into segments. I <u>sprinkled</u> the grapefruit segments with sugar. I <u>allowed</u> them to stand at room temperature for 30 minutes. I <u>grated</u> enough rind from two lemons to give 2 tablespoons. I <u>squeezed</u> the juice of 2 lemons. I added the grapefruit and melon balls, then <u>puréed</u> everything in a blender. I <u>added</u> enough water to give half a litre of liquid. I <u>stirred</u> well. I <u>tasted</u> and <u>added</u> sugar. I <u>served</u> the cocktail in frosted glasses. I <u>sprinkled</u> the glasses with lemon grind. I <u>garnished</u> the cocktail with green mint leaves and a slice of lemon.

5

1 While I was clearing the breakfast table my husband left for work. 2 While I was doing the ironing I was watching television. 3 While I was taking the dog out for a walk I was thinking about a nice birthday present for my mother-in-law. 4 I remembered that I had to pick up clothes at the dry cleaner's while I was putting the dirty clothes into the washing machine. 5 While I was making the beds I was listening to the radio. 6 While I was working in the garden the postman rang the doorbell. 7 While I was cleaning the windows it started raining. 8 While I was hoovering the flat I realized it was time to think about dinner. 9 While I was looking through my cookery book I discovered a nice recipe for fish and chips. 10 While I was peeling the potatoes and cutting them into sections my mother dropped in for a cup of tea. 11 While I was laying the table my husband came home from work. 12 While I was opening a bottle of wine he was sitting at the table and looked forward to his dinner.

7

1 didn't call; 2 fell asleep; 3 was; 4 wore; 5 wore; 6 prepared; 7 cleaned; 8 left; 9 had; 10 drove; 11 took; 12 had; 13 felt; 14 woke me up; 15 returned; 16 went; 17 talked; 18 spent; 19 looked

8

say, says, saying, said
choose, chooses, choosing, chose
try, tries, trying, tried
do, does, doing, did
have, has, having, had
eat, eats, eating, ate
hope, hopes, hoping, hoped
supply, supplies, supplying, supplied
begin, begins, beginning, began
develop, develops, developing, developed
agree, agrees, agreeing, agreed
argue, argues, arguing, argued

3. Czasy *Past Simple* i *Present Perfect*

1

1 bought; 2 paid; 3 spent; 4 heard; 5 read; 6 had; 7 made; 8 fed; 9 travelled

2

1 been; 2 chosen; 3 robbed; 4 hidden; 5 eaten; 6 drunk; 7 seen

3

1 because I have been watching television all night. 2 because I have been spending too much time sitting at the computer. 3 because I have been eating too many garlic and onion canapes. 4 because I haven't been getting enough sleep. 5 because I have been doing too many stretching exercises. 6 because I have been eating too many chocolates. 7 because I have been smoking too many cigarettes. 8 because I have been drinking too much. 9 because I have been walking around in high heels all day. 10 because I have been sunbathing all day. 11 because I have been walking in the rain. 12 because I have been carrying heavy shopping bags.

4

1 have lived; 2 lived; 3 moved; 4 have been able to; 5 have attended; 6 hasn't smoked; 7 saw; 8 has seen; 9 went; 10 have been; 11 have been; 12 hasn't turned up

5

1 had, has recovered; 2 stayed, have made; 3 have lost, haven't found; 4 haven't seen; 5 haven't you (*lub:* have you not) come; 6 have ... finished; 7 Have... been, visited

6

1 have lived; 2 have lived; 3 is; 4 was; 5 is; 6 isn't working; 7 have you been; 8 have been; 9 began; 10 have you changed; 11 have had; 12 left

7
1 have been asking; 2 have been arguing; 3 haven't been listening; 4 have been trying; 5 have been neglecting

4. Czas *Past Perfect*

1
1 had been trying; 2 had been searching, had been wearing; 3 had been raining, had forgotten; 4 had arranged, was waiting, wasn't turning up; 5 was shopping, had forgotten; 6 was enjoying, have forgotten, hadn't forgotten; 7 was walking, had parked

2
1 By the time the other guests arrived he had eaten most of the party sandwiches. 2 He was sick because he had eaten too much. 3 His girlfriend was very angry and decided to ignore him all evening because he had forgotten to dance with her. 4 A horrible stain appeared on the white table cloth when he had spilt some red wine. 5 He couldn't go home by car and had to walk home because he had drunk too much at the party. 6 Nobody wanted to drive him home because he had annoyed so many people at the party. 7 He got soaking wet because he had forgotten to put on his coat and it was raining. 8 By the time he remembered that he carried a raincoat in his rucksack he had caught a cold. 9 He had walked ten miles in the pouring rain before a car stopped and offered him a ride. 10 By the time he arrived home the rain had stopped. 11 He couldn't open the door to his flat because he had lost his keys. 12 All of a sudden he remembered the spare key under the doormat when he had rung his neighbour's door bell. 13 He only suffered from a slight hangover the next morning because his friendly neighbour had made him a pot of coffee.

5. Formy czasu przyszłego

1
1 are going to, will; 2 are going to, will; 3 will; 4 are going to; 5 is going to; 6 will; 7 will (*lub:* is going to); 8 is going to, will (*lub:* is going to); 9 will, will; 10 is going to (*lub:* will), is going to (*lub:* will), will (*lub:* is going to), will (*lub:* is going to)

2
1 are having; 2 are having; 3 are playing; 4 are attending; 5 are giving; 6 are meeting; 7 are appearing; 8 are leaving; 9 are giving; 10 are arriving

3

1 are taking, closes, takes; 2 are going, starts; 3 are visiting, arrives; 4 is starting, starts, ends; 5 am ... staying, leaves; 6 are having, is; 7 am going, have; 8 are buying, cost, are

4

1 Will you go out; 2 will be going; 3 will get on (*lub:* will be getting on); 4 will you recognise; 5 will have (*lub:* will be having); 6 will he know; 7 will be wearing; 8 will he pick; 9 will be meeting; 10 will you be doing; 11 will be having; 12 will go; 13 will enjoy; 14 will be; 15 will have (*lub:* be having)

5

1 Will you open the window, please? 2 Will you close the window, please? 3 Will you get us some tea or coffee, please? 4 Will you speak up, please? 5 Will you ring for a taxi, please? 6 Will you excuse me, please? 7 Will you pass on a message, please? 8 Will you remind me to phone the baker's, please? 9 Will you sign the letter, please? 10 Will you send off the invitations, please?

6

1 will have had; 2 will have worked; 3 will have reached; 4 will have been; 5 will have started; 6 will have faded away; 7 will have gone; 8 will have tried; 9 will have gone; 10 will have decided; 11 will have become

6. Strona bierna

1

1 is served; 2 are boiled; 3 are prepared; 4 are fried; 5 is served; 6 is served

2

1 Our perfume is sold in <u>flasks</u>. 2 Whisky is stored in <u>barrels</u>. 3 Whisky is bought in <u>bottles</u>. 4 Milk is filled in <u>cartons or bottles</u>. 5 Marmalade can be bought in <u>jars</u>. 6 Crisps are packed in <u>bags</u>. 7 Bottled beer is delivered in <u>crates</u>. 8 Our catfood is delivered in <u>tins</u>. 9 Chewing gum is sold in <u>packets</u>. 10 Ice cream is offered in <u>tubs</u>. 11 Margarine is bought in a <u>tub</u>.

3

1 they; 2 it; 3 they; 4 it; 5 it; 6 they; 7 it; 8 it; 9 it; 10 they; 11 it

4

1 They are jotted down by the writer. 2 It is written by him. 3 They are fleshed out by him. 4 It is finished by him. 5 It is sent to the editor of his local newspaper. 6 They are printed in the weekend edition by the editor. 7 It is offered to a publisher by the author. 8 If he likes it, it will be published as a hardcover book. 9 Later, it is offered by the bookshops. 10 They are sold by the shops in the first year. 11 It is translated into many languages by leading literary translators.

5

1 It is believed that the novel will be reviewed by critics. 2 It is known that the property will be bought by a Hollywood film producer. 3 It is reported that the author will be asked by the producer to turn the novel into a film script. 4 It is understood that the film based on the novel will be released by a distributor. 5 It is alleged that the film will be loved by cinemagoers all over the world. 6 It is said that the Nobel prize for literature will be awarded to the author by the jury. 7 It is understood that the Oscar in the category Best Film Production of the Year will be won by the Hollywood film producer.

6

1 The opera “Porgy and Bess” was composed by George Gershwin. 2 Many famous churches and other buildings in London were designed by Sir Christopher Wren. 3 England was conquered by William the Conquerer. 4 The miniskirt was created by Mary Quant. 5 The part of Scarlett O’Hara in “Gone with the Wind” was played by Vivian Leigh. 6 The films “Lawrence of Arabia” and “Doctor Zhivago” were directed by David Lean. 7 The play “King Lear” was written by Shakespeare. 8 Australia and New Zealand were discovered by James Cook. 9 The steam engine was invented by James Watt. 10 The phrase “Ich bin ein Berliner” was coined by John F. Kennedy.

7

1 He is said to have been a spy for the KGB. 2 to have had a nervous breakdown. 3 to regularly use the personal services of Madame Fifi. 4 to have left him. 5 to live with a male model twenty years younger than herself. 6 to have been facelifted ten times over the past two years. 7 to spend a fortune on clothes. 8 is thought to allow her to marry him because she is rolling in money. 9 is known to have had an affair with Lord Sinclair’s younger daughter and to have dropped her when the other woman came along. 10 is reported to have given a live interview on television talking about all the details of their love life. 11 is said to be not capable of keeping anything to herself.

7. *Gerund* a bezokolicznik

1

1 Missing; 2 Being; 3 Falling; 4 Making; 5 Keeping; 6 Having; 7 Educating; 8 Dancing; 9 Drowning; 10 Looking; 11 Killing; 12 Knocking (*lub:* Knockin')

2

1 going to the cinema regularly. 2 reading the Financial Times every day. 3 on supporting the World Wildlife Fund and similar organisations. 4 going to Old Trafford to see my favourite team playing. 5 of moving to the United States. 6 trying tap dancing myself. 7 of reading novels and short stories. 8 in knowing more about other painting techniques. 9 on learning languages. 10 to organising my next trip around the world. 11 doing nothing or lying in bed and watching old Hollywood movies on television. 12 hanging around in cafés and meeting friends.

3

1 to spend; 2 to improve, to improve; 3 to be getting; 4 to develop; 5 to be; 6 to adopt; 7 to come up; 8 getting; 9 reducing; 10 dismissing, to go, to be able

4

1 used to believe, thinks, having; 2 used to be, is; 3 used to live, is; 4 used to eat, is; 5 used to love, suits; 6 used to hate, drives; 7 used to prefer, enjoys; 8 used to call, is, thinks

8. Imiesłów

1

1 Having been woken up by the sound of the alarm clock I get up. 2 Having taken a shower I get dressed. 3 Having breakfast I watch breakfast TV. 4 Driving to work I listen to the news on the radio. 5 Having worked from 9 to 5 I go home. 6 Having eaten something I go to the local pub. 7 Drinking 2 pints of beer I talk to colleagues and friends. 8 Having come home I set the alarm clock. 9 Thinking about what happened during the day I fall asleep.

2

1 Being such a narcissist; 2 Being such a scaremonger. 3 Being such a coward; 4 Being such a bore; 5 Being such a pessimist; 6 Being such a gossip; 7 Being such a fusspot; 8 Being such a yes-man

3

1 come, leaving; 2 crawling; 3 touch; 4 howling; 5 lock; 6 climbing; 7 whisper; 8 burning; 9 swearing

9. Zdania z *if*

1

1 if; 2 when, If; 3 If, When, if; 4 If; 5 If; 6 When, if; 7 if, when; 8 if If, When, when

2

1 If I didn't have to work, I would come to your party. 2 If it wasn't looking like it's going to rain any minute, we could go for a walk. 3 If I didn't have this terrible headache, I could go out with you. 4 If I weren't always so busy, I would visit you more often. 5 If I hadn't arranged to meet my parents, I could have lunch with you today. 6 If you weren't always talking with your mouth full, I would have dinner with you. 7 If I didn't have visitors this weekend, I could babysit for you. 8 If my place wasn't in a complete mess, I would ask you to come upstairs for a drink. 9 If I hadn't promised my girlfriend to go shopping with her, I could help you with your packing. I0 If we were more alike and had more in common, I would marry you.

3

Yes:

1If you like the combination of teamsports, bodychecks and ice-skating, ice-hockey is the type of sport I would recommend. 2 If you admire people like Boris Becker and Andre Agassi, tennis seems to be your kind of sport. 3 If altitude sickness is a problem for you, you shouldn't try paragliding or parachuting or hang gliding. 4 If you are very tall, playing basketball or doing the highjump would be a good idea. 5 If you like horses, you should go in for horse racing or other equestrian sports. 6 If you have good stamina and like long-distance running, I recommend marathon running. 7 If you like fast cars and are obsessed with speed, motor racing is your cup of tea. 8 If you prefer team sports and games that go on for hours if not for days, I recommend cricket. 9 If you like rough sports, you should join a rugby club or play American football.

No:

1If you don't like the combination of teamsports, bodychecks and ice-skating, ice-hockey isn't the type of sport I would recommend. 2 If you don't admire people like Boris Becker and Andre Agassi, tennis doesn't seem to be your kind of sport. 3 If altitude sickness isn't a (*lub:* is no) problem for you, you should try paragliding or parachuting, or even hang-gliding maybe. 4 If you aren't very tall, playing basketball or doing the highjump wouldn't be a good idea. 5 If you don't like horses, you shouldn't go in for horse racing or other equestrian sports. 6 If you don't have good stamina and like long-distance running, I don't recommend marathon running. 7 If you don't like fast cars and aren't obsessed with speed, motor racing isn't your cup of tea. 8 If you don't prefer team sports and games that go on for hours if not for days, I don't recommend cricket. 9 If you don't like rough sports, you shouldn't join a rugby club or play American football.

4

1 If I hadn't watched, would have had; 2 If they hadn't shown, wouldn't have spent; 3 If I had had, would have studied; 4 If I had worked, would have covered; 5 If I had learned (*lub:* learnt), would have been; 6 If I hadn't had, would have slept; 7 If I had been able, wouldn't have made; 8 If I hadn't followed, wouldn't have failed; 9 If I hadn't watched, wouldn't have written

10. Czasowniki pomocnicze

1

1 Joe is said to drink three bottles of whisky every day. 2 He is said to eat ten hard-boiled eggs for breakfast. 3 He is said to sleep on a bed of nails. 4 Such torture is meant to gradually kill off all feelings of pain. 5 He is supposed to have robbed fifty banks when he was younger. 6 The bank robberies were meant to show the whole world that rules and regulations were not for him and that he is in a class of his own. 7 He is said to have 30 children. 8 This was meant to prove that he was a real womanizer. 9 He is said to have killed a lion with his bare hands. 10 Joe's father Jim is said to have been a hunter in Africa and a famous bullfighter in Spain. 11 Jim was to be an ardent admirer of Ernest Hemingway. 12 And later Jim was to be the hero of many little boys – including his own son. 13 A film producer is supposed to do a documentary about Joe's many adventures. 14 Joe is said to publish some of his poems next year. This is intended to show that he's got brains not just brawn. 15 Joe intends to write his memoirs. 16 He is supposed to do a promotional tour to sell the book. 17 This was supposed to be the start of his second career as a writer.

2

1 – F; 2 – E; 3 – E; 4 – E; 5 – F; 6 – E; 7 – F

3

1 Would you ask your mother whether you may lend me some money? 2 May my brother borrow your car? 3 May I use your pocket calculator? 4 I may play the piano between 3 and 6 o'clock in the afternoon.

4

1 mustn't, must, is not allowed, are not allowed; 2 can, are not allowed; 3 must, mustn't; 4 are not allowed, must, is not allowed; 5 are allowed, mustn't, must; 6 mustn't; 7 can; 8 mustn't, is not allowed

5

1 I should have worked harder. 2 I should have attended classes more regularly. 3 I shouldn't have missed so many lessons. 4 I should have done my homework every day. 5 I should have gone out less. 6 I should have listened to my professor's lectures more carefully. 7 I shouldn't have overslept so often. 8 I shouldn't have always been late for classes. 9 I should have spent the weekends studying rather than partying. 10 I should have tried to avoid last year's mistakes. 11 I should have convinced myself that school isn't so bad after all.

6

1 mustn't, must (*lub:* have to); 2 mustn't, needn't; 3 mustn't; 4 mustn't; 5 mustn't, needn't

11. Mowa zależna

1

Patricia told me that

1 she had wonderful news. 2 the day before (*lub:* the previous day) she had had a pregnancy test done. 3 she was three months pregnant. 4 the baby will be due in March next year. 5 she should have known herself because every morning she had woken up feeling ill. 6 she had felt sick in the mornings during the first couple of days of her pregnancy. 7 she had given up smoking when she found out. 8 she had been reading many books about how to be a good mother. 9 they were going away for a few days because she needed a rest. 10 eventually she was going to give up work. 11 I could come and babysit for her if I liked.

2

Jill said that

1 John had asked her to marry him two months before. 2 she had been in love with him for many years. 3 she had said yes. 4 they were getting married on 5th June. 5 that (day) would be the happiest day of her life. 7 they would spend their honeymoon on the Bahamas.

She asked me if

6 I would be able to come to their wedding.

3

poziomo: state, admit, reply, explain, add, answer
pionowo: say, tell, explain, remark

5

1 what her (*lub:* their) holiday had been (*lub:* was) like, it had been (*lub:* was) marvellous and that they had had (*lub:* had) a great time.
2 where she (*lub:* they) had gone (*lub:* went), they had gone (*lub:* went) to the Greek island of Rhodes. 3 who she had gone (*lub:* went) with, she had gone (*lub:* went) with her husband. 4 where exactly they had stayed (*lub:* stayed), they had stayed (*lub:* stayed) at a small hotel. 5 what the weather had been (*lub:* was) like, the weather (*lub:* it) had been (*lub:* was) great and that they had had (*lub:* had) sunshine every day. 6 how they had spent (*lub:* spent) their time, they had gone (*lub:* went) for walks in the evening and had done (*lub:* did) a lot of sunbathing.

6

1 whether (*lub:* if) we are free next Saturday. 2 whether (*lub:* if) 7 pm is too early. 3 whether (*lub:* if) we would like to have dinner at their place. 4 whether (*lub:* if) we are interested in last year's photographs, too. 5 whether (*lub:* if) we'll come by car or whether (*lub:* if) we'll take the underground. 6 whether (*lub:* if) we want her to draw a map to show us how to get to their house.
7 whether (*lub:* if) we'll bring our (*lub:* the) kids.

7

1 they were not only serving drinks, but also food? (*lub:* they were serving drinks and food? *lub:* they were serving also food?) 2 it wasn't a fancy dress party and that nobody was wearing fancy clothes. 3 there would be live music. 4 nobody was giving (any) presents to the hosts.

8

1 that we might have to wait five or ten minutes at the entrance. 2 to queue at the end of the line. 3 not to jump the queue. 4 not to take bags or umbrellas into the museum. 5 that we needn't (*lub:* didn't need to, didn't have to) worry about our belongings – their cloakroom was never unattended. 6 not to leave (*lub:* that we weren't allowed to leave) the marked path. 7 that we could take photographs provided we didn't use a flash. 8 that we had to follow the directions of their personnel.

> Przeczytaj list, w którym akapity (**A-G**) zostały przemieszane. Uporządkuj akapity tak, aby tworzyły spójną całość. Rozwiązanie wpisz z zamieszczoną tabelkę (**1-7**).

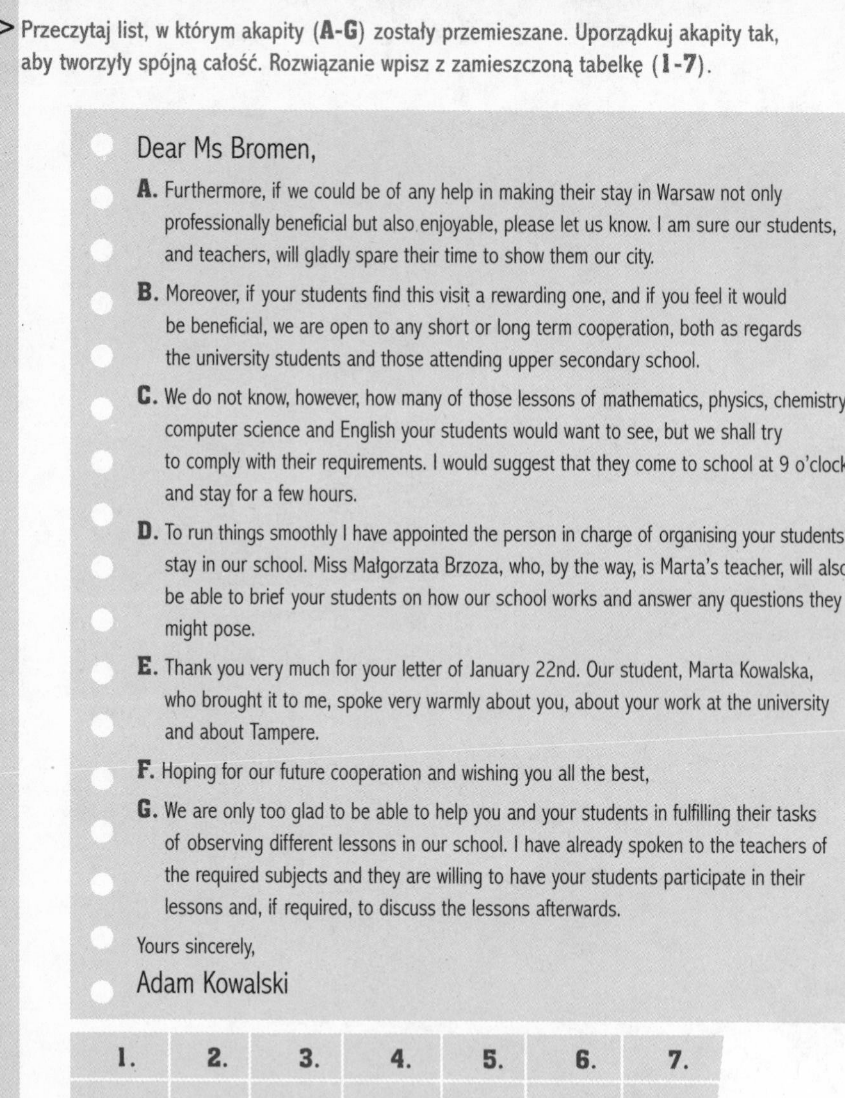

Dear Ms Bromen,

A. Furthermore, if we could be of any help in making their stay in Warsaw not only professionally beneficial but also enjoyable, please let us know. I am sure our students, and teachers, will gladly spare their time to show them our city.

B. Moreover, if your students find this visit a rewarding one, and if you feel it would be beneficial, we are open to any short or long term cooperation, both as regards the university students and those attending upper secondary school.

C. We do not know, however, how many of those lessons of mathematics, physics, chemistry, computer science and English your students would want to see, but we shall try to comply with their requirements. I would suggest that they come to school at 9 o'clock and stay for a few hours.

D. To run things smoothly I have appointed the person in charge of organising your students' stay in our school. Miss Małgorzata Brzoza, who, by the way, is Marta's teacher, will also be able to brief your students on how our school works and answer any questions they might pose.

E. Thank you very much for your letter of January 22nd. Our student, Marta Kowalska, who brought it to me, spoke very warmly about you, about your work at the university and about Tampere.

F. Hoping for our future cooperation and wishing you all the best,

G. We are only too glad to be able to help you and your students in fulfilling their tasks of observing different lessons in our school. I have already spoken to the teachers of the required subjects and they are willing to have your students participate in their lessons and, if required, to discuss the lessons afterwards.

Yours sincerely,

Adam Kowalski

1.	2.	3.	4.	5.	6.	7.

KLUCZ 1E 2G 3C 4D 5A 6B 7F

ZADANIE 2 >POZIOM PODSTAWOWY

> Przeczytaj poniższy tekst. Na podstawie informacji zawartych w tekście zdecyduj, które zdania podane w tabeli są zgodnie z treścią tekstu (**True**), a które nie (**False**). Zaznacz znakiem (**x**) odpowiednią rubrykę w tabeli.

CHOCOLATE

Chocolate has always been number one among all sweets. Everyone knows it is fattening, but it is still desirable. Nine out of ten people in Britain regularly eat chocolate, and women are those who buy the most. Some experts believe that the answer to our obsession with chocolate lies in the chemical content of chocolate, but others think that it is because of psychology.

There is no scientific evidence that chemical substances contained in chocolate make us eat it. It is the sweetness, flavour, texture and calories which make it so attractive. We have an inborn preference for sweet things, and chocolate is the most familiar and available everywhere.

There are many varieties of chocolate, including assorted chocolates, bars of different shapes and flavours but also Smarties, After Eight chocolates and Maltesers, to mention but a few. We associate chocolate with pleasure, rewards, gifts and love. We also use it for emotional comfort.

Most bars of chocolate have a cocoa solid content of about twenty percent; the other main ingredients are sugar, vegetable fat, and, in the case of milk chocolate, milk solids. Those who are fans of 'real chocolate', which is slightly bitter in taste and which can contain up to 70 per cent cocoa solids, and no milk, claim that it is a much healthier option. It is lower in fat and calories and has a specific intensive flavour which makes you less likely to get addicted to. However, most tastes are not so sophisticated and, believe it or not, in Britain the top-selling bar is currently Kit-Kat.

	True	False
1 Most people prefer eating chocolates to other sweets.		
2 We eat chocolate only because it is sweet.		
3 Everybody agrees that chemical substances in chocolate make it desirable.		
4 Men and women are equally fond of chocolate.		
5 Eating chocolate is something special.		
6 All types of chocolate contain milk.		
7 People consider bitter chocolate to be more addictive.		

>> KLUCZ 1. true 2. false 3. false 4. false 5. true 6. false 7. false

ZADANIE 3 >POZIOM PODSTAWOWY

> Przeczytaj sześć wskazówek, o czym należy pamiętać zanim przystąpi się do egzaminu. Przyporządkuj tytuły do poszczególnych akapitów. Wpisz litery (**A-G**) w odpowiednie miejsca. Jeden tytuł nigdzie nie pasuje.

SOME SUGGESTIONS BEFORE TAKING EXAMS

1______ Better leave early in case of traffic jams as you must be on time for all examinations. Latecomers will not be admitted into the examination hall.

2______ Before entering the room you will be asked to provide proof of your identity (for example: your identity card, passport, or the like). This has to be shown at every examination session.

3______ You are advised to leave all your 'lucky' things at home as you must have on your desk only the materials and equipment necessary for the papers you are taking.

4______ You must not take part in any unfair practice or break the rules in any way when taking the examination. You must not talk or disturb other candidates once the examination has started.

5______ Any candidate using or attempting to use a crib, dictionary, spell-checker, calculator, cassette recorder or mobile phone will be disqualified. Mobile phones must be switched off and placed with personal belongings in the area shown by the supervisor.

6______ There is a snack bar in the waiting lounge where you can refresh yourself before or after the exams, but remember that you must not smoke, eat or drink in the examination room.

A. Be honest and behave properly.
B. No drinks or food are allowed in examination halls.
C. Mobile phones must be left outside the room.
D. Be punctual.
E. Electronic equipment must not be used.
F. Remember about necessary documents.
G. Toys and gadgets should be left at home.

>>KLUCZ 1D 2F 3G 4A 5E 6B C – nigdzie nie pasuje

ZADANIE 4 >POZIOM PODSTAWOWY

> Przeczytaj poniższy tekst. Zdecyduj, w których akapitach (**1-5**) znajdziesz odpowiedzi na poniższe pytania (**A-F**). Jedno pytanie nie pasuje do żadnego akapitu.

TEACHING – A PROFESSION TO TALK ABOUT

1______ Education and the teaching profession are constantly in the focus of public attention. It is a profession of which we all have experience and often talk about.

2______ For many, schooldays are remembered with fear and stress, while others say they were the happiest days of their lives. What we can remember of the days spent in class include teacher's anger when we were late or skipped classes or, at the other end, school trips, praise for work well done and very good results in exams.

3______ Teachers can leave a life-long impression on pupils – the strict maths tutor with a register book on the table, or the geography teacher talking about her holidays on the Bahamas. Unfortunately, a bad time at school and low pay may put many people off taking classroom teaching as a career. The truth is, however, that most teachers are extremely happy with their jobs and can't imagine doing anything else. They ignore unfavourable remarks about long holidays, early finishing and weekends off because, for a really dedicated teacher, professional life does not end in the classroom.

4______ Many teachers say that they have tried many jobs since leaving university, but none of them is as rewarding and creative as teaching. 'As a teacher, you are paid to be yourself, to be truthful and convincing, to show by the way you behave what kind of person you are', says Catherine Roffee, a history teacher at a school near Manchester. 'You really can make a difference to people's lives.'

5______ What is difficult is the self-discipline. There are certain 'musts' like open evenings, parents' evenings, report writing, lunchtime and afternoon meetings, preparing work, marking essays and examination papers, attending post-graduate teacher training courses. The list of hidden tasks is endless. Yet the priorities are obvious – the top one is the students. If they want to talk to you, you must listen. Most importantly, you must enjoy the company of young people. As Ms Roffee says, 'the greatest thing you can give them is your time'.

A. What do we remember best from the time we were at school?
B. Are women better teachers than men?
C. Can teachers continue their education while they work?
D. Which features of character are important for a teacher's job?
E. What is one of the most popular topics of conversation?
F. Are the majority of teachers satisfied with their jobs?

KLUCZ 1-E 2-A 3-F 4-D 5-C B – nigdzie nie pasuje

ZADANIE 5 >POZIOM PODSTAWOWY

> Przeczytaj fragment artykułu. Z podanych odpowiedzi (**1**-**4**) wybierz właściwą, zgodną z treścią tekstu. Zaznacz jedną z czterech możliwości zakreślając literę **A**, **B**, **C** lub **D**.

MADAME TUSSAUD'S

Everybody who visits London knows who Madame Tussaud is – or rather was. A wax figure of the old lady is standing at the entrance to her own exhibition centre.

Born in 1760, she learnt the art of making life-size portraits in wax when she was a young girl in France. She survived the French Revolution by making wax models of its victims. In 1802 she came to England and by 1835 Madame Tussaud's was already one of the famous London sights. What was the secret of her success? Her portraits were lifelike and convincing. She paid great attention to detail, for example to the clothes her wax figures wore.

The process of creating a wax figure is very long. Over the years, hundreds of celebrities have made their way to Madame Tussaud's to be received in the studio where the sculptor makes precise measurements and photographs the subject's head from every possible angle. It requires a lot of patience and excellent artistic skills.

How do the organizers decide which people to include in the exhibition? Every year they run a popularity poll which helps them to choose. Also, they ask the visitors to the exhibition to say who their hero or heroine is. And the list of famous people who have been chosen for the display is really breathtaking. It includes famous actors and actresses, singers, astronauts, party leaders and other politicians; most loved people such as Princess Diana but also most hated ones like Hitler or Osama Bin Laden. So if you want to rub shoulders with kings and queens or the latest pop stars, Madame Tussaud's is the place to visit.

New models are being produced all the time, while others are quietly removed from the display. When they take the model away, it is not melted immediately. Instead, it is taken to a special storage room for a period of time as sometimes it is difficult to predict who may return to the political or artistic arena and therefore must be brought back to the exhibition. Actually, Madame Tussaud's is more than just an exhibition. It is also an excellent index of popularity and status of people in the public eye. Every year the exhibition is visited by some two million people who queue up to look at these portraits of the famous as well as the infamous from all walks of life.

1. Why did Madame Tussaud become so popular?
- A. Because she was rich.
- B. Because she was an artist.
- C. Because she created an exhibition centre.
- D. Because her wax figures were so natural.

2. When a person for a model has been chosen, he or she
- A. needn't come to the centre.
- B. must be measured.
- C. must be precise.
- D. must have artistic skills.

3. Who helps to decide which celebrity is going to have a wax figure made?
- A. Famous people.
- B. Madame Tussaud.
- C. Ordinary visitors.
- D. Sculptors and artists.

4. Most old models are
- A. immediately destroyed.
- B. temporarily stored.
- C. immediately melted.
- D. temporarily damaged

KLUCZ 1D 2B 3C 4B

> Przeczytaj trzy legendy (**1-3**), a następnie dopasuj do każdej dwa lub trzy spośród podanych poniżej tematów.

(1) The legend of gold fish

Once upon a time in the valley of the rising sun all people were very upset. A lot of rain had fallen and ruined their rice harvest. The people were worried that they would be hungry.
One night, a little girl called Cherry Bloom had a strange dream. Next morning, she did precisely what she heard in the dream: she wrote a letter to the king who lived far away, in a castle on the banks of the same river, telling him what had happened to the harvest. The dream told her to paint one of her pet fish gold to make it look more attractive, tie the letter to it, and place it in the river. A fisherman found the golden fish, and gave it to the king as a present. The king read the letter, and sent rice to the hungry people. Cherry Bloom was so grateful that she sent another gold-painted fish to the king; and that is how the first goldfish was born!

(2) The legend of the dragonfly

Many years ago, a magic dragon lived in a cave near a very quiet lake. He was very lonely because it was too quiet for a dragon. A fairy, who was living nearby, felt sorry for him and visited him every day. But once, when she knelt by the lake to drink some water she slipped and fell in. She didn't have her magic wand with her to save her and she didn't know how to swim. She shouted for help as loudly as she could. The dragon heard her from the other side of the lake. He had no time to run or fly and save her, so he blew with his magic hot fiery breath on to the lake, turning all the water into steam, and the fairy into a misty-winged, sparkling insect. People call this insect a dragonfly.

(3) The legend of the pine tree

Once, the fairy of the forest got very angry with the trees. They were all quarrelling which of them had the best leaves. 'Mine are the biggest', said the birch. 'Mine give the deepest shade', said the oak. They all laughed at the little pine, making fun of it and saying it wasn't a real tree at all, as it had needles instead of leaves. The forest fairy turned herself into a bird and asked each tree if she could build her nest in their branches. Each tree refused, except for the pine, which welcomed her. She climbed to the top, changed back into a fairy, and punished the other trees by making them lose all their leaves in winter.

Which legend talks about:

A. a close friendship
B. giving help
C. punishment
D. living conditions
E. a natural disaster
F. an accident
G. bad behaviour

KLUCZ 1B,D, E 2A, B, F 3B, C, G

ZADANIE 7 >POZIOM PODSTAWOWY

> Przeczytaj, list, w którym akapity (**A-I**) zostały przemieszane. Uporządkuj akapity tak, aby tworzyły spójną całość. Rozwiązanie wpisz w zamieszczoną tabelkę (**1-9**).

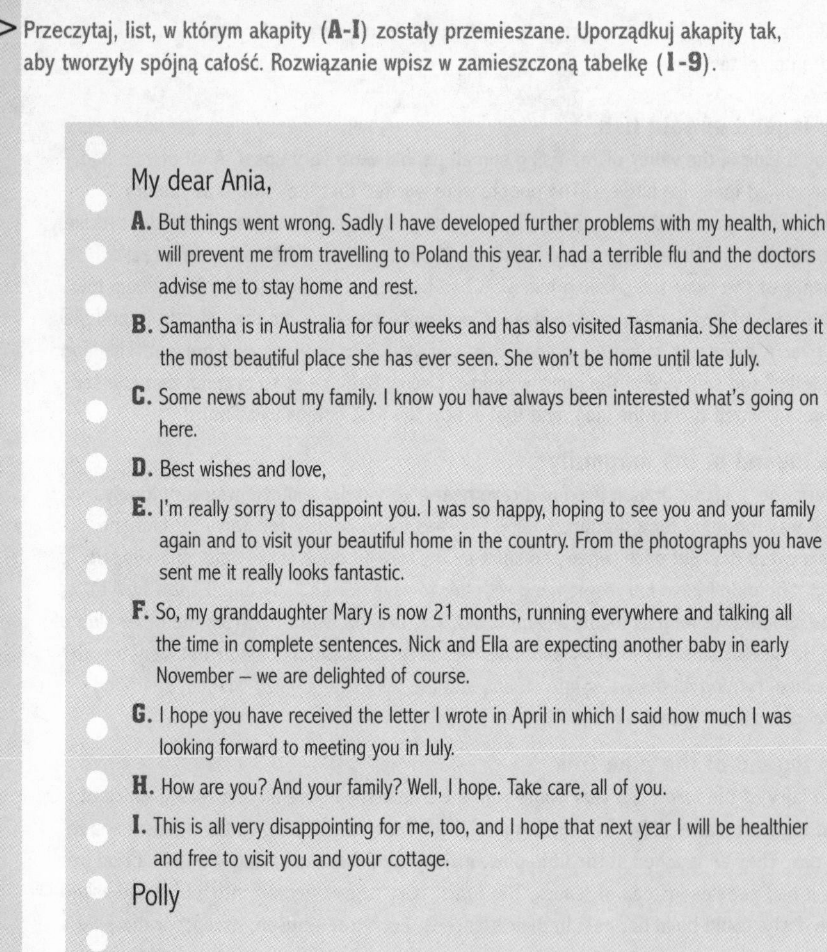

My dear Ania,

A. But things went wrong. Sadly I have developed further problems with my health, which will prevent me from travelling to Poland this year. I had a terrible flu and the doctors advise me to stay home and rest.

B. Samantha is in Australia for four weeks and has also visited Tasmania. She declares it the most beautiful place she has ever seen. She won't be home until late July.

C. Some news about my family. I know you have always been interested what's going on here.

D. Best wishes and love,

E. I'm really sorry to disappoint you. I was so happy, hoping to see you and your family again and to visit your beautiful home in the country. From the photographs you have sent me it really looks fantastic.

F. So, my granddaughter Mary is now 21 months, running everywhere and talking all the time in complete sentences. Nick and Ella are expecting another baby in early November – we are delighted of course.

G. I hope you have received the letter I wrote in April in which I said how much I was looking forward to meeting you in July.

H. How are you? And your family? Well, I hope. Take care, all of you.

I. This is all very disappointing for me, too, and I hope that next year I will be healthier and free to visit you and your cottage.

Polly

1.	2.	3.	4.	5.	6.	7.	8.	9.

KLUCZ 1 G 2A 3 E 4I 5C 6F 7B 8H 9D

> Przeczytaj poniższy tekst. Z podanych odpowiedzi wybierz właściwą, zgodną z treścią tekstu. Zaznacz jedną z czterech możliwości zakreślając literę A, B, C lub D.

PANCAKE RACE

One of the main events of Shrove Tuesday at Olney in Buckinghamshire in England is the pancake race. The Olney pancake race dates back to the Middle Ages. It was probably first run there in 1445 and has continued ever since, with occasional lapses and revivals. One such lapse occurred, for obvious reason, during the Second World War, but in 1948 the custom was restarted and has not since suffered interruption.

The competitors are housewives who must be inhabitants of Olney, or the nearby Warrington. The rules require them to wear aprons and to cover their heads with a hat or scarf. The course to be run is from the village square to the parish church, about four hundred and fifteen yards. A bell rings twice before the race, once to warn the women that it is time to make their pancakes, and again to call all of them to gather in the square with their pancakes on their frying-pans. Finally, the Pancake Bell is rung for the third time to start the race. Usually it is sounded at about eleven o'clock in the morning. Originally, the bell had nothing to do with the pancakes. It was rung to remind people of going to church to confess their sins in preparation for the holy season of Lent preceding Easter.

The pancakes have to be tossed three times during the race, and some, inevitably, land in the road. This, however, does not disqualify the runner, who is allowed to pick the pancake up and toss it again. The winner is given a prayer-book as a prize by the vicar.

Although it has been just a local custom of Olney, the news of it reached a small town of Liberal in the United States. Its inhabitants decided to run a pancake race of their own over a similar distance and challenged Olney to an international speed contest. The housewives of Olney, with hundreds of years of practice behind them, accepted the challenge with some confidence, but their rivals across the Atlantic proved speedier than expected and won the race.

1. The pancake race:
- A. has been run since 1948.
- B. has never been run since the Second Word War.
- C. started in the Middle Ages.
- D. was continued in 1445.

2. The competitors:
- A. must borrow aprons.
- B. must have their heads covered.
- C. mustn't wear aprons.
- D. must cover their hats with scarves.

3. The bell rings to:
- A. warn women against the race.
- B. announce the winner.
- C. begin the race.
- D. stop the women making pancakes.

4. A competitor:
- A. can toss her pancake once.
- B. must leave the lost pancake.
- C. can lose one pancake.
- D. must toss her pancake several times.

5. Housewives at Olney:
- A. lost the international race.
- B. did not believe they could win.
- C. had less experience than those at Liberal, USA.
- D. ran faster than their rivals.

KLUCZ 1C 2B 3C 4D 5A

ZADANIE 9 >POZIOM PODSTAWOWY

> Przeczytaj poniższy tekst. Na podstawie informacji zawartych w tekście zdecyduj, które zdania podane w tabeli są zgodnie z jego treścią (**True**), a które nie (**False**). Zaznacz znakiem (**x**) odpowiednią rubrykę w tabeli.

TOKYO – A CITY WORTH VISITING

Apart from earthquakes, which may happen any time, there is not much to fear in Tokyo. No mugging, no pickpockets – you can, and most Japanese do, walk around with all your credit cards or a lot of cash in your pocket. If you leave your wallet behind somewhere, more likely than not it will be returned to you. And you need not worry about being cheated in the shops or bars. What's more, women can walk down the darkest back streets in Tokyo. No whistling, not even a 'hello darling'. There is not even much risk of catching a cold. The white masks that people wear are not, as the legend goes, to protect them from air pollution, but to protect a passer-by from their germs.

So here you are at Narita Airport after a 17-hour flight from Europe and eight hours' jetlag from London. You may not realize that you have just come to the most civilized country in the world though at first, while you drive 66 traffic-filled kilometers that separate Narita from Tokyo, it may not look attractive with its ugly concrete blocks, factories, power lines, etc. No need to be worried, however. Tokyo, when you reach it, is not only the safest but one of the most exciting cities in the world, with lively, most modern architecture, lots of greenery and, last but not least, friendly people.

You will quickly discover that language is not the problem you were expecting. Everyone in Japan learns to read and write English at school and, at least in the main tourist areas, can manage to say a few words. If in difficulties, seek out a schoolchild or student. Most – when they recover from shock and giggles – will be delighted to have the chance to practise their English. Eating out is easy, too. You do not have to speak Japanese, you just point to the plastic food samples with the prices in the restaurant's windows. They really look like real food!

The chances of getting lost in Tokyo are rather high. After all, the streets were initially designed like a maze to cheat enemy invaders. The best way to get to know any city is to walk its streets. However, this is not recommendable in Tokyo because the distances are huge and there is really much to see. Rather than putting yourself in the hands of a taxi driver (they often refuse to understand English), it is worth mastering the complexity of the subway system. Like everything in Japan, the ticket machines work and the trains run on time.

	True	False
1. The only thing to be afraid of in Tokyo are earthquakes.		
2. People in Tokyo are honest and helpful.		
3. Tourists are well protected from air pollution.		
4. At first Tokyo seems to be an ugly place.		
5. You can easily communicate in English everywhere.		
6. Tourists should know Japanese to buy meals at restaurants.		
7. For tourists Tokyo underground is the best means of transport.		

KLUCZ 1. true 2. true 3. false 4. true 5. false 6. false 7. true.

> Przeczytaj poniższy tekst, z którego usunięto 4 zdania. Wpisz w każde z miejsc (**1-4**) literę (**A-E**), którą oznaczone jest brakujące zdanie. Jedno z podanych zdań nie pasuje do tekstu.

MARIANNE O'BRIAN: A PASSIONATE ENVIRONMENTALIST

Route to the present job.

Marianne O'Brian is an environmental investigator at the Environmental Investigation Agency (EIA) in Dublin. She studied modern languages at Oxford Trinity College and speaks Russian, Spanish and French. After graduating she moved to Ireland to work as a translator for Greenpeace for a year. Later, she became an assistant to the director of Greenpeace in Spain for eighteen months. (1) ____________. She left Greenpeace to work as a producer and reporter for a TV news company for two years and then joined EIA to work on a project to discover what was happening to the seals population off Siberia.

Marianne's day.

'An investigation takes three or four weeks', she says. 'I went with a cameraman, a photographer and a guide to a remote part of the Siberian coast to document animal abuse, particularly the use of sea mammals for food at industrial fox farms'. (2) ____________ They often had to wake up at 4 o'clock in the morning to go out with the Eskimo hunters in boats and observe how they hunted and what happened to the meat after the animal was killed. 'On an investigation, my job is to gather and evaluate information which involves finding the right people to talk to and deciding how much I can rely on what they told me', she adds. Before going to Siberia Marianne contacted people who had been to the area and asked what they had seen. (3) ____________ 'Once there we travelled around, trying to persuade villagers and people working on the fox farms to talk to us. We often used hidden cameras. We often had no running water and I got very cold. We usually went to bed at 10 pm.'

Future plans.

Now Marianne is working on a series of seven television films based on her investigations. (4) ____________ She also writes articles on the area she visited and on the plan to turn it to an international park. The idea is to promote the EIA which has been very effective for ten years and is supported by some 7,000 members.

A. She also read a lot on the subject.
B. One is about her project in Siberia, and she's worked on the script and voice-overs.
C. The cramped conditions prevented her from writing her report every day.
D. The team took tents and lived on fish, dried food and bread from local villages.
E. She then moved on to Greenpeace International and investigated dumping nuclear waste in Russia for three years.

KLUCZ 1E 2D 3A 4B C – nigdzie nie pasuje

ZADANIE 11 >POZIOM PODSTAWOWY

> Przeczytaj poniższy tekst. W pierwszej części zadania przyporządkuj poszczególnym jego częściom tytuły oznaczone **A-E**. Jeden z tytułów został podany dodatkowo i nie pasuje do żadnej części. W drugiej części zadania z podanych czterech możliwości wybierz właściwą.

UNIVERSITY OF CAMBRIDGE

A_____ Most colleges at the University provide a room in the college for their students for at least two of the three years which is the normal length of the undergraduate course. Rooms in college can be luxurious 'sets' in ancient college buildings or small modern bedsitters.

B_____ Students can eat in the dining-hall and use the college bar and common room. Professors usually have comfortable chairs, whereas undergraduates have to sit on benches. Dinners in the newer colleges are more informal and democratic.

C_____ Daily timetables of undergraduate students depend very much on their subjects. Those studying natural or medical sciences and engineering have their mornings occupied with lectures and practical laboratory work. In contrast, students in most arts subjects can arrange their time more or less as they please.

D_____ Two weeks after the end of examinations is Cambridge's social season. Races are rowed on the river. This is also the time of traditional balls, the expensive and formal college dances which last all night. Large numbers of plays and concerts are staged, many in the open air, and there are parties all day long.

E_____ Degrees are given in ceremonies known as 'congregations'. All undergraduates receiving degrees have to wear formal academic dress with a hood trimmed with white rabbit fur to signify their BA status. Three years later, at another ceremony, they can become MAs, entitled to wear a hood trimmed in white silk.

Część 1.

1. Organization of studies.
2. Formal clothes.
3. Examination terms.
4. Events at the end of an academic year.
5. Accommodation.
6. Meals.

Część 2.

1. The text:
   A. shows good and bad sides of life at Cambridge University.
   B. explains how to get to Cambridge University.
   C. gives information for future students.
   D. describes the campus.

2. The text is part of:
   A. a newspaper article.
   B. a leaflet.
   C. an advertisement.
   D. a notice.

KLUCZ **Część I** A5 B6 C1 D4 E2 punkt 3 nigdzie nie pasuje **Część II** 1C 2B

> Przeczytaj nformacje turystyczne o Parku Narodowym Yosemite. Zdecyduj, które akapity (**A-F**) zawierają informacje, których poszukujesz (**1-9**). Akapity mogą zawierać więcej niż jedną z wymaganych informacji.

YOSEMITE NATIONAL PARK

A Anthropologists believe that Indian people occupied Yosemite Valley 4,000 years before the Spaniards colonized California in the late 18th century. Tales about the Valley and its waterfalls led to the first tourist party in 1855 and the first publicity. Since then the number of visitors quickly rose.

B Yosemite National Park is dedicated to the preservation of wildlife and the ecological system that supports it. There are 1,500 different species of plants in the Valley, from a mysterious -looking fungus to giant sequoias. Currently, Yosemite Valley is a home to approximately 75 mammal species. The most likely to be seen by visitors are the mule deer, black bears, coyotes, squirrels and chipmunks. All the animals within the park can be dangerous.

C Various tours of the Valley are offered throughout the year, including moonlight tours that run late May through September. Enjoy a walk or lecture with a park ranger. The Happy Isles Centre offers ranger program, Indian cultural exhibits and kid's activities corner. Many programs, facilities and trails are accessible for wheelchairs, with assistance.

D Each year, over 4 million people visit Yosemite National Park. Please help the National Park Service in their efforts to make the Park also available to future generations. Please remain on the trails and do not remove or damage any part of the natural and historic features in the Valley. Also, place litter and recyclables in the appropriate bins. Dogs are allowed only on trails of the Yosemite Valley floor and must be on a leash at all times.

E Free shuttle buses operate every day of the year. Because traffic can become heavy, we encourage our visitors to park their cars and ride the free shuttle service. Motor vehicles are not allowed on trails under any circumstances. Bicycles are allowed only on the roads and paved bicycle paths. However, if you are a horse lover at heart, two-hour guided trips are given to various park locations. Reservations can be made at the stables or at the tour desks.

F Each year many people hurt themselves here. To avoid injury – be sensible, think before you take a plunge in a stream and never swim upstream of a waterfall. Never feed the animals. If a bear appears on a trail, keep a safe distance from it. Do not come close or feed the bears. Store the food so that it cannot be seen or smelt by them.

In which paragraph can you find information about:

1. attractions for children?
2. rules of behavior on the trails?
3. the history of the park?
4. different wild animals in the park?
5. safety measures?
6. facilities for the disabled?
7. moving around the Valley?
8. organized visits?
9. rules for pets?

>> KLUCZ 1C 2D 3A 4B 5F 6C 7E 8C 9D

ZADANIE 13 >POZIOM PODSTAWOWY

> Przeczytaj poniższy tekst. Na podstawie informacji zawartych w tekście zdecyduj, które zdania podane poniżej (**1-10**) **NIE** są zgodne z treścią tekstu.

ALIENS ON THE EARTH?

According to many stories, alien creatures have visited the Earth for thousands of years. We try to find traces of their presence on Earth in ancient Greek and Roman tales which say that the Earth was visited by gods from heaven who possessed exceptional powers. Scientists, however, have proved that these stories were myths rather than facts. Nevertheless, people have reported and are still reporting seeing unidentified flying objects and strange non-human creatures who visit the Earth.

Lots of books have been written and films made on UFOs, to mention just 'ET' or '2001: A Space Odyssey'. Yet there is little evidence of seeing a UFO except for the testimonies of the witnesses, and they can hardly prove that what they have seen is true. However, a few stories are more convincing. One such event happened on July 5, 1947, near Roswell in the USA.

That day Dr R. C. Holden, a professor at Texas Tech University, and some of his students were doing archaeological research and found a crash site. They reported to local authorities that they had discovered remains of a strange looking aircraft and several bodies of alien creatures. Immediately, some soldiers from the Roswell Army Field arrived at the site and cordoned off the area. Dr Holden and his students were questioned at the base and given orders not to talk to anybody about their finding because it could be a threat to national security. Military eyewitnesses claim that the craft was about seven meters in diameter and torn at the front, so some of the interior could be seen. They also described several dead bodies which were smaller than humans, had very large heads, long thin arms and eyes much larger than human eyes.

The bodies were put in bags and taken to the military base. Later, they were sent to Washington, while the aircraft was transported to another military base in Ohio where it was supposed to be studied. To date, there is no reliable report on the investigation.

Which of these facts are NOT true?

1. Aliens have always been present in myths and tales.
2. People continue to report seeing creatures from outer space.
3. There is a lot of evidence of aliens' visits on the Earth.
4. Most stories on UFO are convincing.
5. Dr Holden was doing research on UFOs.
6. The area of the crash was blocked from the public.
7. Dr Holden and his students were commanded not to talk about the event.
8. The aliens' aircraft was not damaged.
9. The bodies of aliens were examined by Dr Holden.
10. The results of the examination have been presented to the general public.

KLUCZ 3 4 5 8 9 10

> Przeczytaj list Toma i Sandy do przyjaciół. Zdecyduj, które ze zdań umieszczonych poniżej (**1-9**) zawierają informacje niezgodne z tekstem.

Hi there everyone!

Time for our annual letter to keep you informed on what has been a busy year. We are still in a state of chaos from the big move. The house is not yet finished and there is always lots of work to do in the garden. However, slowly but surely we are getting there.

The year began with a new job for Sandy, though still with the National Trust. She was tired of working in an office so she has become Custodian of the Old Post Office at Tintagel. Steep learning curve, hard graft getting ready for the start of the season, busy with 40,000 visitors in seven months, and plenty to do after the season! We are all very glad here she made the change.

The year was further complicated by my resumption of geological activities. I got a job in Botswana, two months at first and then a further six weeks, after a month off in July at home. With Sandy working and myself in Botswana all the jobs on the house and garden were put on hold. By the end of the autumn we were in need of a holiday, so as soon as we could find a gap in Sandy's busy schedule we took off for the US. It was the first time for both of us, and very impressive, too. We started off by spending a few days with our old friends Keith and Paula in Washington DC. We then flew to Phoenix, hired a car and toured Arizona, dropping in on cousin Nancy for a quick visit over Thanksgiving. We toured a bit of the state and saw some superb scenery: Apache Lake, Superstition Mountains, Sunset Crater, Grand Canyon and Rainbow Bridge. Sandy shot 13 rolls of film to prove how impressive our tour was! All very stunning, and in the case of Grand Canyon – staggering! Accommodation at the bottom is generally booked for months in advance, so when I enquired I was surprised to discover that they had a vacancy. So we just had to do it! It's a long haul: 10 miles down on a rough track with the inevitable 10 miles back – uphill all the way.

The weather throughout our holiday was superb; mostly warm, sometimes hot and always sunny except for the morning of our Grand Canyon descent. Temperatures reached 20 degrees, and when we arrived at Heathrow it was only 1 degree! But within a day or so UK warmed up to very comfortable temperature and US was all in snow – even Arizona had snow! We had timed our trip to perfection!

Love to You All

Tom and Sandy

Which sentences are NOT true?

1. Tom and Sandy moved to a new house.
2. Sandy's new job is very challenging.
3. Tom works mostly in Britain.
4. They went to the USA when Sandy could get a holiday.
5. While in the US they mostly visited their cousins.
6. Sandy is not keen on taking photographs.
7. It's not so easy to get accommodation at the bottom of the Grand Canyon.
9. They are very enthusiastic about their trip to the US.

>> KLUCZ Zdania 3, 5 i 6 zawierają nieprawdziwe informacje.

ZADANIE 2 >POZIOM ROZSZERZONY

> Przeczytaj dziewięć porad psychologa, jak być zadowolonym z wykonywanej pracy. Przyporządkuj tytuły do poszczególnych akapitów. Wpisz litery (**A-L**) w odpowiednie miejsca. Dwa tytuły nigdzie nie pasują.

DR MARY BRIDGES ADVISES...

1_____ Try and see the humorous side of office events and share it with others. It has been long stated that work is most effective if employees are happy and light-hearted.

2_____ Take responsibility for your own personal development and ask to attend appropriate internal or external training courses.

3_____ This is often misunderstood for being aggressive. But in fact this is all about respect. It involves stating what you want from people and opens lines of communication to let other people express their own needs and opinions.

4_____ Try to involve yourself in tasks that may cause you initial anxiety. You'll be surprised at your ability to cope with them and develop your skills.

5_____ Ensure that you're on top of your work, not the other way round. Start cleaning up your desk. It's amazing how efficient you feel when your desk doesn't look like it's doing about ten things at once, even though you are.

6_____ Work on your strengths and be more comfortable with who you are. Identify your achievements and don't be embarrassed about letting colleagues and your boss know you've managed a project or task successfully.

7_____ Don't commit tasks to memory, write them down and strike them out when accomplished. Set tasks every morning to give you a clear picture of what you have to achieve during the day and which tasks are the most pressing.

8_____ Try feng shui. Plenty of fresh flowers, daylight and less clutter will help you organize your thoughts. Also playing music to suit your mood is proven to make you more productive.

9_____ Don't be limited by your routine. Take an alternative route to work or go somewhere different at lunchtime. Accept organizational changes with enthusiasm – it's best to view changes as opportunities rather than as threats.

A. Do the things you least enjoy first.
B. Make fun a priority.
C. Variety is the spice of life.
D. Seek regular appraisals.
E. Face your fears.
F. Create calming environment.
G. Be assertive.
H. Make lists.
I. Stay focused and set goals.
J. Manage your time effectively.
K. Know yourself.
L. Improve your skills.

KLUCZ 1B 2L 3G 4E 5J 6K 7H 8F 9C (A i D – nigdzie nie pasują)

ZADANIE 3 >POZIOM ROZSZERZONY

> Przeczytaj poniższy tekst. Na podstawie informacji zawartych w tekście zdecyduj, które zdania podane w tabeli są zgodnie z treścią tekstu (**True**), a które nie (**False**). Zaznacz znakiem (**x**) odpowiednią rubrykę w tabeli.

Bristol – The South & West Exhibition Centre

Participation in international trade fairs is an efficient way for producers to showcase their products to export markets. The advantages include audience concentration, face-to-face communication and the opportunity to meet and get to know new business partners. Compared with other methods of selling and promotion, advertising through direct mail, sales literature, the general press and specialist journals or television commercials, trade fair participation offers a far less expensive but equally effective and targeted platform.

Six reasons why your firm absolutely needs to attend trade fairs at the S&WEC:

> **Information:** the opportunity to present key issues and obtain in-depth knowledge of current and future developments,
> **Contacts:** make new business contacts and strengthen existing ones,
> **Decision-makers:** meet leading companies and their spokespeople,
> **Short distances:** one of the most modern exhibition centres in the world enables you to include any number of appointments into a short space of time,
> **Special events:** the opportunity to offer and/or attend special presentations, discussions and forums in any of our conference rooms,
> **Facilities:** 5 spacious and air-conditioned exhibition halls, 20 separate conference rooms of variable size, 5 restaurants, 3 cafeterias, 6 snackbars. The centre is also within easy reach of the city, main railway station and airport. All in all, the ideal venue to make participation enjoyable and successful.

Contact our service manager.
All further information is available on our website with its download service
www.exhib.sandwec-bris.htm

(based on 'Reading Business' Langenscheidt)

	True	False
1. International trade fairs can give you better knowledge of your prospective partner.		
2. Advertising campaigns in the media are less recommendable because of costs.		
3. Attending trade fairs require a thorough knowledge of your business partners.		
4. Short distances between stands and conference rooms facilitate professional contacts.		
5. S&WEC center is most suitable because it is far from the noise of the city centre.		
6. You can get more information on the Centre from the Internet.		

>>KLUCZ 1. true 2. true 3. false 4. true 5. false 6. true

ZADANIE 4 >POZIOM ROZSZERZONY

> Przeczytaj poniższy tekst. Z podanych odpowiedzi wybierz właściwą, aby otrzymać logiczny i gramatycznie poprawny tekst. Zaznacz, zakreślając kółkiem, jedną z czterech możliwości.

ONCE A BUSY DOCK...

In the early nineteenth century, St. Katharine Dock was a hive of industry – sailing ships returning from all corners of the world and stevedores unloading valuable cargoes of ivory, marble, wool, rubber, wine and tea (1)________ storage in the waterside warehouses. With the advent of larger ships and the development of more appropriate docks down the river, St. Katharine Dock became (2)________ important as a trading post.

Today, many of the original buildings have been imaginatively (3)________, creating a world of fascination embracing history, beauty, pageantry and entertainment – a breathtaking sight for the visitors and an idyllic marina for the yachtsmen.

This brochure gives you a summary of all the (4)________ attractions of the area, which you may wish to see or visit at your (5)________ on different occasions. But to encapsulate it all into an exciting and complete day out, we would suggest you arrive by bus or tube, stroll (6)________ St. Katharine's Way past the World Trade Centre and start the day by enjoying a relaxing breakfast at the strikingly modern Tower Thistle Hotel overlooking the yacht marina. Right by the Hotel is Tower Bridge, one of London's most (7)________ landmarks. Wander through the exhibition illustrating building of the bridge and view some of the few remaining examples of Victorian hydraulics. Along Riverside is the HMS Belfast – the largest cruiser (8)________ built for the Royal Navy – now a floating Naval Museum with seven decks to explore and special exhibitions to see. Then make (9)________ the Tower Pier and choose one of the most relaxed ways of seeing London's most important monuments – from the deck of the Thames pleasure (10)________ which can take you up stream to Westminster or down stream past the colourful riverside pubs to the architectural glories of Greenwich. After lunch wander along fascinating boutiques and shops which make window (11)________ and gift hunting a real pleasure. To complete your daytime sightseeing spend some time in the living history of All Hallows Church and visit the Brass Rubbing Centre. Make your visit to St. Katharine Dock a (12)________ memorable one.

1.	on	for	from	in
2.	so	more	most	less
3.	reinforced	refurnished	renovated	redecorated
4.	main	few	huge	some
5.	free	spare	leisure	holiday
6.	below	down	off	behind
7.	unknown	pretty	seen	famous
8.	never	ever	always	once
9.	down	up	out	for
10.	yachts	buses	boats	vehicles
11.	visiting	buying	shopping	staring
12.	quiet	most	real	really

>> KLUCZ 1. for 2. less 3. renovated 4. main 5. leisure 6. down 7. famous 8. ever 9. for 10. boats 11. shopping 12. really

> Przeczytaj informacje dotyczące egzaminów. Usunięto z nich siedem istotnych informacji (**A-G**). Dopasuj te informacje do pięciu tytułów. Do niektórych można dopasować więcej niż jedną informację.

UNIVERSITY OF CAMBRIDGE *Local Examinations Syndicate*
INFORMATION

1. Make sure you attend on time.
> Know the date, time and place of your examinations.
> Arrive at least 15 minutes before the start of each examination.
> If you arrive late for any of the papers, report to the Supervisor or Invigilator.

2. Provide what you need.
> Take into the examination room the pens, pencils and rubbers which you need for the examination.
> Correction fluid must not be used on computer answer sheets.
> Leave anything which you do not need or which is not allowed either outside the examination room or as instructed by the Supervisor.

3. Examination instructions.
> Listen to the Supervisor and do what you are asked to do.
> Read carefully and follow the instructions printed on the question paper and on the answer sheet.

4. Advice and assistance.
> If during the examination you are in doubt what you should do, raise your hand to attract attention. The Invigilator will come to your assistance.
> If on the day of the examination you feel that your work may be affected by ill health or any other reason, tell the Supervisor or Invigilator.

5. Leaving the examination room.
> You may not leave the examination room without the permission of the Invigilator.
> You must not leave the room within ten minutes of the end of an examination.
> When you leave the examination room you must leave behind the question paper, your answer paper, any other paper used for rough work clearly crossed through and any other materials provided for the examination.

(This material is taken from the Cambridge ESOL 'Notice to Candidates', 2003; it is not the full text of the Notice and may not be the most recent version © UCLES, 2003)

A. If you have used loose sheets of paper for answers, you must place them in the correct order and fasten them together before you leave.
B. If you miss any of the papers without good reason, you will not normally be given a grade.
C. You may not borrow anything from another candidate during the examination.
D. Tell the Supervisor or Invigilator at once if you think you have not been given the right question paper or if the question paper is incomplete or badly printed.
E. You must not ask for, and will not be given, any explanation of the questions.
F. Do not make a noise near the examination room.
G. Fill in any details required on the front of your question paper and on your answer sheet before the start of the examination.

>> KLUCZ 1B 2C 3D, G 4E 5A, F

ZADANIE 6 >POZIOM ROZSZERZONY

> Przeczytaj poniższy tekst. Na podstawie informacji zawartych w tekście zdecyduj, które zdania podane w tabeli są zgodnie z treścią tekstu (**True**), a które nie (**False**). Zaznacz znakiem (**x**) odpowiednią rubrykę w tabeli.

WATER SUPPLY PROBLEMS ON THE ISLAND OF MILOS

The population of the beautiful island of Milos is approximately 7,000. During the holiday period in the summer this number increases to over 700,000. As a result of the tourist boom the island is suffering from an acute water shortage. The groundwater level has receded significantly and sea water has now begun to pollute it. To provide drinking water for the island it has become necessary to transport to Milos over 300,000 tons of mineral water in bottles and 240,000 tons of water in tankers every year. The cost of doing this is gradually becoming so high that it started to prevent people from buying adequate amounts of water. The tourist industry has resulted in environmental damage and the pursuit of pleasure has brought pain to the land.

But all is not yet lost. There is a project which promises not only to help the island but to create an example of positive thinking and proper approach to environmental problems with the aid of new, environmentally-friendly technology. In cooperation with the Greek government and aided by European Community funds, the German insurance group Gerling has launched a partly private, partly public project to help solve the problem of the shrinking supply of drinking water on the island. They plan to run a special desalination plant to produce drinking water from the sea. It will be the first project of its kind, and it has won support from the European Union thanks to its innovative nature. The result will be not only a plentiful water supply for the island, but also the possibility of providing irrigation for local agriculture, which will result in better crops.

In time the groundwater level will recover and the situation hopefully come back to normal.

(adapted from 'Reading Business', Langenscheidt)

	True	False
1. The number of people on the island increases during summer time.		
2. There is not enough fresh water to drink.		
3. Milos doesn't need to buy water somewhere else.		
4. The large number of tourists has caused damage to the environment.		
5. The Greek government alone will solve the problem.		
6. European Community backs the desalination project.		
7. The project will also help local farmers in their work.		
8. The situation is bound to be even more difficult in future.		

>> **KLUCZ** 1. true 2. true 3. false 4. true 5. false 6. true 7. true 8. false

> Przeczytaj poniższą informację. Z podanych odpowiedzi wybierz właściwą, aby otrzymać logiczny i gramatycznie poprawny tekst. Zaznacz, zakreślając kółkiem, jedną z czterech możliwości.

MIDSUMMER DAY

Midsummer's Day, June 24, and the longest day of the year, June 21, have been celebrated (1)______________ the earliest times. In many countries of Europe bonfires are lit at dusk. When the fires have subsided, people dance around and leap across them to encourage the sun to move (2)______________ the heavens and ripen the crops. To ward off disease and witchcraft, the ashes are kept as lucky charms.

In England, Stonehenge in Wiltshire is (3)______________ its midsummer associations. This monument, which is made of a circle of stones, dates back at least 5000 years.

It is thought to have been an important religious centre for Neolithic and Bronze Age people. Its design is spectacular. The major axis of the circle is carefully aligned with the midwinter and midsummer sun. Historians believe that ancient tribes (4)______________ the place to record the advent of the summer solstice, and that later civilisations used it to predict the timing of sunrise, moonrise and the eclipses. When archaeologists dug into the outer circular bank surrounding the stones, they discovered cremated human bones buried in holes. Stonehenge remains a place of pilgrimage today. (5)______________ the past 80 years or so, modern Druids have celebrated the midsummer sunrise there.

Since the 1970s, endless convoys of travellers have gravitated to the site. They made the news for trying to hold a midsummer festival there. This went (6)______________ the wishes of English Heritage Trust – a conservation body – which fears that such large crowds could damage the monument. The conflict has not been resolved entirely.

1. for	than	since	before
2. beyond	by	down	across
3. known as	famous for	famous about	known because
4. applied	treated	used	made
5. For	During	By	Over
6. along	with	against	across

≫KLUCZ 1. since 2. across 3. famous for 4. used 5. For 6. against

ZADANIE 8 >POZIOM ROZSZERZONY

> Przeczytaj fragment ulotki informacyjnej o kursach edukacyjnych w Londynie. Dopasuj kursy wymienione w punktach **1-9** do miejsc oznaczonych literami **A-H**, wstawiając odpowiednią literę obok numeru pytania. Jedna litera nie pasuje do zadania, a niektóre mogą być użyte więcej niż jeden raz.

LONDON EVENING CLASSES

There's a lot you can learn in London, and the capital's after-hours' curriculum cannot fail to entice even the most reluctant students. For proof, flick through Floodlight, the evening-class bible, which lists every subject on offer.

The London Tarot Centre offers tarot training, psychic training and astrological training with a galaxy of ethereal evening classes to choose from. Fees are set at £350 per course.

For a vocational qualification in massage, reflexology or aromatherapy, try The South London School of Massage in Acton Town, with fees of around £400 for a six-month course starting in the summer. Whitton Adult College also offers courses in hypnotherapy, homeopathy, reflexology and aromatherapy to look after your body and treat it in a non-conventional way.

For wannabe chefs, the choice of evening classes offering expert tuition in mouth-watering vegetarian, Indian, Chinese and Afro-Caribbean cookery classes are on offer at Chelsa Adult Education College, as are courses in baking, cake decorating and entertaining. For the dinner party perfectionists, the world famous Lisen's School of Food and Wine at Park Grove holds evening classes and holiday courses for interested amateurs and enthusiastic hobby chefs with fees from £15 to 200 for short courses.

London university colleges offer many options for studying by post – providing all the benefits of university teaching expertise without requiring you to commit yourself to graduation. Evening classes on offer include a global selection of languages and thus The Royal College of London offers evening sessions in French, German, Spanish, Italian, Portuguese, Russian, Greek, Mandarin, Japanese and Arabic up to seven levels. Courses start in May, October and January, last a minimum of ten weeks and cost between £110 to £450. Your local adult education colleges will probably also offer everything from beginners' Czech to business Mandarin. For more creative expression, why not use your evenings to develop latent talents? London offers a full programme of artistic courses. Just browse Floodlight.

Where can you:

1. improve your knowledge of exotic cuisine
2. study not necessarily to get a degree
3. study at different levels
4. learn to foretell the future
5. be taught alternative medical treatment
6. stay at home, but learn nevertheless
7. find advertisements of classes you are looking for
8. train to be a non-professional cook
9. learn how to make people enjoy themselves

A London university colleges
B Floodlight
C The Royal College of London
D Whitton Adult Centre
E School of Massage and Reflexology
F Tarot Centre
G Lisen's School of Food and Wine
H Chelsa Adult Education College

KLUCZ 1 – H, 2 –A, 3 – C, 4 – F, 5 – D, 6 – A, 7 – B, 8 – G, 9 – H, litera E nigdzie nie pasuje

ZADANIE 9 >POZIOM ROZSZERZONY

> **Część 1.** Przeczytaj poniższy dialog. Uzupełnij pozostawione w nim luki (**1-17**), przekształcając czasowniki w nawiasach, tak aby otrzymać logiczny i gramatycznie poprawny tekst. Wymagana jest pełna poprawność ortograficzna wpisywanych form czasownikowych.

A: Can I speak to Mr. Jerry?

B: I'm sorry, but Mr. Jerry (1)__________ (just go) out, and he (2)__________ (not be) back until tomorrow.

A: Excuse me, but I'd like to ask you a question, if you don't mind. I have never seen Mr. Jerry but as I (3)__________ (come) up the stairs, I (4)__________ (meet) an elderly gentleman who (5)__________ (just leave) the office.

B: Yes, that (6)__________ (must, be) him. If you (7)__________ (come) earlier, you (8)__________ (be able) to speak to him.

A: I wish (9)__________ (come) earlier, but unfortunately I (10)__________ (not know) he (11)__________ (leave) the office before three o'clock.

B: Yes, he (12)__________ (must, go) to a conference today. If you wish to see him soon, please give me your telephone number and I (13) __________ (phone) you as soon as Mr. Jerry (14)__________ (come) in tomorrow morning.

A: Well, this is rather difficult. You see, I don't know if I (15)__________ (be) in my office tomorrow. But if Mr. Jerry (16)__________ (be) here on Thursday, I (17)__________ (try) to contact him.

> **Część 2.** Przeczytaj uważnie poniższe zdania. Z podanych odpowiedzi (**1-7**) wybierz właściwą, tak aby otrzymać logiczne i gramatycznie poprawne zdanie. Zaznacz jedną z czterech możliwości, zakreślając literę **a**, **b**, **c** lub **d**.

1. I __________ leave my coat in the cloakroom.
   a) prefer b) would better c) would rather d) like more to
2. My brother has not been given promotion, __________ is a pity.
   a) that b) which c) what d) who
3. I'm going to the optician to __________.
   a) test my eyes b) test me my eyes c) have my eyes tested d) have tested my eyes
4. She bought two crystal __________.
   a) glasses of wine b) wine glasses c) glasses for wine d) glass wines
5. __________ her blindness, she was able to recognize his face.
   a) In spite b) Despite c) Although d) Even though
6. Give him your telephone number __________ he gets lost.
   a) whether b) perhaps c) unless d) in case
7. The teachers at the school __________ with flu one after another.
   a) went down b) went off c) went out d) went under

KLUCZ **Część I** 1. has just gone, 2. will not be, 3. was coming, 4. met, 5. was just leaving, 6. must have been, 7. had come, 8. would have been able, 9. had come, 10. didn't know, 11. would leave, 12. had to go, 13. will telephone, 14. comes, 15. will be, 16. is, 17. will try **Część 2** 1c, 2b, 3c, 4b, 5b, 6d, 7a

ZADANIE 10 >POZIOM ROZSZERZONY

> **Część 1.** Uzupełnij poniższy tekst, wpisując po jednym wyrazie w każde wolne miejsce, tak aby otrzymać logiczny i gramatycznie poprawny tekst. Wymagana jest pełna poprawność ortograficzna wpisywanych wyrazów.

THE DAY I WILL NEVER FORGET

I will (1)________________ forget that night. It was my 7th birthday and I do not (2)________________ to tell you what it meant to me. I had been waiting for that day (3)________________ a long time, like every small child who is used (4)________________ waiting for his own birthday.

Finally came the moment I (5)________________ expected so much. The official ceremony seemed to be over, which did not (6)________________ me unhappy anyway. It was half past nine when I noticed my father taking out a huge packet with a pink ribbon (7)________________ top.

You will never guess what was inside. An enormous glass elephant I had been dreaming about (8)________________ ages. It looked as it was alive. I had never thought I could get something (9)________________ brilliant.

Suddenly I heard a terrible noise. In the very same moment all lights in the house went (10)________________. I was so scared that I dropped my new toy which broke (11)________________ pieces. I could not help crying. There was (12)________________ point trying to make me feel happy. I was screaming so loudly I woke up the neighbours sleeping in (13)________________ nearest house. Nothing could replace my elephant, (14)________________ the illustrated book about the wild nature in Africa I got with the animal. (15)________________ my mum promised to buy me a similar elephant as soon as possible I was not satisfied anyway. I did not stop weeping, (16)________________.

What else can I say? I did not sleep that night. My birthday turned (17)________________ hell because of one stupid energy breakdown. Not only (18)________________ I lose my present, I also became ill. At no time was I so unhappy. And it (19) ________________ to be the happiest day in my life! What (20)________________ irony.

> **Część 2.** Wykorzystując wyrazy podane drukowanymi literami, uzupełnij każde z niedokończonych zdań tak, aby zachować znaczenie zdania wyjściowego. Nie zmieniaj podanych fragmentów i formy podanych wyrazów. Wymagana jest pełna poprawność ortograficzna wpisywanych fragmentów.

1. They managed to solve that difficult problem.
   SUCCEEDED
   They ________________________________ that difficult problem.
2. May I come in?
   MIND
   Do ________________________________ come in?
3. Sally may phone so I'd better stay at home tonight.
   CASE
   I'll stay at home ________________________________.

4. It's a pity I don't remember answering his letter.
WISH
I ______________________________ his letter.

5. You're too young to decide about it yourself.
ENOUGH
You're ______________________________ to decide about it yourself.

6. I would advise her to tell the truth.
RATHER
I ______________________________ the truth.

7. Even though they dislike her, they agreed to help her.
DESPITE
______________________________ they agreed to help her.

8. Perhaps Betty went to Brussels.
MIGHT
Betty ______________________________ to Brussels.

9. I've never seen such a breathtaking scenery.
MOST
This ______________________________ seen.

10. They say people here believe in rain gods.
ARE
People here ______________________________ in rain gods.

>> KLUCZ **Część 1** 1. never 2. have 3. for 4. to 5. had 6. make 7. on 8. for 9. so 10. out 11. into 12. no 13. the 14. even 15. Although 16. either 17. into 18. did 19. was 20. an
Część 2 1. They succeeded in solving that difficult problem. 2. Do you mind if I come in? 3. I'll stay at home in case Sally phones. 4. I wish I remembered answering his letter. 5. You are not old enough to decide about it yourself. 6. I'd rather she told the truth. 7. Despite their dislike for her, they agreed to help her. (Despite the fact that they dislike her.........) 8. Betty might have gone to Brussels. 9. This is the most breathtaking scenery I have ever seen. 10. People here are said to believe in rain gods.

ZADANIE 11 >POZIOM ROZSZERZONY

> Przeczytaj poniższy tekst. Uzupełnij pozostawione w nim luki (**1-10**), przekształcając wyrazy podane w nawiasach tak, aby otrzymać logiczny i gramatycznie poprawny tekst.

GLOBALISATION

As the world gets smaller and the population larger, the rich get richer and the poor get poorer. True? If it is, then multinational companies are to blame for hindering the governments of the world in their task of protecting the environment, relieving (1)_______________ **(poor)** and improving the health of the population. Big business is seen as the devil in disguise pushing democracy aside in pursuit of bigger and bigger profits on an international scale with no (2)_______________ **(responsible)** to any government or custodial body. However, on closer analysis, there are several factors which may expose this line of thought as naive and mistaken. First of all, multinational companies are far more open to (3)_______________ **(criticize)** than small business enterprises, simply because they are so large and (4)_____________ **(power)**. They take up a larger space in the public eye. Secondly, to condemn big business would be to condemn capitalism as a whole and to ignore the benefits it has brought since its development at the beginning of the 18th century. (5)_______________ **(Live)** standards and general well--being have improved beyond recognition as a result. Thirdly, it seems that their actual power is overestimated. Latest studies (6)_______________ **(conclusion)** that most multinational companies do not in fact have a global strategy and that only a very few such as Nestle and Unilever can really call themselves globally (7)_______________ **(significance)**. Besides, over 15% of multinationals are losing money and are having to redefine their policies. And finally, it is simply not true that multinationals are independent of governments. They rely on them to provide legal and (8) _______________ **(finance)** measures of support. Proof of this came after the September 11 tragedy. Far from being independent, multinational airlines demanded governmental help. So maybe multinationals and big business are not so bad after all? At least we cannot lay the blame for all the world's problems at their door. The problems are too complicated for that. On the other hand, it would be (9)_______________ **(equal)** naive to believe that big business did not use global structure to its own (10)_______________ **(economy)** advantage. Business is business after all.

(adapted from 'Reading Business' Langenscheidt)

>> KLUCZ 1. poverty 2. responsibility 3. criticism 4. powerful 5. living 6. conclude 7. significant 8. financial 9. equally 10. economic

ZADANIE 12 >POZIOM ROZSZERZONY

> Przeczytaj poniższy tekst, z którego usunięto 6 zdań. Wpisz w każde z miejsc (**1-6**) literę (**A-G**), którą oznaczone jest brakujące zdanie. Jedno z podanych zdań nie pasuje do tekstu.

Matthew Cuthbert enjoyed the drive. It was a pretty road, running along between farms and fir woods. The air was sweet with the scent of many apple trees in bloom, and the meadows seemed full of mists of pearl and purple. Matthew was an odd-looking person with long iron-grey hair that touched his shoulders and a full, soft brown beard which he had worn ever since he was twenty.

(1) _________ He thought he was too early, so he tied his horse in the yard of the small hotel and went over to the railway station. The long platform was almost deserted. (2)_________ Matthew, barely noting that it was a girl, went past her as quickly as possible without looking at her. He was afraid of women except his sister, Marilla, because he had an uncomfortable feeling that women were secretly laughing at him. (3)_________ 'The train came in and was gone half an hour ago', the station master answered. 'But there was a passenger dropped off for you – a little girl. She's sitting out there'. 'I'm not expecting a girl', said Matthew calmly. 'It's a boy I've come for. He should be here. Mrs Alexander Spencer was supposed to bring him over from Nova Scotia for me.' (4)_________ 'Mrs Spencer came off the train with that girl and asked me to look after her till you came. She said you and your sister were adopting her and that you would come to take her home. I haven't got any more orphans hidden here. Maybe they were out of boys and sent a girl instead', he added.

Matthew did not know what to do. (5)_________ Slowly he turned to the little figure thinking how he should behave. When the girl realized he was coming to her, she stood up and held out her hand saying in a clear, sweet voice: ' I suppose you are Mr Matthew Cuthbert of Green Gables. I'm very glad to see you. I was beginning to be afraid you weren't coming for me tonight. But I was quite sure you would come for me in the morning.' Matthew took the little trembling hand in his and immediately decided what to do. (6)_________ He would take her home and let Marilla do that. 'I'm sorry I was late', he said shyly. 'Come along. The horse is over in the yard. Give me your bag.'

(adapted from 'Anne of Green Gables' by L. M. Montgomery)

A. He stopped the station master and asked him if the five-thirty train would soon arrive.
B. He wished that Marilla was with him to help in this strange situation.
C. He could not tell this child with the shining eyes that there had been a mistake.
D. The station master looked rather surprised.
E. When he reached Bright River there was no sign of any train.
F. She wasn't at all afraid and was looking around with great interest.
G. The only person in sight was a girl who was sitting on a pile of boxes at the far end waiting for something or somebody.

>> KLUCZ 1E 2G 3A 4D 5B 6C F – nigdzie nie pasuje

ZADANIE 13 >POZIOM ROZSZERZONY

> Przeczytaj fragment opowiadania. Z podanych odpowiedzi (**A-F**) wybierz właściwą, zgodną z treścią tekstu. Zaznacz jedną z czterech możliwości, zakreślając cyfrę 1, 2, 3 lub 4.

In 1928, when I was nine, I belonged to an organization known as the Comanche Club. Every schoolday afternoon at three o'clock, twenty-five of us Comanches were picked up by our Chief outside the boys' exit of the school, on 109th Street near Amsterdam Avenue. We then pushed our way into the Chief's reconverted commercial bus, and he drove us (according to his financial arrangement with our parents) over to Central Park. The rest of the afternoon we played football or baseball. Rainy afternoons, the Chief took us either to the Museum of Natural History or to the Metropolitan Museum of Art.

Saturdays and most national holidays, the Chief picked us up early in the morning and drove us out from Manhattan into the wide open spaces of Van Cortland's park or the Palisades. If we had athletics on our minds, we went to Van Cortland, where the playing fields were good size and where we could not meet a baby carriage or an old lady with a cane. If our Comanche hearts were set on camping, we went over to the Palisades.

When he was not with the Comanches, the Chief was John Gedsudski, of Staten Island. He was an extremely shy, gentle young man of twenty-two or three, a law student at N.Y.U and altogether a very memorable person. He was a fair umpire at all our sporting events, a master fire builder, and an expert first-aid man. Everyone of us, from the smallest to the biggest, loved and respected him.

Every afternoon, when it got dark enough for a losing team to stop playing, we Comanches relied heavily and selfishly on the Chief's talent for storytelling. By that hour we were usually an extremely tired group of boys and fought each other – either with our fists or our shrill voices – for the seats in the bus nearest the Chief. The Chief climbed into the bus only after we had settled down. Then, in his modulated tenor voice, gave us the new part of 'The Laughing Man'. Once he started narrating, our interest grew. 'The Laughing Man' was just the right story for a Comanche.

(adapted from J. D. Salinger ' The Laughing Man')

A. Every day after school the boys
1. went home.
2. met their Chief.
3. stayed at school.
4. took the school bus.

B. If the weather was good the boys were taken to
1. Natural History Museum.
2. Amsterdam Avenue.
3. Central Park.
4. Metropolitan Art Museum.

C. Each trip was
1. paid for by the Chief.
2. paid for by the boys' parents.
3. sponsored by the school.
4. sponsored by Comanche organization.

D. At Van Cortland the boys
1. played various games.
2. played football.
3. did camping.
4. walked with babies and old ladies.

E. The boys' Chief wanted to become
1. a baseball player.
2. an umpire.
3. a lawyer.
4. a first-aid man.

F. Each evening, when they stopped playing, all the boys
1. sat calmly round the fire.
2. were hungry and wanted the Chief to give them supper.
3. were too tired to listen to the Chief.
4. were fighting to sit close to the Chief.

KLUCZ A2 B3 C2 D1 E3 F4

PHRASAL VERBS A SELECTION

break down	stop working	zepsuć się
break into	enter illegally	włamać się
bring up	raise, educate	wychować
call back	return a phone call	oddzwonić
call off	cancel	odwołać
call on	pay a short visit	wpaść, odwiedzić
carry on	continue	kontynuować
come across	find by chance	natknąć się
come into	inherit	odziedziczyć
come round/to	regain consciousness	oprzytomnieć
come up	mention	napomknąć
count on	rely upon	polegać
cut down on	reduce	ograniczyć
fall for	start loving	zakochać się
fill in/out	complete (a form)	wypełnić (formularz)
fill up/out	make full	napełnić
find out	discover information	dowiedzieć się
get across	communicate	zrozumieć
get by	survive/live	radzić sobie, wyżyć
get down	depress	zasmucać
get down to (work)	start (working)	zabrać się (do pracy)
get off (the bus)	leave (a bus)	wysiadać (z autobusu)
get over	recover	dojść do siebie
get through to	make contact by phone	dodzwonić się
give away	distribute/reveal	rozdawać/wydać (sekret)
give in	surrender	poddać się
give out	distribute	rozdawać
give up (smoking)	stop doing	rzucić coś (palenie)
go off	explode	wybuchnąć
go on	continue	kontynuować
go out with	have a romantic relationship	chodzić z kimś
go up	increase	wzrastać

>>

grow up	become an adult	dorastać
hold on	wait	zaczekać
keep on	continue, persist	kontynuować
keep up	maintain the same level	zadążyć
let down	disappoint	zawieść, rozczarować
let off	not punish	puścić wolno
live up to	meet expectations	sprostać oczekiwaniom
look after	take care of	opiekować się
look down on	consider sb inferior	patrzeć na kogoś z góry
look for	seek	szukać
look into	investigate	badać (sprawę)
look up	find in a dictionary	szukać w słowniku
look up to	admire, respect	podziwiać, szanować
make for	head for	skierować się (ku)
make out	see with difficulty, understand	zrozumieć, połapać się
make up	invent	wymyślić coś
pick up	learn a little	załapać trochę
put down	kill an animal to end its suffering	uśpić zwierzę
put off	postpone	przełożyć na później
put through	connect on the phone	połączyć (przez telefon)
put up	give (temporary) accommodation	przenocować kogoś
put up with	tolerate, endure	tolerować, znosić
run out of sth	finish, consume	skończyć się, zabraknąć
set off	start a journey	wyruszyć w podróż
sort out	organise	uporządkować
speak up	speak louder	mówić głośniej
split up	stop a relationship	zerwać (z kimś)
take after	resemble	być podobnym do kogoś
take in	deceive	oszukać, nabrać kogoś
take off	leave the ground	wystartować (o samolocie)
take over	gain cotrol	przejąć (firmę)

take up	begin a new activity	zacząć coś uprawiać (np. sport)
talk over	discuss	omówić
tell off	critise, scold	nakrzyczeć na kogoś
think up	invent sth	wymyślić coś
turn down	refuse	odmówić
work out	do a calculation	wyliczyć
wrap up	put warm clothes on	ubrać się ciepło, opatulić

IRREGULAR VERBS A SELECTION

be	**was/were**	**been**	być
begin	**began**	**begun**	zaczynać (się)
bite	**bit**	**bitten**	gryźć
break	**broke**	**broken**	łamać
bring	**brought**	**brought**	przynosić
build	**built**	**built**	budować
buy	**bought**	**bought**	kupować
catch	**caught**	**caught**	łapać
choose	**chose**	**chosen**	wybierać
come	**came**	**come**	przychodzić
cost	**cost**	**cost**	kosztować
cut	**cut**	**cut**	ciąć
dig	**dug**	**dug**	kopać
do	**did**	**done**	robić
draw	**drew**	**drawn**	rysować
drink	**drank**	**drunk**	pić
drive	**drove**	**driven**	prowadzić (samochód)
eat	**ate**	**eaten**	jeść
fall	**fell**	**fallen**	upadać
feel	**felt**	**felt**	czuć
fight	**fought**	**fought**	walczyć
find	**found**	**found**	znaleźć
fly	**flew**	**flown**	latać
forget	**forgot**	**forgotten**	zapominać
get	**got**	**got**	dostać
go	**went**	**gone**	iść
grow	**grew**	**grown**	rosnąć
have	**had**	**had**	mieć
hear	**heard**	**heard**	słyszeć
hit	**hit**	**hit**	uderzyć
hurt	**hurt**	**hurt**	ranić
keep	**kept**	**kept**	trzymać

>>

know	**knew**	**known**	wiedzieć
lay	**laid**	**laid**	kłaść
learn	**learnt/learned**	**learnt/learned**	uczyć się
leave	**left**	**left**	opuszczać
lend	**lent**	**lent**	pożyczać (komuś)
lose	**lost**	**lost**	zgubić
make	**made**	**made**	robić
mean	**ment**	**ment**	znaczyć
meet	**met**	**met**	spotkać
pay	**paid**	**paid**	płacić
put	**put**	**put**	kłaść
read	**read**	**read**	czytać
ride	**rode**	**ridden**	jechać (na rowerze)
ring	**rang**	**rung**	dzwonić
run	**ran**	**run**	biegać
say	**said**	**said**	mówić
see	**saw**	**seen**	widzieć
sell	**sold**	**sold**	sprzedać
send	**sent**	**sent**	wysłać
set	**set**	**set**	ustanowić
shake	**shook**	**shaken**	potrząsać
shoot	**shot**	**shot**	strzelać
show	**showed**	**shown**	pokazać
shut	**shut**	**shut**	zamykać
sing	**sang**	**sung**	śpiewać
sit	**sat**	**sat**	siedzieć
sleep	**slept**	**slept**	spać
speak	**spoke**	**spoken**	mówić
spend	**spent**	**spent**	spędzać
stand	**stood**	**stood**	stać
steal	**stole**	**stolen**	kraść
swim	**swam**	**swum**	pływać

take	**took**	**taken**	brać
teach	**taught**	**taught**	nauczać
tell	**told**	**told**	mówić
think	**thought**	**thought**	myśleć
throw	**threw**	**thrown**	rzucać
understand	**understood**	**understood**	rozumieć
wake	**woke**	**woken**	budzić
wear	**wore**	**worn**	nosić
win	**won**	**won**	wygrywać
write	**wrote**	**written**	pisać